Praise for

When Teams Collide

"*When Teams Collide* should become required reading for anybody managing people in the globalized workplace... Richard Lewis's "insider's perspective" is reflected in well-researched comparative case studies and a remarkable set of 24 profiles of hypothetical individuals from as many countries. Rarely does one come across a business textbook that can just as easily serve as entertaining and rewarding bedtime reading, with its blend of entertaining stories and profound lessons."
Tim Cullen, Programme Director, Oxford Programme on Negotiation, Saïd Business School, Oxford

"Because we serve many of the world's largest multinational companies, we know that the ability to build effective global teams is an important skill of an executive. At Deloitte, we ascribe much value to this skill set, and have made it an important component of Deloitte's Next Generation CFO Academy curriculum, the foundation of which is built upon the three pillars of success – Leadership, Influence, and Competence. Knowing how to team and make decisions in an international environment is critical to the development of 'next generation' CFOs. Richard Lewis's book, *When Teams Collide*, explores these concepts in a very effective and engaging manner, providing meaningful, real-life examples to illustrate the international dimensions of building effective teams. This book is an educational resource for both aspiring and current CFOs."
William J. Ribaudo, Managing Partner and Dean, The Next Generation CFO Academy, Deloitte & Touche LLP

"Richard Lewis has outdone himself, no small feat. *When Teams Collide* synthesizes much of his earlier, excellent work while also furthering those efforts by grounding his LMR framework firmly within real life, real people, and real situations... The insights are almost innumerable."
Tim Flood, PhD, Associate Professor, Management and Corporate Communication, University of North Carolina

"Richard Lewis has written an extraordinarily useful book. A main quality of the book is the many business cases and individual stories and examples illustrating how our cultural lenses impact our understanding of social processes. These cases are conveyed with great insight, warmth and humor."
Atle Jordahl, International Director, Norwegian School of Economics (NHH)

"This book is a MUST for every business team leader who plans to start doing business in a new cross-cultural environment... The old saying "Do in Rome as the Romans do" is still very valid when added to Richard Lewis's own cross-cultural experiences over 50 years and in 150 countries. This book will help you to avoid major and costly mistakes as team leader."
Markku Vartiainen OBE, President, Finnish-British Chamber of Commerce

When Teams Collide

To
Dr. Francesco Ingrassia

When Teams Collide

Managing the International Team Successfully

Richard D. Lewis

NICHOLAS BREALEY
PUBLISHING

London • Boston

This revised edition first published in 2012 by Nicholas Brealey Publishing
An imprint of John Murray Press

An Hachette UK company

12

British Library Cataloguing-in-Publication Data
A catalogue record for this book is available from the British Library.

ISBN 978-1-90483-835-7
eBook ISBN 978-1-90483-837-1

Printed and bound by Clays Ltd, Elcograf S.p.A.

John Murray Press policy is to use papers that are natural, renewable and
recyclable products and made from wood grown in sustainable forests. The logging
and manufacturing processes are expected to conform to the environmental
regulations of the country of origin.

Nicholas Brealey Publishing
John Murray Press
Carmelite House
50 Victoria Embankment
London, EC4Y 0DZ, UK
Tel: 020 3122 6000

Nicholas Brealey Publishing
Hachette Book Group
Market Place Center, 53 State Street
Boston, MA 02109, USA
Tel: (617) 523 3801

www.nicholasbrealey.com

Contents

Foreword

Working in a team has been a challenge since time immemorial. While it is not easy in a familiar – monocultural or narrowly technical – environment, the challenge grows exponentially when borders are crossed and varying cultures and personalities enter into a collision course.

The inevitability of this challenge is actually a blessing, as unpleasant as dealing with it might be (the truth will set you free, but first it will make you really mad). This is not only because of the goals that will be achieved, but mainly because of the resulting personal and professional growth, as well as organizational maturation. While solving their (mostly manmade) problems, individuals and groups ultimately transcend the limitations imposed by their upbringing and social conditioning, and learn to know and utilize each other's way of thinking and doing things.

The paradox here is that in order to succeed we need to go beyond culture. Before that, though, we obviously need to understand what cultural differences entail.

Richard D. Lewis, one of the leading authorities in the field of applied cross-cultural studies, became acutely aware of the issues with respect to intercultural communication and interaction through personal experiences during his career-long investigation of how people with striking differences get along. His insights were reflected in the hugely popular *When Cultures Collide*, where he furthered the ideas of E.T. Hall and proposed an original framework for assessing the cultural preferences of individuals, teams, groups, nations, and regions.

During the application and validation of the Lewis Model in various settings around the world, Lewis and his colleagues gained an enormous amount of evidence about what it takes to work and lead across cultures. It was only natural to summarize this evidence in a book dedicated to teams: *When Teams Collide*.

The title of this book leads to three immediate expectations: it is about teams of all kinds that have to deal with the invariably different work preferences of their members; it is about a practical approach to diversity beyond culture; and it is about a broader context of successful cooperation across and beyond borders. In other words, this book is a robust attempt to depict, explain, and offer a concrete way of dealing with the complexity of human interaction in professional settings.

How many attempts of this kind have we known? Quite a few. A basic internet search would inevitably produce a myriad of papers, articles, chapters, and books dedicated to the subject of working in a team, managing a team, surviving in a team, etc. Most of the attempts to tackle the "team issues" are either fragmented (one issue at a time) or narrowly specialized (e.g., the Belbin approach), which is normal for any kind of research, but seems insufficient for those who need practical guidance for daily challenges, either in small (team) or large (organizational) settings.

Lewis found a way to approach the challenge. He chose a holistic scan of the ingredients of teams' success, which takes into account team members, team leaders, the operating context, and, most importantly, the reality of cross-cultural business conduct.

This book is built on the proven foundation depicted in *When Cultures Collide*. Moreover, it has been applied thousands of times in institutions in various domains – private, governmental, international, nonprofit, and academic. The continuity here is not just a matter of sticking to your guns or understanding only what you know (which unfortunately, especially in the area of cross-cultural studies, is often the case). It provides a way to reflect on the fundamental differences in world cultures and their individual variations.

The Lewis Model is intuitive and easily comprehensible. It offers a dynamic, tripartite cultural categorization in which linear-active, multi-active, and reactive features of a person or a team become a roadmap to a better understanding of self and others. The explanatory power of the model is considerably enhanced by a carefully crafted framework of cultural universals and their variations: communication and interaction patterns, leadership styles, meeting patterns, empathy, trust, and business ethics. The visuals – a trademark of the Lewis approach to knowledge creation and dissemination – make it so much easier to navigate the often muddy waters of intercultural relations.

The richness of the context, the power of the visuals, and the detailed nature of the case studies make the book appealing to a wide audience. The seamless narrative style means that it is readable and easily accessible to those without a deep background in international business or cross-cultural issues.

Lewis offers 11 "items of knowledge" that must be acquired and utilized for successful teamwork across cultures. While most items seem intuitive enough, this is the first time they have been compiled as a matrix of mutual understanding and successful business conduct.

Each item (or area), from cultural categorization of team members (and the team itself!) to team organization, communication, leadership, ethics, and trust, is backed by thorough case studies. The storytelling (much revered nowadays in leadership education) is exemplary and makes the reading not just enjoyable but truly educational – one feels that one is having a conversation with the author, who shares valuable information and passes on wisdom. There are no simulations, hypothetical situations, or made-up characters. The whole story is a mirror of the life-long learning of a gifted observer.

In essence, the book sets out what we must do and why. Most importantly, it offers a way to do it (which is where most authors fall short).

Throughout the book, Lewis offers both generalized and specific observations about different cultures, which suits both types of curiosity: epistemological and practical. Therefore, readers who are looking for specific behavior in an unfamiliar cultural setting will be rewarded as much as those looking for eternal answers to eternal questions.

As trivial as it sounds, it is not a challenge for different people to interact, unless they have a common business to attend to. That is when goodwill and presuppositions of cultural awareness swiftly disappear. The grip of one's cultural identity is too strong; the desire to elude it is too irresistible... As S. Johnson put it, "the chains of habit are too weak to be felt until they are too strong to be broken."

To reach out to our colleagues and counterparts, we must aim beyond cultural borders; to succeed, though, we must start with culture(s) – learning about self, others, and self and others together. Richard Lewis offers us an invaluable route for negotiating the difference.

Dr. Iouri Bairatchnyi,
Former Director, Cross-Cultural Programme,
World Bank, Washington, DC

Introduction

The expansion of multinational organizations, conglomerates, and even medium-sized firms into as many as 200 markets worldwide means that international teams are rapidly becoming the central operating mode for global enterprises. Estimates put the number of such teams at between 2 and 3 million at the beginning of the twenty-first century.

Mergers, acquisitions, the opening of foreign subsidiaries, and exploiting fresh markets are heavily dependent on newly created teams. Thousands of new projects require the creation of teams to meet different challenges, develop new products, resolve persistent conflicts, or examine the latest techniques, and many of these teams possess technical expertise in a variety of fields, especially in R&D. Others deal with sales and marketing, accounting and reporting, finance and budgeting. Teams may be large or small, homogeneous or diverse, mobile or static, real or virtual.

The responsibilities and the sheer number of important tasks entrusted to teams mean that their members need to be equipped with a plethora of qualities and characteristics. To begin with, they must be quick off the mark. They need to make fast decisions, particularly since they are often mobile teams that may be together for only two or three days at a time. They are expected to be innovative or even avant garde: they may be breaking new ground, and dealing with colleagues, partners, or opponents who have unorthodox, atypical, or unsettled views and attitudes (new Russians, debuting Chinese, ex-Soviet – perhaps Islamic – entrepreneurs from countries such as Kazakhstan or Azerbaijan). They get involved in alliances that have the potential for significant profits and a significant degree of friction. They have to meet new challenges with enthusiasm and have enough confidence to deal with chaos. They must acquire international experience fast (if they succeed, they become company stars).

A high-performance team generally consists of a small group of people with complementary skills who are committed to a common goal and working approach. When successfully integrated, its members also care for one another's personal growth and success. They must know more than head office and be willing to take a stand if their recommendations are disregarded. They must familiarize themselves with local (marketing and ethical) conditions and adapt the company style accordingly. The team itself must be sufficiently diverse and its members must use their diversity to good effect, cultivating it and becoming its champions if challenged by a monocultural head office. In all of this they must be properly led and managed.

Managers of international teams should be key figures in the company as a whole. They should be experienced in cross-border business, adaptable, unbiased, flexible but fair, a motivator, an HR expert, and something of a psychologist. If they are linguists (with the multiple horizons that more than one language offers), all the better. They must be able to relate equally well to head office and to the different views and aspirations of team members; they must be chameleon-like in facing them (adapting to each personality); they need to be able to distinguish quickly between (internal) conflicts and pseudo-conflicts. Quite clearly, they have a difficult and sensitive task.

There is no simple way of training someone to manage an international team and leaders originate from many countries and cultures. Nevertheless, there are 11 basic items of knowledge that the leader of an international team must acquire and utilize. These are summarized below and are further elaborated in successive chapters of this book.

Categorizing cultures

The Lewis LMR model divides cultures into three categories:

✧ Linear-active
✧ Multi-active
✧ Reactive

Linear-active people tend to be task-oriented, highly organized planners who complete action chains by doing one thing at a time, preferably in accordance with a linear agenda. Speech is for information and depends largely on facts and figures.

Multi-active people are loquacious, emotional, and impulsive and attach great importance to family, meetings, relationships, compassion, and human warmth. They like to do many things at the same time and are poor followers of agendas. Speech is for opinions.

Reactive people – good listeners – rarely initiate action or discussion, preferring first to hear and establish the other's position, then react to it and formulate their own opinion. Reactives listen before they leap. Speech is for creating harmony.

Team managers need to distinguish early on which category each team member belongs to and adapt their own stance accordingly.

Depending on their nationality and upbringing, each team member is situated in a "cultural anchorage" in which they are comfortable. When the captain of a sailing vessel finds an anchorage that suits him, he is reluctant to leave it, irrespective of his plan. He is gratified if the anchorage is stable, safe, and unencumbered. One can say the same about people and cultures. Most people are satisfied with their cultural characteristics. Strangers may find Finnish culture dull, Italian too emotional, and Russian or Nigerian too volatile (possibly chaotic) – but that is the way these people like it. They live that way and have done for centuries. They don't want to leave their cultural anchorage. This makes it difficult for the manager of an international team to convince a colleague to change anchorages, for instance to encourage an Italian to be as disciplined and systematic as a German, or a Japanese to speak out directly and make quick decisions like an American. Managers need to harness and synergize diversity rather than eliminate it.

Besides taking into account differences in cultural categories and national characteristics, managers would do well to recognize fault lines, which have considerable significance in some states. It is well known that northern and southern Italians are very different in character and behavior, for example. The cultural fault line is around the latitude of Rome. Some countries have several fault lines between regional behaviors, for instance Russia, China, Spain, and the USA, but it will suffice if the team manager can quickly identify the main "tectonic plates" between Parisians and *les gens du Midi*; Prussians and Bavarians; Castilians and Catalans; Flemings and Walloons; Finnish and Swedish Finns; New Yorkers and Southerners; and, particularly, the fault lines between the north and the south of England, as well as the Scots, Welsh, and Irish (north and south).

Sometimes fault-line preferences transcend national boundaries. For example, people in the north of England and Scotland empathize splendidly with Norwegians and Finns, those in the south of England with Danes, Dutch, and southern Swedes.

Organizing the team

Having identified its members' cultural characteristics, the team must be organized from the outset to maximize the great potential that the cultural mix offers. National strengths, weaknesses, insights, and blind spots must be considered; taboos and cultural black holes must be taken into account. In addition, the *raison d'être* of the team must be clarified.

Speaking the language

Each team has a lingua franca – probably, but not necessarily, English. Whatever the choice, the team leader would do well to consider the possibilities offered by the medium of that language. These include clarity, politesse, humor, charisma, exactness, ambiguity, vagueness, expressiveness, exhortation, minimalism, understatement, hyperbole, euphemisms, and coded speech. Each language has its own strengths – English humor, French exactitude, Spanish vigor, German logic, Italian elegance, Japanese courtesy and face-saving mechanisms, Chinese ambiguity (leaving options open). Team leaders may legitimately exploit such traits. This book examines English as the most likely international medium, but Spanish, Chinese, French, Portuguese, Swedish, Russian, Arabic, and even Turkish may be convenient for some groupings. The team language, with native and nonnative speakers communicating in it and manipulating it, is one of the most interesting elements of international teamwork.

Leading the team

Having built an international team whose members have suitably complementary strengths, the question then arises: Who leads it? Do some nationals take up the mantle of leadership more easily than others? This is a difficult question to answer. Certainly, some cultures produce individuals who relish the prestige and power of leadership. French, Spanish, and South American managers are good examples. They manage autocratically and tend to make irreversible decisions. Others, like Canadians, British, and Swedes, feel that they are good at arbitration and tend to seek agreement among those present rather than impose personal decisions. Americans are essentially people of action and see their role as maintaining momentum. Finns use facts skillfully and seek sensible conclusions. In the end, good leadership depends more on individual personality than a particular passport.

Profiling team members

Team members are often characterized by a considerable degree of easy internationalism, tolerance, and cultural sensitivity. They will, however, bring with them their own national values, taboos, and perspectives. By familiarizing themselves with their colleagues' differing profiles and worldviews, team leaders can promote synergy among the individuals they seek to integrate and control.

Recognizing speech styles

Among the tasks of managers are the necessities of instructing, motivating, and leading their subordinates. They may often lead by example, but as far as motivation and issuing directives are concerned, their success will be heavily dependent on language. Different languages are used in various ways and with a variety of effects. Hyperbolic American and understated British English clearly both inform and inspire staff with a distinctive allure and driving force. Managers of all nationalities know how to speak to their compatriots to best effect, since there are built-in characteristics in their language that make it easy to convey ideas to its native speakers. In fact, they are only vaguely aware of their dependence on the linguistic traits that make their job easier, so becoming aware of them can make a real difference.

Communicating in English

Whatever the team members' national communication style may be – reticent or loquacious, open or closed, formal or informal – it is likely that they will have to project that style into the team language, which as we have seen is most likely to be English. Even though individuals may possess linguistic competence, another minefield lies ahead: which English? British and American English have their own nuances and their own brand of self-expression. For speakers of other languages, the British are the harder to follow. This is not because their pronunciation is less clear, but on account of the hidden agendas in British speech.

Using humor

A sense of humor is a powerful weapon in a manager's arsenal. Whether leaders consider themselves humorous or not, it will be a factor in controlling the team. However, humor crosses national boundaries with difficulty, especially when heading east, while in Anglo-Saxon countries humor is used systematically. Most international teams develop their own special brand of humor, which may signify their "coming of age" as a team.

Making decisions

Decisions often have to be taken rather quickly, as time may be limited. A decision-making process is clearly required. Yet, even what at first seem to be the most straightforward of discussions can run into dispute or deadlock. When such situations occur between nationals of the same culture, the momentum can usually be regained through the use of a well-tried mechanism. Deadlocks can be broken, for instance, by a change of negotiators, a shift in venue, an adjournment of the session, or a repackaging of the deal. Arab teams will take a recess of prayer and come back with a more conciliatory stance; Japanese delegations will bring in senior executives "to see what the problem is"; Swedish opponents will go out drinking together; and Finns will retire to the sauna. Such options are not always available in international teams. Moreover, cultural difference can mean that the nature of the deadlock is misconstrued by all parties.

Behaving ethically

International teams of several types – those promoting trade in different countries, launching new products, entering new markets in connection with joint ventures, sales and purchasing teams in general, or those involved in license procurement, patents, and expatriate placement – are frequently confronted with dilemmas in trying to achieve their objectives. In a diverse and multicultural team, managers will on occasion be in dire need of guidelines as to how to proceed through a veritable labyrinth of traditional, established ways of contracting business. These vary in every culture and there are no internationally accepted definitions of either ethical behavior or corruption. There are many gray areas such as child labor, abortion, treatment of immigrants, or genetic engineering, and one issue that an international team will have to meet head-on and with some frequency is facilitation payments.

Building trust

Trust is arrived at in different ways, often based on different criteria. Some people instinctively trust their own nationals, at least in general. This applies to Danes, Finns, Swedes, and Norwegians and, to a somewhat lesser extent, to Germans, Canadians, and Japanese. These nationalities also show reasonable trust in others until it is shown that the trust is misplaced. Most Latins and other multi-actives, on the other hand, only accord trust when they see that it is merited. Within a multinational team it is essential that the manager create trust quickly. It may help to know that reactives respond well to consistent courtesy, multi-actives to ready compassion, and linear-actives to word–deed correlation.

1

Categorizing Cultures

Human behavior, in social and business life alike, varies significantly around the world and is subject to a substantial number of influences – genetic, political, economic, and religious are just some of them. The discovery in 2001 that all human genes are remarkably alike (we share 99.9 percent of our genes with others) led to genetic determinism taking a back seat in its significance for behavior. Similarly, the failure of the theories of economic determinism (Marxism among them) to become reality in the last decades of the twentieth century left a clear field for the acceptance of cultural determinism as the primary and dominant crucible for molding our conduct.

Diversity and compatibility

The collective program or agenda for our behavior is set by our cultural group through the influence of parents, teachers, peers, and societal preferences and restraints, aided and abetted by written and unwritten rules and regulations. Often, but not always, the cultural group is synonymous with a nation-state, so we may talk about French or German or Japanese culture. As there are significant variations of behavior within the borders of some countries (for instance Bavarians and Prussians, Milanese and Sicilians), there exist more cultural groups than nation-states. Strictly speaking, there are 200–300 national or regional mindsets, commanding general uniformity of allegiance from their adherents. That is to say, most Scots are usually content to display the well-known characteristics of the northern British, while New Yorkers revel in their distinctive brand of Americanness.

These cultural programs are the repositories of rich diversity, yet, like genetic species, they are more homogeneous than one

would expect. Increased international contact, especially in the field
of commerce, has familiarized business people with the customs
and communication styles of trading partners, of staff in overseas
subsidiaries, and of colleagues in international teams. They have
noted that they get on better with some than with others. Often
they learn to adapt sufficiently to the preferences of the other party.
In effect, they adopt a cultural stance that facilitates understanding and empathy. Few people are able to change their behavior at
will to react to someone else's worldview, but regular contact with
a variety of nationalities soon makes one realize that they fall into
three broad categories, as outlined in the Introduction:

✧ Those in the *linear-active* group follow linear agendas, planning
  ahead step by step, completing action chains, and achieving
  clearly defined goals with some precision.
✧ Those in the *multi-active* group enjoy doing many things at
  once, are warm, loquacious, emotional, and impulsive, and are
  very concerned with relationships.
✧ Those in the *reactive* group are introvert, respect-oriented listeners who are accommodating, courteous, and amenable to
  consensus and compromise.

In general, nationalities within a particular category understand
and tolerate one another fairly readily. There may be some national
friction (for instance between Japanese and Koreans or Hungarians
and Slovaks), but a common categorical wavelength facilitates
intercourse. The corollary of this is that people from different categories often frustrate and annoy each other. This is most common
between linear-active and multi-active people (Nordic abhorrence
of Latin gesticulations or verbosity, for example). People in the
reactive category tend to have less confrontation with the other
two groups (because they react and accommodate by instinct), but
they too have their own silent agenda that can be quite judgmental.

The good news is that no human being belongs solely to
one category. The most linear Swiss or German will have some
multi-active emotion or excitability buried somewhere below the

disciplined exterior. Japanese – *ne plus ultra* reactives – are seduced by linear thinking in their manufacturing processes and financial dealings. Multi-active Italians from Milan will tell you how Germanic they can be (or would like to be). Impassive, reactive Koreans can explode into rage (like Turks) at the drop of a hat. One's individual traits may also contradict the norms of national programming. Emperor Meiji was an unusually charismatic Japanese; Winston Churchill belied the British stiff upper lip tradition by weeping frequently in public.

These deviations – or aberrations – are good news because they indicate that human beings are fundamentally open to a diversity of persuasions and beliefs. Table 1.1 overleaf, showing linear-active, multi-active, and reactive variations, demonstrates that traits are strung out along three different axes, implying possible rapprochements to different mindsets. While one-category characteristics may be prevalent with some nationalities (linear Swiss, multi-active Brazilians, reactive Vietnamese), this does not mean that they cannot benefit from insight into other mindsets. For instance Indians, naturally loquacious and emotional, not only have eastern wisdom and courtesy, but supplement these qualities with a good understanding of the west.

Members of international teams have great advantages in developing inter-category synergy and promoting and cultivating compatibility. Their contacts are multicultural, frequent, and varied. They are not walled in, either physically or mentally, by the parochial constraints of an ever-present HQ. They flit around, acquire versatility and adaptability, and qualify as cosmopolitan.

If they are perceptive, their horizons widen quickly. Europeans begin to see some of the things that Japanese see, though they were mysterious before. Self-awareness heightens all round.

The table of linear-active, multi-active, and reactive characteristics can be used as an assessment tool of your own cultural traits. If you select a trait from each horizontal trio and give yourself a score of one for each, you will arrive at three separate column totals of linear, multi-active, and reactive qualities. A score of, for instance, 10-6-8 could then be plotted inside the triangle in Figure

LINEAR-ACTIVE	MULTI-ACTIVE	REACTIVE
Talks and listens in equal degrees	Talks most of the time	Listens most of the time
Rarely interrupts	Often interrupts	Never interrupts
Confronts with facts	Confronts emotionally	Never confronts
Dislikes losing face	Has a good story	Must not lose face
Uses official channels	Seeks out key person	Uses network
Follows linear agenda	Diverges frequently from agenda	Follows circular agenda
Frank, direct	Indirect, manipulative	Indirect, courteous
Truth before diplomacy	Diplomatic, creative truth	Diplomacy before truth
Limited body language	Lots of body language	Hardly any body language
Cool	Excitable	Inscrutable
Promotes product	Promotes personal relationships	Promotes inter-company harmony
Completes action chains	Completes human transactions	Harmonizes by action at appropriate times
Partly conceals feelings	Displays feelings	Conceals feelings
Speech is for information	Speech is for opinions	Speech is to promote harmony
Punctual, time dominated	Relaxed about time	Focuses on doing things in the correct order
Has individual goals	Has intimate-circle goals	Has company goals
Task oriented	People oriented	Very people oriented
Does one thing at a time	Does several things at once	Reacts to partner's action
Respects facts and figures	Respects oratory, expressiveness, charisma	Respects age, wisdom, experience
Plans ahead step by step	Plans grand outline	Reacts to others' plans
Defines problems and solves in quick sequence	Goes for all-embracing solutions	Prefers gradualist solutions
Separates business and personal life	Intertwines business and social	Links business and social
Bad orders can be discussed	Bad orders should be circumvented	An order is an order
Admits own mistakes	Finds an excuse	Hides, covers up mistakes

Table 1.1   The three major cultural categories

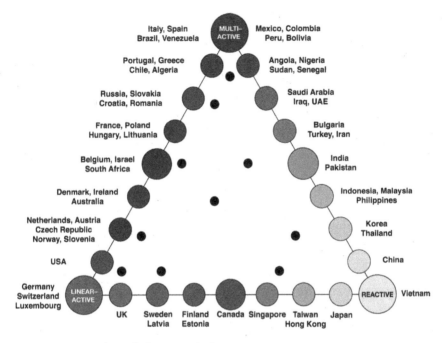

Figure 1.1 Cultural characteristics

1.1. Based on more than 25,000 tests, this is a kind of triangular "league table" showing the relative placements of major countries in terms of their degree of linearity, multi-activity, or reactivity. If two or more nations are bracketed together, such as France and Poland, it does not mean that the two cultures are completely similar. What it does mean is that French and Polish people are roughly the same in their linear-active or multi-active traits. At the top of the diagram where eight multi-active cultures are located, Mexico, Colombia, Peru, and Bolivia are on the right-hand side, as they have large Indian populations that give them reactive tendencies. The ones on the left reflect more their Latin character. Americans and Australians are more extrovert than British; Danes are more talkative than other Nordics; Finns have several Asian traits; Singapore and Hong Kong are more westernized (= linear-active) than Japan or China. Koreans and Thais are the most excitable of the East Asians; India is midway, combining multi-active loquacity with Oriental courtesy; laid-back Canada and bicultural Belgium are the other cultures in median positions. Geographical proximities and climatic similarities are visibly influential in determining cultural categories.

When plotting individual characteristics on this diagram, team members find that they are positioned close to or distant from others. Proximity indicates a high degree of compatibility, even though your own most prevalent category might be different. Those plotted close to the linear-active–reactive axis might share qualities of the "strong silent" type. Those close to the multi-active–reactive axis will certainly share strong relationship orientation. Those near the center of the triangle might well have balanced attitudes that would serve them well as mediators, chairpersons, or team leaders. Compatibility is harder to achieve among individuals who are plotted right in the corners of the triangle, though they may have sterling qualities in their own right and be effective leaders.

Further globalization of business and national interests is likely to initiate a homogenization of customs, habits, fashions, tastes, and behavior. It would be a mistake to think that such a rapprochement will be accomplished quickly, however. As yet there are few signs of major nations or religions abandoning their basic cultural traits or credos, and thousands of years of conditioning will be extremely difficult to reverse. The evident Americanization of some countries at micro level (dress, food, fashion, music, sport) is a red herring. At the macro level, national, regional, tribal, and religious cultures remain deeply embedded. Greater compatibility will happen, but it is likely to be a gradual, persistent process, encouraged by the ideal of the global village, and achieved through sensible analysis of one's own cultural baggage as well as by sympathetic study of the diverse preferences and aspirations of the three cultural categories.

Figure 1.2 shows a selection of nationalities on a linear-active/multi-active scale and includes a "league table" of linear and multi-active professions. (Reactive nations are left out of this comparison, since they have a natural inclination toward compatibility with others.) What this figure indicates is that an individual's behavior is affected simultaneously by their nationality and their vocation or profession. Swiss are normally very linear in their thinking, but so

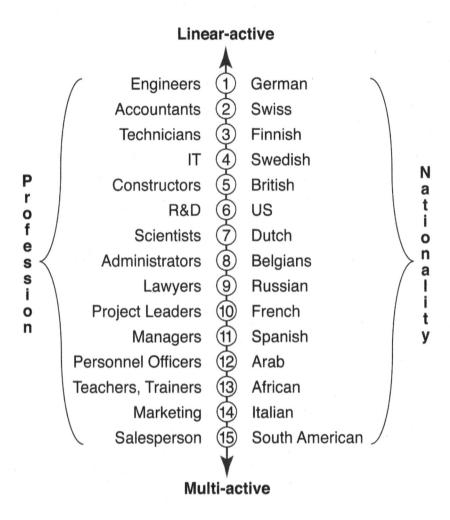

Figure 1.2 Linear-active/multi-active scale

are engineers. Indians may indulge in flexible or situational truth, but so do salespeople. These influences may conflict: an excitable Argentinean may, on a daily basis, have to submit to cold accounting disciplines. A factual German will have to dig deep into their imaginative qualities to find creative marketing strategies. On the other hand, people may be hit by "double whammies." Finnish engineers find little in common with Brazilian salespeople, for instance.

Using the linear-active/multi-active scale, one can make a quick assessment of compatibility between individuals by adding the scores for profession and nationality, for example:

German technician   1 + 4 = 5
French HR officer   10 + 12 = 22
Italian salesperson (male)   14 + 15 = 29

Women are generally more multi-active than men, so one can add at least two points:

British administrator   5 + 8 + 2 = 15
Italian salesperson (female)   14 + 15 + 2 = 31

Figure 1.3 shows that people may be close to each other or far apart on a factual/emotional or national/cultural scale.

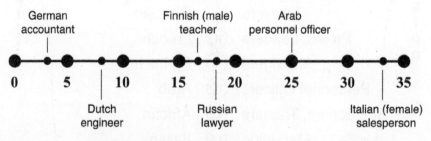

Figure 1.3   Compatibility

German accountants have little trouble communicating with Dutch engineers; neither do American managers (17) with Swiss trainers (15). When the gap widens to 10 points, then communication breaks down. Swedish constructors (9) working with Peruvian project leaders (25) have a hard time. Recently I had to address a communication problem between a Finnish head office and the company's distribution outlets in France, Spain, and Italy. Nordic scientists (10) were trying to advise Latin salespeople (25–29) and relations were persistently adversarial. The use of Finnish salespeople (18) as intermediaries alleviated the problem.

In the context of international teams, compatibility of outlook is often more easily achieved, as frequently the assembled team is a project group. Swiss, Swedish, Dutch, and French R&D people talk the same language, as do American and Belgian accountants. Marketing groups have lively and creative meetings whatever nationalities are involved. Engineers without a common tongue often get on famously, sketching diagrams for each other when words are not enough. Women often understand each other well, irrespective of their origins; all-male nonspecialist teams experience more friction. American managers and salespeople often chafe at Latin, Asian, even British lack of pace. Nordics find Italians and Spaniards too wordy, French too prickly. Swedes and Swiss are often seen as pedantic or finicky. In general, however, team members tend to get used to each other's idiosyncrasies and, after numerous and regular meetings, settle for knowing when to "agree to disagree." Skillful team leaders are invaluable.

Diversity – bonus or drawback?

The term "brain drain" was frequently employed in the twentieth century. The huge discrepancy between the salaries and rewards of Americans and Europeans meant that the drain had only one direction – it flowed into the United States. In the late 1940s and especially in the 1950s, a large number of skilled Britons, benefiting from the common language, were attracted to US companies, particularly in scientific and technological fields. They were not the only ones: disillusioned Germans, oppressed Czechs, Poles, and Hungarians, ambitious Taiwanese, and many others enriched American thinking in areas as diverse as science, chemistry, engineering and manufacturing, medicine, and academic studies.

The subsequent burgeoning prosperity of countries such as Germany, Japan, France, and occasionally Britain slowed down this flow, though continuous US booms meant that it was never halted. In the 1980s and 1990s, however, the brains started to come back to where they had originated. Germans, Swedes, and Britons with 20 years' experience of US methods found themselves useful and effective in Europe, either as representatives of US companies setting up there or in powerful European firms. The advent of the Single Market gave American companies great incentives to establish European bases, often in the UK. The myth of superior

US management techniques was debunked and Japanese, German, Swedish, Swiss, and British management styles proved at least as effective as American, frequently better.

A positive outcome of these international exchanges was the realization that diversity among decision-making executives could be a bonus rather than a drawback. This is by no means an open and shut case, however. Ask a Swede which makes a stronger team, one comprising six Swedes or one consisting of a Swede, a German, an Italian, a Spaniard, a Japanese, and an American, and they will probably go for the six Swedes. A Finn would tell you that anything is better than six Swedes and would go for diversity. This is partly because an incredibly successful and rapidly expanding company like Nokia cannot possibly find the engineers and executives it needs from the minuscule Finnish labor market.

French executives confident of their intellectual superiority over others, Americans convinced of US business success, and Japanese complacent about both tend to favor teams and working groups composed of their own nationals. Swiss, Danes, Finns, Belgians, Dutch, Canadians, Australians, Indians, overseas Chinese, and even British are quick to see the advantages of multinational (and therefore multicultural) teams. Nationals of small countries, especially those that are prosperous (Denmark, Finland, the Netherlands, Switzerland, Singapore) have no choice: they must recruit where they can. They also happen to be the countries that have acquired most cultural sensitivity, as they needed to develop commercial relations with big states. Overseas Chinese and Indians have long been expert at functioning in international environments and bring valuable experience and adaptability to international teams. They can often star in this context. Canadians, Australians, and Brits have sufficient cultural diversity in their home labor markets to have gained familiarity with the pros and cons.

Figure 1.4 shows us how such a team (perhaps also including a few deviants and eccentrics) can be versatile in performance.

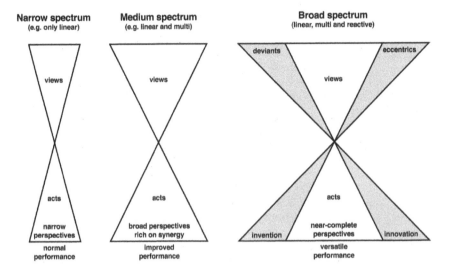

Figure 1.4   Diversity, versatility, and excellence

Finding cultural anchorages

These three cultural categories refer to people organizing their
lives in completely different ways. They are all human beings, but
they differ fundamentally in behavior just as much as three animals
would, say a dog, a cat, and a horse. Like these three domesticated
animals, they have three distinct agendas. This is what we mean by
cultural diversity. In certain circumstances it is as difficult for one
category to understand the intentions or aspirations of another as
it would be for a cat to understand the hopes or disappointments of
a horse (possibly the two animals would sense each other's feelings
better through intuition, sense of smell, and sharp observation).
This is made clear in Table 1.2 overleaf.

While two people from the same category can understand the
other's motives most of the time, people from different categories
do not. An Arab interacting with a Norwegian would have a common interest in oil, but virtually no other point of contact. Their
views on religion, food, art, women, rules, government, society,
human rights, rearing of children, laws, and history would not
intersect. When the business discussion was ended, they would

Dog	Alliance with humans – committed Dependent on humans for food and shelter Faithful Obedient Manipulates humans by body language and eye contact Humble (pleading expressions) Does not mind losing face Extrovert Goes for walks with owner Sees it as its duty to defend owner's property against intruders Hostile to cats and some other animals
Cat	Alliance with humans – tenuous Less dependent on humans for food and shelter, but manipulative when it wants them Fidelity questionable Shows of affection sporadic Often disobedient Introvert, often inscrutable Proud, never loses face Demanding rather than pleading Disdains dog's obedience to and dependence on humans Does not go for walks with owner Does not see it as its duty to defend owner's property against intruders
Horse	Alliance with humans Dependent on humans for food and shelter Stronger and bigger than humans but tolerates their dominance Tolerance includes working, being ridden and perhaps raced Usually friendly and approachable Sensitive, often nervous Good memory Sociable, with a herd instinct

Table 1.2 Animal agendas

have no common language and even if they had, they would not know what to talk about.

The three basic categories of human being have sharply contrasting lifestyles. There are over 200 separate nationalities and a greater number of regional cultures, but due to certain instinctive, geographical, and historical circumstances, people have chosen one of the three routes to organize life. Though many individuals and some nationalities are hybrid, there is a compelling common denominator of behavior in each category that makes them soul-mates and enables us generally to forecast what they will do.

Thus the family has paramount importance in all Latin cultures but enjoys the same position in other multi-active cultures such as India, the Arab countries, and African societies. Truth is seen as scientific and unalterable in linear-active societies as far apart as the USA, Germany, and Australia. Courtesy and the concept of face are dominating features of reactive behavior all the way from Rangoon to Tokyo.

In general, human beings organize their lives around two core features: values and communication. These elements usually remain remarkably constant in a person's behavioral make-up, principally because the human, faced with the trials and vicissitudes of life, is pushed strongly toward seeking security in traditional behavioral refuges. These are the cultural anchorages described in the Introduction.

Like mariners who consider they have found a safe anchorage, a cultural group is reluctant to relinquish it and is likely to retain their berth in it for centuries (or millennia). Seventh-century Norse Vikings interacting with the disciples of Mohammed would have found no more commonalities with them than do their modern counterparts. Experts on Chinese history affirm that the street scene in a rural Chinese town differed little in the twentieth century from one in the days of the Ming Dynasty.

The effective management of an international team requires team leaders to be acutely aware of the distinctively different life-organization styles in which each of the three categories is anchored. Unless they make certain concessions or adaptations regarding these lifestyles, discord will continually raise its head. On the other hand, equal awareness of the common denominators within each category will help in forecasting behavior.

The linear-active anchorage

Linear-active people believe that they can control life, taking basically rational decisions, using incontrovertible facts or logic. They make plans according to a time schedule that they draw up, believe in, and adhere to. They assume that all other people will recognize

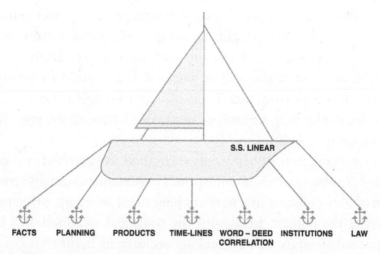

Figure 1.5 The linear-active anchorage

the same facts, accept and respect them, and make decisions in consequence. Linear-actives distinguish clearly between facts and human aspirations and, while not disparaging the latter, are reluctant to allow them to influence, interfere with, or distort linear reality. Success and prosperity are natural consequences of orderly, rational planning. Economic decisions are best kept separate from subjective feelings.

Rules, regulations, and laws form a great part of the framework within which linear-actives operate and though these are recognized as man-made, they are seen as largely beneficial for the maintenance of an orderly society. Legal restrictions in such matters as taxes, traffic regulations, marriage, divorce, breach of contract, deceit, libel, piracy, violence, and so on should be applied to everyone without exception.

Linear-active parents are protective of their families and provide for their children in terms of both education and material support. The schooling they provide will enable their children to make their own way in life. Through hard work, law-abiding behavior, and general integrity, they will replicate their parents' success. In order for children to have freedom of decision and to be able to develop their own initiative, the bonds between them and their parents tend to loosen after the age of 16. This contrasts sharply with the nature of familial bonds in multi-active and reactive societies, where there are years more dependence.

Linear-active people are largely influenced by Protestant values concerning the work ethic, honesty, strait-laced morality, and social justice. Human rights, democratic institutions, and respect for material advancement (including money itself) are important issues in linear-active societies. This implies hatred of debt and paying bills promptly.

Power distance is kept at a minimum, as adherence to facts and figures enables specialists to state their opinions boldly, even though they may contradict the opinions of superiors. Brainstorming sessions are consequently more successful in linear-active environments than in multi-active or reactive ones.

Pursuit of one's career and the workplace itself are important stimuli for linear-actives and counterbalance the focus on the family, which is less intense than in the other two categories. Family issues are not closely intertwined with working life in linear-active societies to the extent they are in such countries as Italy, India, or China. The state and efficient officialdom earn more respect among linear-actives, who devote a considerable amount of time to institutions such as clubs, societies, and associations, as well as the company for which they work.

The multi-active anchorage

Multi-active people also believe that they can control life, yet less on the basis of applying facts and figures (which may not always be to their liking) and more through exploiting human hopes and feelings, using willpower, feats of persuasion, and often charisma. Multi-actives do not believe that facts based on scientific truth always correspond to reality. Multi-active truth is always contextual and is in the ear of the listener, just as beauty is in the eye of the beholder.

In multi-active societies, success and prosperity depend less on the work ethic in a rational framework than on human connections in a networking mode. Contacts are valued, both horizontal

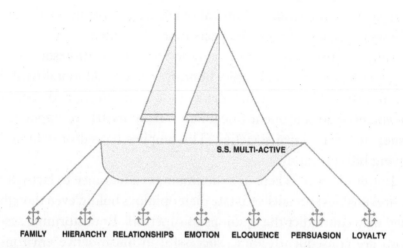

Figure 1.6 The multi-active anchorage

and vertical (across or up and down the hierarchy), and are often maintained throughout life by the demonstration of loyalty and closeness. As long as the strength of these bonds is reciprocated, loyalty will intensify to the extent that in the event of the friend committing a misdemeanor, they would be shielded against third parties, including the authorities or even the police. This behavior is sometimes described as particularist as opposed to universalist (the same rules apply to all).

Laws and regulations are man-made in multi-active eyes. They are not necessarily disobeyed, but are often freely interpreted, "bent," or circumvented as a matter of course. Basically, "the law is an ass."

Multi-active people do not adhere to schedules, programs, and agendas with the dutiful fidelity shown by linear-actives. Multi-actives believe that good decisions, including business ones, are made at times that are optimal to the situation – for instance when people are in a good mood or momentarily inspired or stimulated. This moment may not necessarily coincide with a fixed meeting, deadline, or agenda. Consequently, punctuality and timekeeping are less important in the multi-active world than in the linear-active one. Linear-active people do not forgive this attitude easily, since they organize a significant part of their life and activity around time.

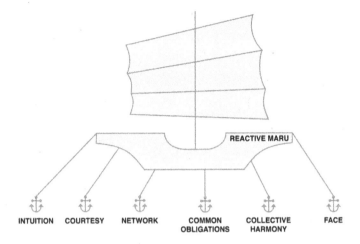

Figure 1.7 The reactive anchorage

The reactive anchorage

Reactive people, many of whom are Asians, do not believe that they are in control of their destiny. They do not have the multi-actives' faith in powers of persuasion (even less in charisma), neither do they see life in terms of the factual truth so adhered to and admired by linear-actives. For reactives, there is no absolute truth. Truth is invariably situational or contextual. Opposites (right and wrong, good and bad, black and white, appearance and reality) may both be correct at the same time. This reactive flexibility regarding the circumstantial nature of events may derive from religious or philosophical sources, superstition, or a combination of all three. It is based on humility regarding the (limited) power of the individual and an innate respect for the collective group, the forces of nature, and the "circular" rhythm of events (seasons, birth, death). Reactive people seek less to control events than to live in conformity with them (natural forces, historical developments, past precedents).

At the personal level, reactive people are polite and accommodating, prioritizing harmony of views over winning arguments. They invite interlocutors – especially foreign ones – to speak first and give their viewpoint. This enables them to modify their own stance and give a reply that will perhaps be less controversial or adversarial than an opening statement might have been. Reactives "look before they leap" and generally seek gradualist solutions, as opposed to linear-active quick "logical" ones or multi-active inspirational ones.

The communication challenge

One of the chief tasks of a team leader is to align the differing views of the members of the team. Certainly they must attempt to reconcile divergent values (such as directness vs. diplomacy, punctuality vs. a flexible attitude to time, scientific vs. contextual truth, and so on), but as the team will in the main be functioning orally, their first task will be to harmonize the communication styles prevalent in the three categories. Modes of communication are more readily visible (and audible) than core values; they present an initial, immediate problem to deal with and solve. However, with a little perspicacious guidance, team members are generally readier to adapt their modes of address than to abandon deeply rooted values.

———◆———

The three cultural anchorages correspond fairly closely to the three cultural categories. Within each category there is general agreement about how one organizes life and about what is important, very important, or, alternatively, trivial. Germans, Americans, and Norwegians see step-by-step planning as productive. Few Italians, Arabs, and Africans would ignore the importance of compassion. Face is vital to the existence of Koreans, Vietnamese, and Japanese. These categorical common denominators do vary slightly (or considerably) at the national level. The cultural habitat of Sweden is similar to that of Norway, but not quite the same. For instance, Norwegians like to think that they plan faster than Swedes. Chinese and Japanese watch their speech carefully to avoid anyone losing face, but the former are occasionally more direct than the latter, while Koreans can occasionally surprise everyone with explosive behavior. Spaniards and Italians are equally emotional about most things, but the former are touchier about national honor.

Lifestyles are grounded in the enduring cultural anchorages, but develop nuances, quirks, and idiosyncrasies as they filter down to national level, and exploit further divergence as they go through regional filters. Ethnic roots may come into play (Basques, Catalonians, Jews, Albanian Kosovars); in some countries, regional cultural traits may have geographical origins (China, Russia, United States) or historical ones (Iraq, Bavaria, Sicily, Nigeria). Some states maintain remarkably homogeneous national cultural habitats (Japan, Finland, Hungary, Australia).

Figures 1.8 and 1.9 give some examples of cultural variation in categories, sovereign states, and regions. It is useful for team leaders to know whether they are managing Castilians or Andalucians, Milanese or Neapolitans, Bavarians or Rhinelanders, Parisians or Marseillais, Californians or Kentuckians, Scots or English, mainland Chinese or ones from Singapore, Malaysia, Hong Kong, Indonesia, Thailand, or Canada!

English	British Celts	Milan	Sicily
cool	emotional	cult of efficiency	cult of loyalty
coded speech	direct speech	affinity with Germanics	affinity with Africa
class conscious	rather classless	big corporations	clans, cliques
factual	artistic	meritocratic advancement	patronage system
phlegmatic	romantic	scornful of south	defends own system well
poor linguists	good linguists	high-tech	agricultural
empire builders	emigrated to settle	law abiding	authorities co-exist with Mafia

Figure 1.8 Examples of regional agendas

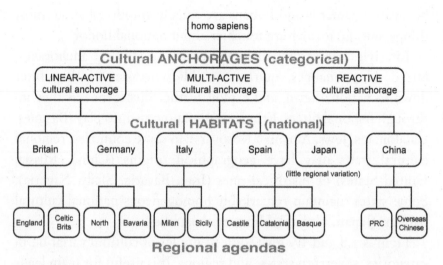

Figure 1.9 Cultural anchorages, cultural habitats, and regional agendas

CASE STUDIES

The following case studies illustrate how two famous international companies faced the issue of cultural diversity in mergers and acquisitions. Americans and Germans both fall broadly into the linear-active category, but DaimlerChrysler failed ostentatiously in training its staff to cope with different cultural styles and habitats. KONE, on the other hand, exhibited singular adeptness at synergizing Finnish cultural traits with those of the numerous foreign firms it acquired.

DaimlerChrysler

In 1998 when the impending merger of Daimler-Benz and Chrysler was announced, it heralded the biggest cross-border industrial merger ever. The rationale was obvious. Chrysler was perennially third in the Detroit Big Three and, despite heroic efforts by CEO Lee Iacocca to revitalize the company, it struggled to maintain its productivity and world ranking. Daimler-Benz – more prestigious and dynamic – was essentially a specialist producer of premium saloons and had made few efforts to widen its product range and customer base.

The amalgamation of the two companies produced an industrial giant with global sales of more than $150 billion, making it fifth among the world's car manufacturers. It was to be a shining example of what globalization could achieve for an adventurous group combining two well-established brand names. A smooth integration of the two famous corporations would enable the group to meet the demands of nearly all segments of the car market, and sales could be expected to increase exponentially.

That phrase "smooth integration" was a key challenge to Daimler-Chrysler as well as the route to success. Certain elements of the Daimler-Benz management were awake to the problems likely to arise in uniting German and American executives and workforces at various levels of activity and responsibility, since German and American mindsets and worldviews differ sharply. There are worse cross-cultural mismatches, but there are also better ones. Wisely, Daimler-Benz appointed a senior executive, Andreas Renschler, to supervise the integration. He had worked for several years in the United States and was sufficiently well versed in both cultures to foresee and hopefully circumvent the cultural difficulties that would undoubtedly present themselves.

We had worked with Mercedes executives and teams in the years between 1975 and 1995. Andreas Renschler contacted Richard Lewis Communications and arranged an initial meeting in Stuttgart to discuss training programs for executives who would be involved in the early stages of cross-border activity. We sent a three-person team to the headquarters in Sindelfingen, two of our English consultants who had lived in Germany and one German-American who flew in from New York. We spent the whole day with Renschler, an experienced and mature individual with a good grasp of cross-cultural issues and a keen insight into American and German behavioral patterns. We were joined during the day by a German HR team, assembled specifically to facilitate the merger.

Communication styles

We made a presentation predicting the likely obstacles in the way of developing a quick understanding. In the early stages of the merger, differences in communication styles would be the first major hurdles to be surmounted. In Germany the primary purpose of speech is to give and receive information. Americans are also factual, but use speech emphatically to give opinions and are more persuasive than Germans. In this respect they often employ hype, which Germans instinctively react against. Americans tend to evince optimism and put forward best scenarios. Germans are more comfortable with a cautious, somewhat pessimistic view that envisages worst scenarios. They want a lot of context before approaching any important decision. The let's-get-on-with-it attitude of the Americans often increases German caution. "Yes, but what happens if…?" is a typically German attitude. Americans are anxious to expound the grand strategy and mop up the details later. They seek simplification of issues to clarify their route to action. Germans have a tendency to complicate discussion ("life is not simple, you know").

Germans' formality is evident in their style of communication. When meeting strangers, they usually enter a room with a serious look on their face, contrasting with the broad Hollywood smiles of the Americans. At this stage Germans may seem stiff and distant to Americans. Surnames are used for years and full titles are expected. Americans go for first names from the start and have an informal way of conducting a discussion, using slang, irony, and kidding, which disconcerts most Germans, especially senior ones. Germans are used to asking serious questions to which they expect serious answers. Americans, fond of humor, often reply in a rather flippant or casual manner. Germans fail to appreciate jokes, wisecracks, or sarcasm during a business discussion. Germans are not fond of small talk and often find Americans chatty. Charismatic Americans view Germans as lacking in charisma and perhaps dull. Germans in fact distrust charisma and instant smiles. As they generally think in silence, they are not sure how to react when Americans think aloud. Are they offering statements or suggestions, or are they try-ing to make their own mind up? Brainstorming is popular with Americans but less so with Germans, who would be reluctant to speak out in front of a superior. German ideas are expressed guard-edly with considerable caution. American speech is quick, mobile, opportunistic. Germans seldom argue with a colleague's remarks. Americans prefer a free-for-all discussion. Their speech is loaded with clichés ("Let's get this show on the road," "I can't fly this by the seat of my pants") or tough talk ("I tell you I can walk away from this deal"); both of these are absent from German speech. American agreements are usually reached by persistent persuasion in open discussion; Germans find agreement through thorough analysis of details, leading to clarification and justification.

Listening habits, too, are part of the communication process. How would Germans and Americans listen to each other? The American audience demands initial entertainment and tends to lis-ten in snatches if they are not amused. The next phase is: "What's new?" Time is money so get on with it. Don't complicate issues – tell it like it is! Slogans and catchphrases are readily absorbed by Americans; Germans don't use them.

The German listener does not yet wish to know about the pres-ent; the past must come first. Consequently, all the context leading up to the deal must be gone into. When this need has been satis-fied, then one can describe the present situation, before edging cautiously forward. Questions in the mind of the German listener are: "Does this sound too simple?" "What happens if...?" "Am I getting the hard sell?" "Aren't we rushing into things?" "Can I have more (technical) information, please?"

Other differences

Diversity in communication styles was likely to lead to early mis-understandings in the merger, but later procedural and structural differences would raise their heads. US corporations usually have strictly centralized reporting. Large German companies often fea-ture decentralization and compartmentalization. Each department reports vertically to its head. Horizontal communication across departments at different levels is practically taboo. Departmental rivalry is much more acute than in the US. In this area, German managers tend to be extremely touchy. Americans are more thick-skinned. Americans go from office to office in a gregarious manner. German offices are strongholds of privacy, usually with doors shut. American managers chase their staff around the building exchanging views ("Say, Jack, I've just had a great idea"). Germans, by contrast, like to do the job on their own, no monitoring until the end of the day. American managers like to shower good executives with praise ("You're doing a heckuva job!"). German staff expect no praise from the boss; they are paid to do the job efficiently.

Germans are class conscious. Senior managers are usually intellectuals. In classless America intellectuals are often called "eggheads." American managers speak out loud. Senior Germans command in a low voice. Americans prize spontaneity, flexibility, and adaptability in reaching their goals. Germans give pride of place to well-tested procedures and processes. If these structures have brought the company so far, why change things?

Renschler and the Mercedes training officers concurred with the points made in our presentation. What should be done in terms of training to facilitate the merger? Our basic reply was that many mergers fail because neither side is sufficiently versed in the historical values, core beliefs, communication patterns, behavioral habits, and worldview of the other. Training would address these issues systematically according to the model we would put forward. An important target in such training is to make one side like the other, which transcends simple knowledge of the other culture.

It was agreed that we would refine our training model to fit the proposed merger of the two companies and would return to Stuttgart a month later with a detailed program.

The training model

When we returned the following month, Renschler had assembled a somewhat larger HR team (six or seven people), including one professor from "DaimlerChrysler University."

They had formed executive teams to tackle various projects in the merger. In Stuttgart the teams consisted largely of Germans, with a sprinkling of Americans and British. Other teams, with more American members, were being formed in Detroit.

Our model envisaged a six-month training period in which teams would be exposed to full-day seminars, workshops, special briefings, and a home-study program. We formalize cross-cultural studies under the following subheadings:

Culture – general

✦ Religion
✦ Cultural classification
✦ Languages
✦ Values and core beliefs
✦ Cultural black holes
✦ Concept of space
✦ Concept of time
✦ Self-image

Culture – communication

✦ Communication patterns and use of language
✦ Listening habits
✦ Audience expectations
✦ Body language and nonverbal communication

Culture – interaction

✦ Concept of status
✦ Position of women
✦ Leadership style

❖ Language of management
❖ Motivation factors
❖ General behavior at meetings
❖ Negotiating characteristics
❖ Contracts and commitments
❖ Manners and taboos
❖ How to empathize

Renschler and his committee were sufficiently pleased with the program. It was agreed that 50–60 percent of the activity would be carried out in Stuttgart, with the aim of familiarizing the largely German teams with American mindsets and business culture, and similar "mirror" seminars would be held in Detroit to help Americans understand Germans. The emphasis throughout would be the fostering of a favorable view of the foreign partner.

As we all agreed on general principles, we discussed a starting date with Renschler. In view of the urgency of the consummation of the merger, he was anxious to begin as soon as possible. There was only one obstacle: the program would first have to be approved by DaimlerChrysler University. The professor on our committee promised to submit the proposal the following week. Soon after, Renschler changed jobs. We never heard from DaimlerChrysler again.

The aftermath

Five years later, after addressing the annual conference of the G100 group in New York, I attended a cocktail party hosted by Jack Welch and Raymond Gilmartin. At this function I met a German DaimlerChrysler board member who had been one of the first Germans to be sent to the United States, where he had worked from 1998 to 2003. He gave me an account of what happened after the merger was completed. The time taken by DaimlerChrysler University to consider the content of a cross-cultural training program resulted in most executive teams being sent from Stuttgart to the United States with no training at all. The cultural clashes we had forecast in 1998 took place in the first few months of joint operations. Differing behavioral habits and attitudes irritated both sides; a situation that was exacerbated by maintenance of the fiction that the amalgamation was a merger of equals while in fact it was nothing of the sort. Daimler could not afford a merger with a jointly owned company based in the Netherlands, since this would have triggered a huge tax charge. This meant that Chrysler had to become part of a German *Aktiengesellschaft*. It was in fact a quiet takeover, in compensation for which the Chrysler shareholders were paid a 28 percent premium over the then market price. Keeping the merger story going was relatively harmless in itself, except that American staff continued to believe that there would be "joint control." It took years to achieve any measure of integration of the two different ways of working. Neither side had been given time or training to study the other's mindset.

It is true that the Germans learned to be less formal and to cut down on paperwork; the Americans, for their part, learned more discipline in their meetings and decision making. German and American commonalities such as work ethic, bluntness, lack of tact, a linear approach to tasks and time, punctuality, following agendas, results orientation, and emphasis on competitive prices and reliable delivery dates created a potential modus operandi, but the two different mindsets led to irritation and misunderstanding on both sides.

The German board member listed dozens of incidents. He opined that the Americans he was working with showed a complete lack of understanding of German values, methods, and working culture. They found that Germans shook hands too much, were often too intense, and followed rigid manuals and rule books that deflated American spontaneity. German meetings were boring, American meetings were exciting; the German drive toward conformity clashed with American invention, innovation, and opportunism. Germans adhered to old traditions and well-tried procedures; Americans preferred a DIY ambience. The Germans who stayed on sought deep friendships, not segmented ones like the Americans (tennis friend, bridge friend, drinking friend, and so on). Americans got annoyed by the German habit of offering constructive criticism. Half the time Germans and Americans just talked past each other. Germans took long holidays, unthinkable in American eyes, especially when there was a crisis, but when difficulties arose, who was in control?

For a year the group had two chairmen, Jurgen Schrempp from Daimler and Bob Eaton, who had been boss of Chrysler. Within a year Eaton was fired and his American successor lasted less than 12 months. DaimlerChrysler's share price fell from $108 in January 1999 to $38 in November 2000. Nobody was quite sure how the combined companies should be run. Cultural differences led to divisions of opinion and methods at all levels. In German eyes, Chrysler was a company with problems in every department, not least productivity. Each vehicle took Chrysler 40 hours to make; Honda and Toyota produce a car every 20 hours. The Germans, with their emphasis on quality, found Chrysler quality control way out of line. Even worse, there was no plan in place to improve it. Chrysler swung from a profit of $2.5 billion in the first half of the merger year to a loss of $2 billion in the second.

The German solution was to import a crack German executive, Dieter Zetsche, to apply German principles to the problem. He set a target of 30 hours per vehicle in 2007; in a five-year plan he slashed spending from $42 billion to $28 billion; he brought new models forward six months more quickly; he shut six factories and cut 45,000 jobs, one third of the total.

Under Zetsche's efficient control, in 2006 Chrysler was perhaps the healthiest car company in Detroit. However, a second important factor emerged from the troublesome acquisition of the American company. The Germans had made the initial mistake that, in order not to be seen as heavy-handed, they had "stayed away" from Detroit. For this reason it took them two years to get to grips with the American company's fragility. Then, when Zetsche concentrated all out on rescuing his ailing colleague, Daimler itself slipped badly. Neglect led to its reputation for quality being dented by unfavorable consumer reports and the company's move down market into Smart cars piled up huge losses.

Ironically, Zetsche himself was moved back to Germany to assume control of the whole group. It was now the turn of the German end of the DaimlerChrysler group to undergo painful restructuring, similar to that which took place in the last four to five years in Detroit. Zetsche joked that since a Chrysler boss (himself) was now running the show in Stuttgart, everyone could at last see clearly that it was a takeover.

KONE

KONE is a highly successful Finnish manufacturer of elevators and escalators. Today over 50 percent of the company's sales come from maintenance and modernization of elevators, escalators, and automatic doors. It embarked on an ambitious program of internationalization at the beginning of the 1970s, buying elevator companies in France (Westinghouse), Germany, Belgium, Italy, Spain, and Austria. It was the first Finnish company to internationalize on a big scale, though Nokia soon followed. The company was controlled principally by the Herlin family. Pekka Herlin and his son Antti are two of the best-known figures in Finnish industry. The current CEO, Matti Alahuhta, is a former prominent Nokia board member who joined KONE in 2005.

In the 1990s, KONE's state-of-the-art machine-roomless Monospace elevator technology was the envy of companies around the world and became sought after by numerous enterprises. One of these was Toshiba, a giant Japanese conglomerate in the field of consumer electronics. Toshiba had long been a household name in Japan and produced everything from advanced electronic and electrical products, information and communications equipment and systems, electronic components, and materials to household appliances. It also produced elevators, but in this area Toshiba was small compared with *keiretsu* rivals such as Hitachi and Mitsubishi, which enjoyed dominant positions in the Japanese elevator market. It had of course occurred to Toshiba that if it could obtain exclusive use of KONE's technology in Japan, it could make rapid

inroads into the market and soon become a big player in a country famous for its extensive construction activities and burgeoning
skyscrapers. KONE, for its part, was well aware of the power of
the Toshiba name and its financial muscle, which would greatly
facilitate KONE's entry into a difficult market.

Initial contacts between the two companies began as early as
1995, when KONE agreed to supply Toshiba with hydraulic elevators for the Japanese market. An early boost to Finnish–Japanese
relations in the industry occurred when the Tokyo Metropolitan
Subway construction company ordered 57 KONE Monospace elevators for a new subway line to be constructed in Tokyo. KONE
supplied the elevators, both companies cooperated on the installa-
tion, and Toshiba took responsibility for maintenance.

Clearly, a joint venture or at least some form of technical agreement beckoned. In 1998, Toshiba invited KONE to send a team
out to Tokyo to discuss possibilities. KONE's executive board,
who rarely did things by halves, decided to go almost en bloc. I
was invited to accompany them as cultural adviser. Three or four
engineers made up the party. The then KONE chairman, Anssi
Soila, led the group, which also included Klaus Cawén, the head
of M&A and Strategic Alliances, who, like the Herlins and myself,
was a keen yachtsman. KONE executive board members included
English, French, German, and Swedish speakers. No one except
myself spoke Japanese, although I made it clear that I would not
use my less than perfect Japanese in any negotiation. Toshiba, in
any case, would carry out the talks in English.

On my advice, Soila agreed to avoid meeting any Toshiba representatives during our first full day in Tokyo, where we were comfortably installed in the Okura Hotel. He telephoned the MD of
Toshiba Lifts, announcing our arrival, and suggested a brief cocktail encounter on the following day around 6 pm. This gave us
almost two full days to rehearse our line of approach and procedural tone, so important in far eastern business.

The dozen of us sat all day in one of the Okura's meeting rooms,
going over the rituals and pitfalls of the Japanese business scene.
The advice I gave them was the same as the routine instructions we

gave for five years to visiting US delegations when I was committee chairman for the American Chamber of Commerce in Japan (ACCJ). It went as follows.

A Japanese company with which you envisage doing business in Japan, whether it be in the form of a joint venture, merger, acquisition, or a technical or trading relationship, will have no desire to start talking business with you soon after arrival. For the first day or two, its main concern is to see that you are comfortably accommodated and have the chance to settle down quietly in a strange environment.

The second or third day after your arrival, the Japanese company will invite you to lunch or dinner at its expense and at a venue of its choosing. There will be a choice of Japanese or western food. The meal will last almost exactly two hours and the Japanese will conclude it by standing up and thanking you for coming. During this first meal or meeting, you must on no account discuss business. There might be the vaguest reference to a future relationship, but in fact it is better if you say nothing at all in this respect.

The purpose of this first meeting, especially given its social nature, is for the Japanese side to have a look at you and begin the slow process of "getting to know you." Their conversation will consist of a string of platitudes that have no meaning except to contribute to the harmony of the occasion. You are also expected to say pleasant things to them – golf, sport in general, weather, celebrities, architecture, art, and culture are all safe subjects. The more mundane the conversation, the better. *What* you say has no importance; *how*, *when*, and *why* you say it are noted more carefully. The Japanese side will be watching you more closely than listening to you. Facial expressions, body language, and general manners – especially courtesy and gentleness – will automatically be noted. Even your physical characteristics will be recorded. Japanese can be uncomfortable sitting close to westerners who are too big, too hairy, or with carrot-colored hair. At all events, what they are doing is trying to make up their minds whether they feel at ease with you and whether they believe they can do business with you over the next 20 years. They think long term.

I told the KONE group that they had several strong cards in their hand. Finns are quiet (almost as much as Japanese), are modest and hardly ever pushy. They are able to convey an air of reliability, even when they remain silent (which the Japanese enjoy). They are not as palpably courteous as the Japanese (who is?), but this is only because they are often too direct in their pronouncements for Asian tastes. However, the Japanese are used to this from their dealings with Americans. Finns are good listeners, which wins many points in Japan. They are also relatively patient. Finnish body language is somewhat similar to Japanese (minimal, virtually nonexistent) and this also puts the Japanese at ease (they get alarmed at Latin or Arab gesturing). In other words, I told them, behave in the quiet manner that is typical of you.

When the second, slightly more formal meeting with Toshiba arrives, don't launch into negotiation even then. On this occasion one acknowledges that there is possibly an agreement in the offing, and that perhaps there are good prospects of fruitful cooperation, but this must be referred to as background scenery, not looked into in any detail at this point. In the ACCJ we found it almost impossible to stop American teams discussing profits, market share, or mechanics of control at the second (and even first!) meeting. This is the American man-of-action way. The Finns are also men of action, but they found no difficulty in putting the brakes on their approach. They even liked the Japanese style.

The KONE team that was drinking in this advice did not consist entirely of Finns. It was one of the most diversified groups I have worked with at board level and consequently was admirably equipped to combine worldviews and perspectives. Its members were as follows:

✦ Anssi Soila, President
✦ Lauri Björklund, SVP, Purchasing and Manufacturing
✦ Klaus Cawén, SVP, General Counsel (Finn-Swede)
✦ Michel Chartron, SVP, Service Business (French)
✦ Jean-Pierre Chauvarie, Area director, Europe (French)
✦ Jussi Itävuori, SVP, Human Resources and Communication

- Raine-Peter Joutsen, SVP, New Elevator Business (Finn-Swede)
- Pekka Kemppainen, SVP, Technology
- Heiko Körnich, SVP, Escalator Business (German)
- Trevor Nink, Managing Director, KONE Elevators Australia (Australian)
- Neil Padden, Area Director, Asia Pacific (British)
- Aimo Rajahalme, SVP, Finance
- Helena Terho, SVP, Quality
- Stefan Björkman, Managing Director, KONE Japan (Finn-Swede)

In the ample time we had available, I was able to describe in some detail to the KONE team the different stages of the Japanese approach to negotiation and reaching agreement. There is a series of preliminaries that must be gone through with sizable Japanese companies:

- The Japanese side hosts visitors at lunch or dinner. Present will be the "contact man" who will attend all meetings. There may be an interpreter and one senior VP. No business is discussed.
- A preliminary meeting with the contact man plus several (new) probably technical Japanese. The background to the deal is discussed in a tentative manner, covering such topics as the market in general, its current state, and competition.
- The first long meeting at which a very senior Japanese will be present, possibly the president if the western company is considered important enough. The purpose of this meeting is to establish the relative status of the major actors on both sides. Being tested are personal reputation and connections, company reputation and connections, size, compatibility, who are opposite numbers, who and what are best, levels of courtesy, pecking order, skill in face protection. The Japanese seek to find out which westerner is best to deal with.
- The next meeting is the one that westerners would regard as the first real business meeting. It is largely technical, inasmuch as the mechanics of cooperation and progress are discussed (still

in a rather tentative manner). Obstacles and possible difficulties
are raised at this point (politely by the Japanese, more openly
and directly by westerners).

✧ The fifth meeting may be a prolongation of the fourth, but is
most likely separate. This is for position taking. The Japanese
will try to establish the western side's position on the main principles, areas of difficulty, and possible sensitive issues. What are
the sticking points? The westerners are asked to state their position first and the Japanese will modify theirs to suit.

✧ Negotiating can begin based on each side's knowledge of the
other's positions. Westerners will try to establish who is right
or wrong, what is good or bad. Japanese steer away from these
(sweeping, hard-and-fast) concepts, not normally seeking western logic. Instead, their thought moves toward an objective in a
sort of spiral. Westerners are confused by frequent non sequi-
turs. Westerners use argument and counter-argument, evidence,
facts and explanation, tackling problems and seeking solutions.
Japanese avoid taking sides, counter-argument, and any kind of
confrontation. They seek agreement not by proving a point but
by "zoning in," in ever-decreasing circles, on what appears to be
a mutually congenial state of affairs. Argument itself, in Japanese
eyes, is seen as a scattered number of points that, through discussion, gradually converge and eventually unify.

This last area proves most difficult in general for Finns. Their
tough history has given them a keen sense of right and wrong, so
they need to adapt to the Japanese way of thinking. However, a
strong Finnish concept is that you don't twist anyone's arm or try
to impose your will on someone else. This principle is shared by
the Japanese.

The KONE team consisted of a balanced group of individuals
who were both perspicacious and experienced. Like many Finnish
business people, they were open to new ideas and concepts, unencumbered by the manuals, systems, or bureaucratic rigidities typical
of some traditional European firms. They could "think outside the
box." Finns are noted for their frequent originality, inventiveness,

and willingness to accept (and perhaps modify) ideas from others. KONE, with its technical innovations and forward-looking executives, has been able to turn out effective international teams whenever the need has arisen.

The subsequent meeting with Toshiba went well and, after going through the various rituals described above, the two companies agreed to form a strategic alliance. As a first step, KONE granted a license to Toshiba to manufacture machine-roomless elevators in Japan based on KONE's Monospace technology.

The alliance was not long in bearing fruit. The KONE team had its eyes not only on the Japanese market, but on Asian markets as a whole. In 1999, one year after clinching the strategic alliance, Toshiba won an order to supply 61 elevators and 50 escalators to the world's tallest building, the Taipei Financial Center in Taiwan. In addition to the world's fastest elevators designed and manufactured by Toshiba, the delivery included 37 elevators powered by the coveted KONE MX40 and MX100 elevator-hoisting machines.

The KONE team has always shown willingness to learn from the company's partners, too. They agreed to start using Toshiba inverters for their own high-rise elevators, and soon after collaborated closely in product development to launch an innovative global escalator.

Cooperation continued apace. In 2001 the two firms signed an agreement to strengthen the strategic alliance through an exchange of shares in KONE Corporation and Toshiba Elevator and Building Systems (TELC). KONE acquired a 20 percent share in TELC, which acquired a 5 percent share in KONE. Board directors were exchanged and the forward-looking Klaus Cawén and Pekka Kemppainen joined the TELC board.

In 2005 a joint venture company, KONE TELC Industries Co. Ltd (KTI), was formed to manufacture escalators jointly in China. KONE owned 70 percent of KTI and TELC 30 percent.

In 2008, 10 double-deck elevators were installed in the Broadgate Tower in London. These were the first double-deck elevators in the world to utilize KONE's Destination Control System. After this start, KONE won major double-deck elevator projects in Shanghai, Abu Dhabi, London, and Chengdu. Further success in Japan followed the latest MX hoisting machine versions matching new Japanese safety codes. Big strategic issues in the alliance continued to be considered.

KONE celebrated its 100th birthday in 2010. What enabled a tiny Finnish company to develop into one of the few global players still going strong after four decades of ruthless consolidation and merging the elevator and escalator industry? From where emanated the courage to take on the once-undisputed giants in the field in the USA, Germany, Switzerland, and elsewhere?

The answer is found to some extent in the foresight, toughness (*sisu*), long-term planning, and pragmatic focus of the Herlin family, who for four generations took the company through two world wars and numerous industrial depressions. Their worldwide success could, however, not have been achieved without the ultra-keen, international outlook that has characterized the company since the 1950s, and especially from 1968 to the present. The international team I collaborated with on the 1998 Toshiba venture opened my eyes to this particular KONE strength (exercised at executive board level). Figure 1.10 illustrates KONE's ongoing commitment to this approach.

Of course, Nokia followed this example and its global success is only too well documented, but KONE's early lead in committing itself to international exploration and growth, principally through acquisition, has few parallels not only in the Nordic region, but in the world at large. (Naturally, acquisitions made in the twentieth century by American conglomerates outnumber all others, but they were largely on account of financial muscle, whereas KONE started acquiring rivals considerably larger than itself.)

KONE shocked the Finnish business community in 1968 when it bought Asea-Graham, Scandinavia's market leader in elevators. Acquisitions in France, Germany, Austria, Spain, and the UK followed rapidly, leading up to the purchase of Westinghouse Europe in 1975. In 1979, after this intense period of internationalization, 80 percent of KONE's revenue came from abroad! I was involved with the company's international training at the time and its

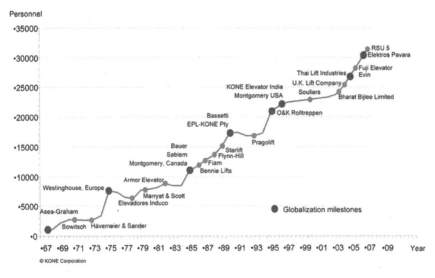

Figure 1.10   KONE: Growth through acquisitions

executives were whizzing in and out of our language training center as if it had a revolving door.

Training was only one of KONE's secrets. From the outset its acquisition teams approached purchased companies with humility, in line with the Finnish trait of being willing to learn from others. Not only was KONE in some cases buying firms larger than itself, its executives, like many Finns, had a healthy respect for the positions and achievements of companies belonging to bigger economies than Finland. Consequently, they made it a principle to give considerable leeway to local management. "Local excellence" became one of their slogans, giving credit to the people on the spot in terms of knowing the market and local idiosyncrasies in commerce. KONE managers did not arrive with the heavy feet typical of many of their US or German counterparts. Finnish international teams have a reputation for being not only humble but also agile and adaptable.

Growth from acquisitions meant that KONE also imported cultural baggage along with the company operations. Local managers were respected, retained, and often fully integrated in the adventurous KONE mentality. The aim was to be the "best in town," and local excellence backed with "global resources" became the firm's organizational philosophy. As early as 1972, Herlin stated, "there is no way that problems spread all over the world can be solved from Helsinki." The company's respectful approach maintained much of the touch and feel of the best features of acquired companies and certainly minimized customer flight.

The acquisition strategy had many merits. The number of competitors was reduced. KONE's private ownership avoided bureaucratic delays. KONE's management is essentially nimble, frequently profiting from economies of scale. These were enhanced by the acquisition of companies with similar technical issues: cranes, container handling, load handling, forest machinery, shipboard cargo handling. After the purchase of Montgomery and O&K Rolltreppen, KONE found itself the world leader in the supply of escalators and auto-walks (with a 20 percent global market share). Service and maintenance divisions, based on the Finnish reputation for quality, have contributed significantly to KONE's profitability. "Care for life" is its slogan in this area.

As the first non-Japanese lift company to penetrate Japan and then China, KONE made a big hit and took a new direction. For instance, half of all escalator orders in the world now originate in Asia, where KONE's Kunshan factory is continually being expanded. The company's ability to retain its preeminence in its cluster of industries is unquestionably due to its creation of enterprising international teams that greatly strengthen cooperation between local outfits (China and France, for example) and global HR.

Matti Alahuhta, KONE's dynamic CEO, who joined the company from Nokia in 2005, touched on the human elements of collaboration where Finnish humility and relaxed management gained the trust of other nationals. The cooperation between local and global teams was made very close and intensive and best practices were shared everywhere. This led to rapid acceleration of growth, for instance in China, where one Finn and one American worked hand in glove with a raft of Chinese managers. Nationality within KONE does not count, Alahuhta pointed out, adding that humor is often introduced in team meetings. In his view, it was important also to *have fun*!

2

Organizing the Team

International teams offer great potential. Their cultural mix provides broader perspectives and more varied insights than a team composed of individuals of one nationality. However, this diversity, by its very richness, makes the group's dynamics more complex. The choice, organization, and mission statement of such teams require careful thought and attention.

First, what is the team's *raison d'être*? What is it supposed to accomplish and over what timescale? How and by whom are the members chosen and how big should the team be? In *Team Roles at Work*, Meredith Belbin offers definite views on this: a small team of strategic managers should service a large number of semiautonomous units run by teams of operational managers. When, where, and how often should the team meet? Should meetings be one or two days, or more? Are there deadlines for achieving objectives? How much autonomy is the team granted? When choosing the team, what criteria are used: professional mix and competence, a rich nationality mix? Will membership keep changing or will it be fairly static?

Once a team has been formed, its modus operandi must be decided. What kind of leader is required – in Belbin's terms, solo leader or team leader? Does the position of chair rotate or not? Who assigns roles and responsibilities? Will each team member have a definite team role or will versatility be preferred? Will there be some seniority among team members? Will the chair be responsible for reporting to HQ? Is the chair closer to HQ or to the team? What can be done together? What can be done between meetings? Are there meetings "outside the meetings" (*à la* Brussels or the UN)? How are the above activities integrated? Does the team spend time socializing before a meeting?

Does the team work to agendas? Who draws them up? How strict are they? Are digressions allowed? How about interrupting

the speaker? Which communication style will prevail: formal/
informal/first or family names/titles/use of humor and so on?
How diplomatic or frank will discussion be? How will decisions be
reached? How will conflicts be resolved? Will brainstorming sessions be a feature? How about internal feedback? How much can
one challenge or contradict the chair? How much autonomy does
the team have from HQ? What happens if HQ disagrees with or
negates the team's conclusions? Who keeps the minutes? What is
each member's vision of success? Will the communication style be
low context (explicit, as in the USA or Germany) or high context
(implicit, as in France or Japan)?

The chair

The modus operandi of a team will probably be influenced by the
nationality of the chair or team leader. Americans will require low-
context discussions with things "spelled out," as they are wont to
say. German chairs will also be low context, elaborating on difficulties when they feel it necessary. French people regard meetings as
occasions where one airs one's views and examines all perspectives.
A French chair will lean toward theoretical discussion, sometimes
disregarding facts that do not fit in with the theories. British chairs
see themselves as arbitrators and take pains to seek wide agreement among team members. They also tend to inject humor into
the conversation and may be seen as somewhat vague and unclear.
Like the Japanese, they tend to hint at what they would like done
rather than give instructions or make forceful recommendations.
Japanese team leaders prioritize harmony over frank discussion
and are not suited to controlling vigorous or controversial proposals made by Dutch, American, or French colleagues. The same
applies to the Chinese, although they can show wisdom and, in the
case of Singaporean or Hong Kong Chinese, sophistication born
of experience. Australian chairs are essentially practical, exercise
easy-going control, and make it clear that colleagues shouldn't take
things too seriously. They also may display occasional irreverence

toward HQ. Canadians and South Africans often lead in a laid-back manner, particularly the former. Swedes pursue consensus at all times, and Finns prioritize economy of expression, being excellent summarizers. Italians and Spaniards, by contrast, are eloquent (wordy) and like to empathize with all (remain popular). The Swiss control meetings well, sometimes coming across as a little fussy. Belgians talk of compromise.

Chairs from all countries may be atypical of their nationality – the more experienced among them will have developed a hybrid cultural stance and show skill in adapting to the views of colleagues. The ideal chair should know first of all the idiosyncrasies of their own culture and perceive how that may affect their view of others. For instance, Finns think that all foreigners talk far too much and the Japanese see the rest of the world as discourteous and impolite, but executives from these countries soon achieve maturity in their judgment of others by being aware of their own blind spots and possible shortcomings.

Knowing their own culture will enable a team leader to appreciate the differences, strengths, and weaknesses of others. It helps if leaders are bi- or trilingual. The more languages they speak, the broader will be their perspective. It is not unusual for Nordic, Dutch, Belgian, and Swiss team members to speak or understand half a dozen tongues. Multilingual chairs are likely to be understanding, tolerant of other worldviews, broad-minded, and charismatic. One might call them international psychologists. Such leaders are able to think in multidimensional terms and deal successfully with ambiguities.

Multilingual or not, the chair must be skilled at utilizing others' diverse strengths, anticipating difficulties and having solutions for them up their sleeve. They may come across as a strong or consultative leader, but they must always be seen as fair and a good listener. One of their tasks is to balance their stance toward both the team and HQ. In front of team members it is best if their attitude to HQ is seen as benign (and loyal) but also critical. They must gain acceptance as team leader through exercising empathy and indicating an unwavering cultural sensitivity. Cultural sensitivity has been defined as the ability to discriminate and experience relevant cultural differences. This leads to inter-cultural competence, which means that the leader's discriminatory skill enables them to communicate effectively no matter which way they are facing in a cross-cultural situation. Some managers possess or acquire cultural intelligence, indicating an outsider's seemingly natural ability to interpret someone's unfamiliar, idiosyncratic, and ambiguous behavior in the same way as a compatriot would.

All of the above is a tall order for leaders of international teams. The compensation for their efforts and diligence is that, if they are brilliant at what they do, they may one day lead the company. There is no better training for that.

Integration

Some teams integrate more quickly than others – usually three or four meetings are enough to enable team members to settle down in terms of goals, ambitions, and procedural style. Much depends, naturally, on the composition of the group and the interplay between different national habits. It is not unreasonable to assume that individuals from similar or almost identical cultures would find little difficulty in resonating with each other, while people from very dissimilar cultures would find it harder to align their views. Surprisingly, a considerable amount of research has been carried out in the last few years revealing that the opposite is often the case.

Why should it be as difficult (or more difficult) to adjust to a similar culture than to a dissimilar one? It seems that someone entering a well-known diverse culture (such as an American going to Japan) will "brace themselves" for cultural shock and for a while enjoy discovering that what they had been told was actually true. They may also be able to create for themselves what Erik Cohen calls an "environment bubble," surrounding themselves with compatriots to share and perhaps soften the so-called culture shock. The American Club in Tokyo, with its compound shape of restaurant and bar, swimming pool, cinema, and social activities, is a good example. It is also not unknown for the host society to show patience and encouragement to "guests in their country," at least for a while. Novelty is always interesting – until it wears off.

On the other hand, people meeting others from a very similar culture (Swedes and Norwegians, Americans and Canadians) may be convinced that their neighbor's behavior will be more or less identical to their own and experience sudden shock when, having to deal with the full social reality of the location, they discover that it is not. The lack of success of Canadian retailers in the USA is held up as an example of how laid-back attitudes irritate a public more attuned to aggressive service. Nordic members of international teams such as those in Nordea (the Scandinavian bank created from Danish, Finnish, Norwegian, and Swedish banks) irritate each other when their similar cultures do not quite calibrate. They do not detect cultural differences readily, as they are not looking for them. When something grates, they tend to attribute the irritation to personal deficiencies – laziness, stinginess, stupidity, and so on. Streetwise, quickly-moving Danes look on consensus-minded Swedes as not only slow, but indecisive. Swedes often judge tight-lipped Finnish males as people who have nothing to say (overlooking their habitual reticence).

Robert Ehrnrooth, a Finnish executive with whom I was well acquainted, took his Swedish counterpart out for a slap-up dinner in Helsinki's best restaurant, serving up vintage wines, a succulent steak, and all the trimmings, expecting that he would be given a suitable break in the following morning's negotiations on the Swede's final price. He was not. He concluded that his Swedish friend was either stingy or short-sighted. Swedes cannot normally be softened up by generous entertaining the night before.

Teams that had both mainland Chinese and Hong Kong members noted that the perceived cultural closeness between them built up an expectation of easy adjustment, which, when not realized, turned into frustration and withdrawal, according to Selmer and Shiu. A study of 36 UK-based companies by Nick Forster reported that English executives had as much difficulty adjusting to similar cultures as to dissimilar ones; and another study by Selmer showed that Americans in international teams in Canada (similar) and Germany (dissimilar) did not reveal any difference in the extent of their adjustment.

While nationalities adapt in varying degrees to other national cultures, there would seem to be a stronger correlation between cultural categories. Thus Americans and Germans (dissimilar cultures) align easily in their linear-active behavior. More strikingly, Italians, Arabs, and Africans (very dissimilar cultures) all subscribe firmly to a range of multi-active characteristics such as the importance of the family, strong people and relationship orientation, compassion, emotion, loquacity, situational truth, charisma, intimate circle formation, seeking out key people for favors, intertwining business and social activities, doing several things at once, and a relaxed attitude to time. Finnish and Japanese cultures, again markedly different, both prioritize good listening, use of silence, distaste of interruption, concealing feelings, inscrutability, minimal body language, and the belief that statements are promises.

Successfully integrated international teams that react nimbly when cultures collide will gain strength from their diversity as globalization roars ahead. They represent a formula that once firmly established is unlikely to be reversed. They are here to stay – and to revolutionize international business.

Heaven and hell

At the end of the day, the success of an international team depends largely on the assignment of roles to its members. We all know the old joke about heaven being where the cooks are French, the police British, the lovers Italian, and the Germans organize everything. Hell is where the British are cooks, the Germans police, the lovers Swiss, and the Italians organize everything. A similar comparison could be made of international project teams. As Chairman of ABB Percy Barnevik once said, "Put everyone in the right place and you have a strong international corporation."

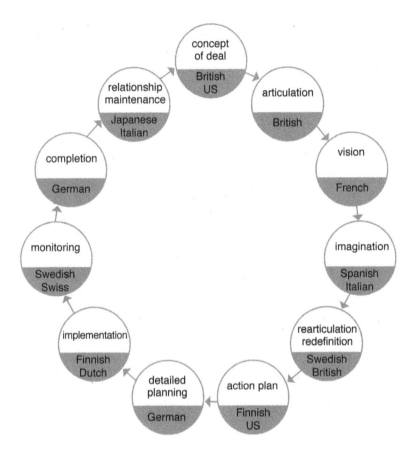

Figure 2.1 International project team 1

Figures 2.1 and 2.2 depict two imaginary international project teams. Do you have any feelings about which might be more successful? (Your opinion will, of course, depend on your nationality and personal cultural tendencies.)

CASE STUDY

When Anglo-American Rolls-Royce Marine bought Norwegian turbine maker Ullstein, it simultaneously acquired Swedish subsidiary Gustavsvik and Finnish subsidiary Rauma. The task of organizing these disparate and often conflictual units into an effective, cohesive team fell to

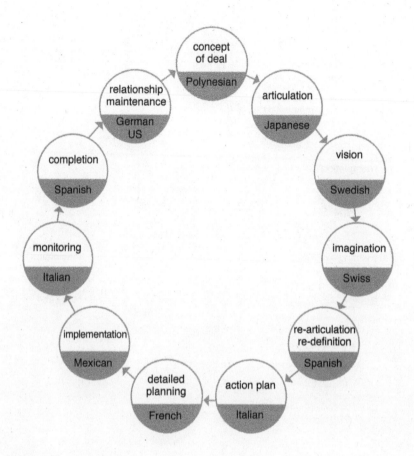

Figure 2.2 International project team 2

the charismatic RRM Chairman, Dr. Saul Lanyado, and his human resources department. It was successfully achieved over a period of six months' intensive cultural training.

Rolls-Royce Marine

While the name Rolls-Royce calls to mind luxury cars and quality aero engines, one of its powerful and profitable divisions is Rolls-Royce Marine, which produces giant turbines to power vessels of various kinds operating among the oil rigs in the North and Norwegian seas.

In 1999, Rolls-Royce Marine bought the hugely successful Norwegian company Ullstein, which had a leading position in the manufacture of turbines in a north European context. Ullstein, furthermore, had two subsidiaries in the same field – Gustavsvik in Sweden and Rauma in Finland. Rolls-Royce, in its turn, had been bought by Ford (US) and had American directors on its board.

Shortly after the takeover of Ullstein, we were contacted by the Rolls-Royce Marine training department, which wished to arrange a dinner appointment with the RRM chairman, Saul Lanyado. Subsequently I had dinner with Dr. Lanyado in the company's executive dining room in London. I found him to be a thoughtful, charismatic figure with bloodlines from several diverse cultures and a wide knowledge and experience of international business habits. He began by saying that the group was grappling with a number of culturally related problems subsequent to the takeover of the Ullstein companies.

I replied that the acquisition of Nordic managers and personnel normally would entail fewer cross-cultural issues than if the new subsidiaries had hailed from Mediterranean or Arab cultures. What problems did Rolls-Royce have with the Nordics (Norwegians, Swedes, and Finns)? Lanyado replied that the Anglos got on quite well with the Nordics, but that the Swedes, Norwegians, and Finns did not get along well with each other. As non-Nordics, both the British and American managers were unfamiliar with intra-Nordic perceptions and issues and were somewhat surprised not only at the national differences, but also at the depth of feeling that surfaced regularly on various issues.

I pointed out that the Norwegians, Finns, and Swedes (not to mention the Danes and Icelanders) had long and different histories in a European context. There had been many invasions, occupations, unions, and divorces. Denmark and Sweden have been at war with each other longer than any other two European nations (152 years). Sweden ruled Finland for over 600 years. The Nordic countries in general work well with each other at a political level (Nordic Council, cooperation inside the EU, and so on), but in international teams this high-level goodwill often disappears. Business methods, even ethical perceptions, differ, and a surprising patriotic rivalry often rears its head. There is a general consensus of opinion concerning such Protestant values as egalitarianism, honesty, punctuality, and equality for women, but the national groups differ sharply in their attitudes toward decision making, action orientation, conflict resolution, communication style, negotiating and selling techniques, outspokenness, charisma, and word–deed correlation. Communicative, confident Danes are often viewed as rather slick by Norwegians, Finns, and especially Swedes; in fact, they are not fully trusted. Action-oriented Finns are exasperated by Swedes' slow decision making and endless meetings. Norwegians admire Finnish bluntness (which is like their own), but distrust the intent of the more diplomatic Swedes and Danes.

Lanyado listened with interest to my remarks. He had several international teams and project groups playing important roles in the consolidation and interpretation of RRM, and wanted to know how we could pursue some development of harmony and mutual understanding. I suggested a day-long seminar, preceded by an after-dinner speech of 45 minutes, outlining the aims of the seminar. Participants would number 30–40 managers who were members of, or who would lead, teams or project groups where four or five nationalities were represented. The aim of the seminar would be to "make Finns, Swedes and Norwegians like each other." This is not so difficult to do, up to a point anyway, in view of the outstanding commonalities that serve as a platform. The points of friction would have to be discussed openly and analyzed. Were we discussing problems or pseudo-problems? Nordics have a lot of common sense and do not normally "go out on a limb" with overly emotive statements or policies.

The first seminar

The program was agreed and in the months that followed we organized a series of half a dozen workshops and seminars with the objectives described above. The first seminar was attended by Lanyado and involved 50–60 team managers drawn largely from the Norwegian, Swedish, and Finnish companies, with a sprinkling of British attendees and one or two Americans.

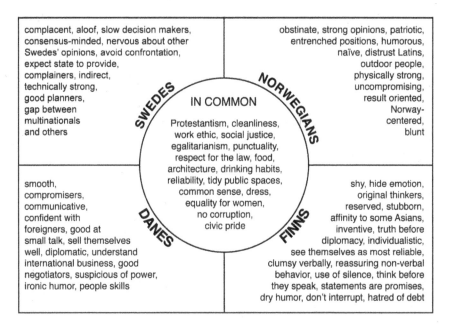

Figure 2.3   Common characteristics, Nordic countries

During the workshop, which was very interactive in character, each participant was encouraged to confront openly the sources of friction between the four major Nordic countries (including Denmark, but excluding Iceland) and to analyze the basic behavioral patterns of Swedes, Finns, Norwegians, and Danes, concentrating on the common characteristics and identifying the behavioral habits that were clearly different and might lead to dissensions.

The participants were divided into eight mixed groups and came up with an analysis, later synthesized, which resulted in the diagram in Figure 2.3.

The diagram was a catalyst for two to three hours' discussion. The commonalities were sharp and clear and provided the basis for fruitful Nordic cooperation and substantial mutual understanding. The basic factor, apart from Protestantism, was *common sense*. The differences were clear and unarguable, but all to some extent acceptable in a commonsensical context.

The participants were very interested in the analyses they themselves had produced. On reflection, it was fairly clear that the four nationalities being studied fell into two groups:

✦ Swedes and Danes
✦ Finns and Norwegians

The first group was characterized by smooth talking, diplomacy, willingness to compromise, ability to articulate, avoidance of confrontation, politeness, and substantial confidence when facing foreigners. The second group was comparatively rough and ready. Truth and frankness trumped diplomacy; loquacity was suspect; obstinacy was justified if backed by facts; statements were promises; word–deed correlation was essential.

Each group came to recognize the other's qualities and strengths. Some synergy was evident. Finns and Norwegians could continue to suspect Swedish and Danish smooth talking, but they could also utilize it in their team's objectives. Finns would have to learn to be patient and respect Swedish consensus building. Norwegians would have to develop an understanding of Danish flexibilities; Swedes might try to speed up a bit; Danes would have to analyze the weight and import of Finnish silence; all would have to synchronize their actions with British conservatism and the American sense of urgency.

Considering integration of the Nordic companies and personnel with the now US–British management led to a subsequent seminar where a comparison was made between the Nordic characteristics and inter-relations and the comparative values and communication styles of the British and the Americans. Where would they be located in the Nordic matrix?

It was not difficult to analyze. The British tendency toward coded (diplomatic) speech, fondness for arbitration, avoidance of confrontation, and repackaging skills put them firmly in the Swedish–Danish camp. The Americans' directness, results orientation, boldness, rough-and-ready toughness, pragmatism, and occasional impatience give them more sympathy for the Finns and Norwegians (see Figure 2.4).

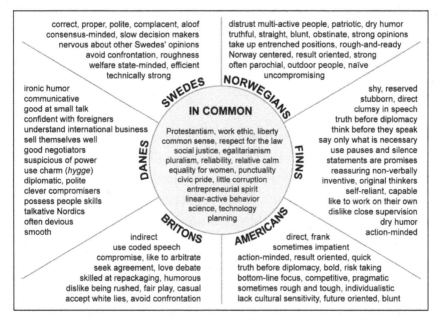

Figure 2.4   Common characteristics, Nordic countries and US/UK

Conclusion

RRM's conscientiousness in addressing cross-cultural issues resulted in a marked improvement of the performance of international teams within the group. It was recognized that although Nordic and Anglo-American values and business methods are relatively compatible, it is important to address seemingly minor differences that can seriously impede efficient team action and general harmony.

3

Speaking the Language

Language is an important factor in an international team. In the great majority of cases the lingua franca will be English, although regional international teams might use another tongue. More than a dozen North African and Middle Eastern states could communicate with each other in Arabic. Argentineans, Brazilians, Mexicans, and Spaniards might well hold meetings in Spanish. A team consisting of a mainland Chinese, a Singaporean, a Hong Konger, and a Taiwanese would confer in Mandarin. After the break-up of the Soviet Union, Turkey explored the possibility of forming a regional trade association among the Turkic-speaking countries in the area, where delegates from Azerbaijan, Kazakhstan, Uzbekistan, Turkmenistan, and Kirghizstan could all communicate in Turkish.

Nevertheless, as we can see by comparing Figures 3.1–3.7, if a company aspires to global reach, English is the most likely vehicle of communication and may well remain so for the first half of the twenty-first century, though sooner or later people wishing to sell into the giant Chinese market may have to do so using Mandarin, by far the world's most spoken language. The strength of English as an international lingua franca depends of course not so much on the fact that more than 400 million people speak it as their native tongue, but on its ubiquitous use as a second language by anything up to a billion speakers.

Americans, Britons, and other Anglos are at a linguistic advantage in an international team. They have to be careful how they exploit this, however. Their relative fluency in comparison to others may give their colleagues the impression that they are being too forceful, or smooth, or even devious. They have to avoid speech that is too locally idiomatic or borders on slang or jargon. In fact, what often happens is that an international team invents its own jargon, which then becomes helpful as it is common to all and

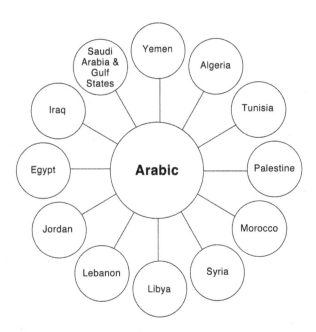

Figure 3.1 Arabic as a lingua franca

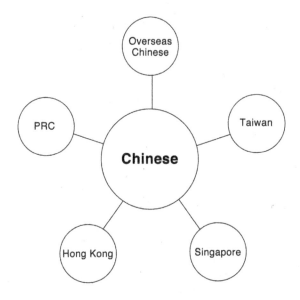

Figure 3.2 Chinese as a lingua franca

Figure 3.3 Spanish as a lingua franca

Figure 3.4 Portuguese as a lingua franca

Figure 3.5 Turkish as a lingua franca

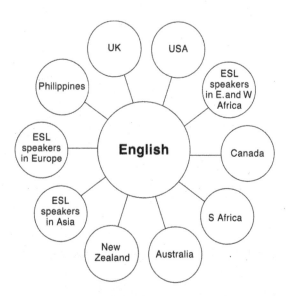

Figure 3.6 English as a lingua franca

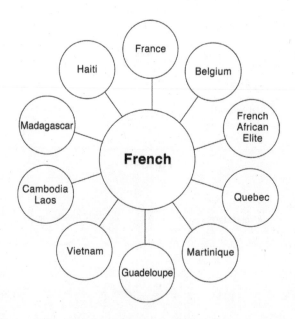

Figure 3.7   French as a lingua franca

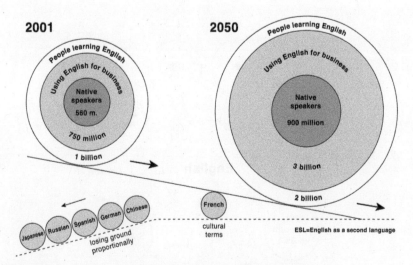

Figure 3.8   The languages of international business

uses key words and expressions that short-cut circumlocutions and vague terminology. A "team language" – a kind of English – develops, to which the Anglos are not necessarily the chief contributors. It is well known that nonnative English speakers understand each others' "English" very well indeed.

This "international vocabulary" is much more extensive than most people realize. Foreign words are used in English when a concept is better or more concisely expressed in another language – faux pas and innuendo are good examples. Britons and Americans with secondary education use numerous words and expressions as if they were English, as shown in Table 3.1.

a fortiori	à la carte	à la mode	à propos	abattoir
ad hoc	ad infinitum	adiós	agent provocateur	al fresco
alter ego	amok	au revoir	bête noire	bidet
blasé	blitz	bon vivant	boudoir	buffet
camaraderie	casus belli	cliché	contretemps	coup
coup d'état	coup de grâce	coup de théâtre	crescendo	cul-de-sac
de facto	de jure	de rigueur	débâcle	débris
début	débutante	déjà vu	dénouement	détente
Doppelgän-ger	double entendre	élite	en bloc	en passant
en route	encore	enfant terrible	entente cordiale	entourage
entrée	entrepreneur	esprit de corps	et cetera	fait accompli
faute de mieux	faux pas	gaffe	gauche	genre
gentil	habitué	hara-kiri	haute couture	haute cuisine
hors d'oeuvre	in situ	innuendo	ipso facto	joie de vivre
kamikaze	kaput	Kiwi	laissez-faire	Lebensraum
Leitmotiv	maître d'hôtel	maîtresse	mañana	mea culpa
mêlée	milieu	modus operandi	ne plus ultra	nouveau riche
nouvelle cuisine	nuance	Ombudsman	panache	par excellence
passé	per se	persona non grata	piano piano	pied-à-terre
primus inter pares	quid pro quo	raison d'être	rapport	rapproche-ment

rendez-vous	riposte	risqué	savoir faire	sayonara
Schaden-freude	sic	simpático	smörgåsbord	sotto voce
status quo	table d'hôte	terra firma	tête-à-tête	vice versa
vis-à-vis	Wanderlust	Weltan-schauung	Zeitgeist	

Table 3.1 Loan words into English

Interestingly, these "loan words" in English are in fact à la mode in other languages. In 2003 I tested their familiarity with German and Swedish business people, who understood, even "claimed" more than 90 percent of them. Speakers of Romance languages have equal familiarity. Even among traveling Asians – overseas Chinese, Malaysians, Indians – comprehension is high, though use is slightly less frequent. It is noteworthy that about 70 percent of these words and expressions are of French origin. This must be a consoling factor to French team members, who find some justification in the claim that French (a former world language) still has considerable international currency. De Gaulle was not so wrong after all!

Global English

The worldwide meanderings of the Anglo-Saxon peoples led to extensive borrowings from languages spoken by those they encountered on their travels and indeed during colonization. English is, however, not the only language that indulges in the use of loan words. With the growing importance of global English, other nationalities are finding it neat, quick, and often appropriate to slot in readily recognizable English words and expressions.

Hardly any language avoids the incorporation of loan words. The Dutch happily use spam, downloader, *een grote hit*, junkmail, mailbox, software, filters, station wagon; the Swedes *sidesteppar* issues; Finns handy (cellphone); Filipinos colgate; Russians *voksal* (from Vauxhall Station); Italians anti-smog day, *dribblare*, *lo stop*, performance; Danes dressman, poleman.

Postwar Germans show little hesitation in borrowing from the language of the victors. Easy acquisitions such as *gefaxt*, *gekidnapped*, *shoppen*, *relaxen*, and *brunchen* are now being followed at a great pace by words inspired by twenty-first-century life, such as *twittern*, *braingestormt*, City Call, Holiday Plus, *der Babyblues*, *eine After-Show-Party*, *eine NO-GO area*, *der Nickname*, *das It-Girl*, *clicken*, *faken*, *fighten*, *flippen*, *jobben*, *mobben*, *outen*; or by business words inspired by the financial crisis, such as *die Bad-Bank*, *Kreditklemme* (credit crunch), *cooken* (a bank's assets), *Konjunkturpaket* (stimulus package), and *Abwrackpraemie* (a car scrappage bonus).

In fact German is less conservative than one might think. Duden, the country's iconic dictionary, lists 5,000 new words that have entered the language in its first new edition for three years. German does cling to its long compound nouns, some of which have been born in the modern era, such as *Vorratsdatenspeicherung* (the saving of data relating to supplies) and *Rechtschutzversicherungsgesellschaften* (legal insurance companies). German international team members tend to express these words in English, though I was once treated to an explanation of *Oberammergauerpassionsfestspieleklosterdelikatalpenkraüterfrühstückskäseschnitten*, which, it appears, is a certain type of sandwich eaten during the Oberammergau Passion Play. Fortunately, this takes place only once every ten years.

German team members like to use English in meetings, often in preference to their own tongue. The reasons they give are that it is quick and appropriate (turnaround, IPO), upbeat (can-do mentality), and motivating (Anglo-American optimism). Germans also feel that using English causes them to switch to Anglo-Saxon attitudes such as togetherness, common sense, relaxing, casual humor, compromise, and a pragmatic way of living, as opposed to a strictly ordered one.

Much to the disgust of the Académie Française, the French have taken on *recordman*, *rugbyman*, *un dancing*, *un smoking*, *un parking*, *un building*, *un meeting*, *un businessman*, *un snack*, *faxer* (to fax), *le weekend*, and so on. Nevertheless, the French have traditionally resented the ubiquitous use of English. Previously the EU did its work 70 percent in French; now it is 70 percent in English. Finland, Sweden, Denmark, Cyprus, Malta, Greece, and Bulgaria pushed for the use of English on entering the EU. In addition, 92 percent of secondary school students in EU countries learn English as a first foreign language at school (compare French 33 percent, German 13 percent). Like the Germans, the French perceive that using English brings with it an Anglo-American way of thinking, along with possibly an erosion of traditional French intellectualism and philosophies. Does a French member of an international team want to change their way of thinking?

While the French are becoming reconciled to the dominance of English due to the virtual empire of the internet and emails, they tend to speak it in an original (and not uncharismatic) way. Monsieur Nerrière, a retired vice-president of IBM USA, stated recently: "In international meetings, we [foreigners] are in the majority so it is we who should determine the official way of speaking English." This is of course happening every day and all over the world. English is splintering: there are hundreds of versions, at least a dozen major ones – American, Australian, Singaporean, Malaysian, Canadian, South African, West African, East African, Filipino, Indian subcontinent, overseas Chinese, and EU English.

In an international team, avoidance of misunderstanding is the key. Colloquial idiom, coded speech, unclear jargon, gobble-degook, understatement, and euphemism will over time be discarded in the interests of clarity. Other neologisms, yet in their infancy, will creep in and multiply. It is very much in the international team manager's interest to be alive to these existing varieties and developing trends. Teams of one or two years' standing very often develop an attractive team version of English that is concise, snappy, appropriate, discerning, original, and often possessing its own brand of team humor. It becomes a kind of team secret – a ready tool for quick understanding, expression, and agreement. This type of parlance will eventually become a new world business language, possibly with different varieties enjoying popularity in separate continents, but a general universal core that new international team members can rapidly acquire. The more varied the nationality composure of the team, the more easily it works.

There is nevertheless some resistance to the linguistic invasion of English, sometimes from unexpected quarters. Iceland is unquestioningly pro-British (it even accepted Britain's time zone, resulting in Reykjavik seeing the sun rise in winter at nearly 11 am), yet it finds Old Norse equivalents for new words and concepts, thus computer is *toelva*, television screen is *skjar*, and AIDS comes out as *alnaemi* (a vulnerable person). Of the Latin countries, only Portugal watches films on television in the English original – Spain, Italy, and France dub them and consequently speak English with a stronger accent. When Defense Minister of India, Jaswant Singh said, "I cannot rest until English is driven out of the country." He is unlikely to get his way any time soon.

The spread of English

English has not always enjoyed such preeminence; indeed, its wide diffusion is a relatively recent phenomenon. The tongue's origins can be traced to the dialects of Germanic tribes who invaded Britain some 1500 years ago: Angles, Saxons, and Jutes. These dialects were later influenced by the Vikings, who arrived between the ninth and eleventh centuries, and by the Normans, who showed up in 1066. This linguistic hotchpotch did not spread anywhere for a few centuries and as late as 1582, Edmund Spenser was told by his teacher that "the English tongue is of small reach, stretching no further than this island of ours, and not everywhere here." French, Spanish, and Latin reigned on the continent, while English developed anarchic tendencies – people minting words and spellings that took their fancy (Shakespeare was the most wildly fanciful of them all).

This linguistic anarchy was called to a rude halt in 1755, when Dr. Samuel Johnson and a team of six clerks composed the first proper dictionary of the English language. This work became the foundation stone of modern English and, as Johnson's biographer

James Boswell said, "conferred stability on the language of the country." This step was taken not a moment too soon, as 40 French academicians were at work to produce a French equivalent (which took them nearly 50 years).

Johnson's work had political significance, with its demonstration of a burgeoning world power displaying its great language. Another politically motivated work made its appearance in 1828: Noah Webster's *American Dictionary of the English Language*. This tome signposted the final act of severance from British rule. The two countries were henceforth indeed separated by the same language.

The dictionary coup de grâce, however, came at the end of the twentieth century. English publishers Bloomsbury published the *Encarta World English Dictionary*, which purports to be "a bible of multiculturalism" for the third millennium. If Webster nicked the American version of the English language from Britain's grasp, the EWED appropriates both Englishes from Anglo-Saxon possession and gives them to humanity (one supposes). The British can be flattered to find that they were at least partly instrumental in creating 3.5 million entries, with 100,000 "headwords," the most frequent global usages, but it is clear they don't own the language any more. Neither, fortunately, do the Americans. International teams, diplomats, cross-border traders, teachers, artists, aid workers, film stars, pop groups, and a host of others will paraphrase, manipulate, twist, corrupt, transform, and ultimately enrich the language of Shakespeare and Dickens. In a few years the Chinese, even the Japanese, will have their turn. There will be many Englishes, some of them mutually intelligible, others not. In international business, a lowest common denominator of comprehension must be created. This is already happening. If one reads learned journals, writes books, communicates from sea or air, or is engaged in sport or artistic events abroad, English has long been to some degree necessary. The language spread exponentially with computer use; the advent of the internet gave it a huge push. A library of information is available at the click of a mouse and 80 percent of it is currently in English.

Can the march of English be stopped? Should it be? As language specialist David Crystal has pointed out, a truly global language is a new phenomenon; there is no precedent. Can it one day be dislodged, as Latin and Greek were? English has reached farther than they did. China and Russia are learning and using English assiduously and this factor, combined with its currency in the Indian subcontinent, means that half the world's population is using it for business, politics, science, and other purposes.

The currency of English in international teams has led to declining interest on the part of Brits, Americans, and Australasians in the study of other languages. In 2000 only nine students graduated from American universities in Arabic. What is happening in effect is that native English speakers are taking it for granted that English has attained an unassailable position in international commerce; it is becoming more and more clear that Asians, Africans, and most Europeans agree with them.

Which is the world's biggest English-speaking country (measured by the number of fluent speakers)? The United States? Correct. And the second biggest? Britain? Canada? Australia? India? The answer is the Philippines, with 75 million speakers. The day may not be far off when Britain will not rank in the top ten English-speaking nations. It is estimated that one billion people are learning English right now. It is only a matter of time before the number of English speakers in Britain is overtaken by those in Canada, South Africa, Nigeria, India, Pakistan, Bangladesh, and the EU, and later, (if lessons go well), feasibly by China, Russia, and even Thailand. The current top 10 English-speaking countries and the potential league table in the next 20–40 years are shown in Table 3.2. The weaknesses of English's potential rivals are illustrated in Table 3.3.

English and globalization have spread hand in hand. Having a global language has assisted globalization and globalization has consolidated the global language.

2010	2030–50?
USA	USA
Philippines	EU
UK	China (inc. overseas Chinese)
Canada	India
South Africa	Philippines
Australia	Canada
India	Australia
EU	South Africa
Malaysia	West and East African élite
West and East African élite	UK

Table 3.2   Top 10 English-speaking countries by number of speakers

Language	Weaknesses
Chinese	Split into three major dialects (Mandarin, Cantonese, Shanghainese) Tone language – difficult to learn Internet favors Roman alphabet
Russian	Break-up of Soviet Union dashed any hopes of its being an international tongue
Japanese	Too vague Culturally delicate Japanese dislike foreigners who speak it well
German	Germans are already too committed to English
French	Culturally useful, will remain a secondary lingua franca
Spanish	Useful, but limited mainly to one continent (why should Chinese, Japanese or Russians learn it?)

Table 3.3   Rivals to English as a world language

CASE STUDY

The successful Finnish bakery described in this case study has prosperous subsidiaries in the Baltic states of Estonia, Latvia, and Lithuania. HQ encouraged its managers to form a closely knit commercial and marketing unit under Finnish direction. Historically, however, these three nations have rarely cooperated effectively, divided as they are by language, religion, and a spirit of independence. English is their lingua franca and provided the only unifying factor in a lively "kick-off" style seminar, typified by occasional flashes of humor and barely disguised mutual cynicism.

Leibur

In 2008 I facilitated a team-building exercise for an old Finnish bakery whose outstanding record in Finland had enabled it to set up and exploit, with considerable success, subsidiary operations in Estonia, Latvia, and Lithuania. The excellence of Leibur bread had guaranteed steady expansion and public acceptance in the three Baltic States, though the administration of the (albeit small) multinational company had not been without certain problems in terms of cooperation and team spirit. The managing director of the Baltic States operation – a dynamic and positively inclined Estonian named Ants Proman – had initiated the workshop, which he foresaw as an annual event to strengthen the conjunction and gung-hoism of his somewhat less than symbiotic colleagues.

In view of the generally harmonic nature of Nordic commercial collaboration between Denmark, Norway, Sweden, and Finland, one might ask why the three Baltic States, with miniscule domestic markets and a total population of little more than 8 million, do not team up at every opportunity? A centuries-long occupation by big foreign powers had come to an end by the fall of the Soviet Union in 1990–91. "Unity is strength" would seem a natural maxim for Estonians, Latvians, and Lithuanians.

In fact, in the past the three nations have rarely cooperated effectively. English, Scots, and Welsh, within the confines of one island, have experienced a similar divergence of aspirations. Lithuanians, an emotional and grandiloquent people, feel more at home with Slavic Poles than they do with Latvians and Estonians. Lutheran Latvians, blond and stocky, are more like northern Germans, who colonized them as early as the thirteenth century. Estonians, also Lutheran and even more reserved, strongly resemble their Finnish cousins and speak a Finno-Ugrian tongue.

Baltic cooperation does exist in substance, though often it is more visible at government level, as opposed to personal relations. The memory of and animosity toward Russian dominance since 1945, as well as periodic threats from the east, are doubtless unifying factors. Estonia and Latvia see eye to eye on defense issues, Latvia and Lithuania cooperate well in the field of nuclear development. All three states view EU membership positively. Differences exist, too: Estonians are keen on joining NATO and want a more proactive role in energy security; Lithuanians would like to shape EU foreign policy toward Russia.

At the personal level, friction between Baltic team members is readily evident. Finns and Estonians, who are perhaps the most alike, nevertheless manage to irritate each other. After "liberation," a constant stream of Finnish business people (and tourists) "invaded" Estonia with the best of intentions. They tended, however, to patronize their southern cousins, having gained the international experience denied to Estonians during the Soviet years. The Estonians, a proud, organized, and individualistic people, do not accept a close comparison with the Finns; they feel they are more European and have more cosmopolitan elements in their culture.

A well-known Finnish writer who has spent time in Finland and Estonia noted the following:

- Finns are seen as humorless and gloomy by Estonians, who are seen as cheeky and cocky by Finns.
- Finns often appear slow and "mulish" to Estonians, who see themselves as "skillful" and "gifted."
- Disciplined Finnish drivers comment on an Estonian "Wild West" traffic culture.
- Law-abiding Finns noticed low legal consciousness in Estonians.
- Finns sulk and grumble in situations that make Estonians laugh.
- The Finnish practice of closing shops on Sundays is seen as puritanical by Estonians.
- Estonians dress smartly and for the occasion; Finns love tracksuits.

✧ Helsinki functions at a low pace; Tallinn pulsates with energy.

✧ Finns are sticklers about punctuality; Estonians have a much more relaxed attitude to time.

✧ Estonians are more formal in forms of address; they find Finns' immediate use of first names rather vulgar and intrusive.

Lithuanians and Latvians speak closely related tongues belonging to the Indo-European group, but barely understand each other, which gives rise to irritation. Finns follow Estonian with great difficulty, but Estonians understand Finnish by dint of having watched Finnish television in Soviet times. The linguistic diversity in the Leibur group tended to keep each nationality sitting with their compatriots. Ants Proman's solution, of course, was for everyone to communicate in English. This they did while I led the discussions, but they tended to lapse into their own tongues quickly afterward. This was in contrast to Nordic teams, who normally stick to English throughout a seminar.

Our workshop dealt with both commonalities and cultural differences among the participants. The group that spoke the least were the Latvians. Phlegmatic throughout, they fielded some snide remarks from the Estonians and Lithuanians with characteristic passivity. One Lithuanian member remarked that in her dealings with Latvians she found them slow, impenetrable, unable to decide anything – in short, infuriating. Estonians hinted more at Latvian stupidity and had several jokes in that vein. Lithuanians made jokes about Estonians whom they saw as cold and impolite (too direct). The complexity of the group was increased by the presence of a Russian minority in each national team.

The Finnish delegates, somewhat senior on the whole, remained neutral among this banter, but, as I discovered later, they had definite views on their colleagues' characteristics. Perturbed by occasional Estonian impertinences, they nevertheless admired their bellicosity toward the Russians, while they deplored the lack of it among the Latvians, who showed great tolerance of their Russian minority. In general, the Finns got on well with the Latvians in an unconfrontational kind of way (slightly bored), but felt quite different culturally from the loquacious, Catholic Lithuanians. One of the Finnish managers who had worked in Vilnius for four years said that he found the people warm, good-humored, stimulating, confident of their glorious past, and with clear goals for the future, but that four years in Lithuania were enough. Why so? He replied that in the end, you find out "they are all foxes."

Largely due to the dynamism and unfailing optimism of Ants Proman and three extremely competent Finnish managers, the long-drawn-out workshop achieved a spirit of congeniality and progressive aspirations. It did not, however, engender the substantial solidarity of purpose that most inter-Nordic teams exhibit. The Finns and Estonians were clear go-getters, but on the whole there was some reticence in the air about future expectations. Tucked in at the top north-east corner of the Baltic, the Leibur group had a comforting geographical compactness about it. Whether this would be matched in future by a corresponding or increasing cultural compatibility would depend on the skill and perhaps stamina of the team leaders.

4

Leading the Team

Having built an international team whose members have suitably complementary strengths, the question then arises: Who leads it? Do some nationals take up the mantle of leadership more easily than others? This is a difficult question to answer. Certainly, some cultures produce individuals who relish the prestige and power of leadership. French, Spanish, and South Americans are good examples. They manage autocratically and tend to make irreversible decisions. Others, like Canadians, British, and Swedes, feel that they are good at arbitration and tend to seek agreement among those present rather than impose personal decisions. Americans are essentially men or women of action and see their role as maintaining momentum. Finns use facts skillfully and seek sensible conclusions. In the end, good leadership depends more on individual personalities than a particular passport.

Nevertheless, different cultures have diverse concepts of leadership. Leaders can be born, elected, or trained and groomed. Others seize power or have leadership thrust upon them. Leadership can be autocratic or democratic, collective or individual, meritocratic or unearned, desired or imposed. It is not surprising that business leaders often wield their power in conformity with the national set-up – for instance, a confirmed democracy like Sweden produces low-key democratic managers; Arab managers are good Muslims; Chinese managers usually have government or party affiliations.

Leaders cannot readily be transferred from culture to culture. Japanese prime ministers would be largely ineffective in the United States; American politicians would fare badly in most Arab countries; mullahs would not be tolerated in Norway. Similarly, business managers find the transition from one culture to another fraught with difficulties. Autocratic French managers have to tread warily in consensus-minded Japan or Sweden. Courteous Asian leaders would have to adopt a more vigorous style in argumentative Holland or theatrical Spain if they wished to hold the stage. German managers sent to Australia are somewhat alarmed at the irreverence of their staff and their apparent lack of respect for authority. Figures 4.1–4.19 show some special and widely varying leadership styles, with managers shown as white circles and employees black.

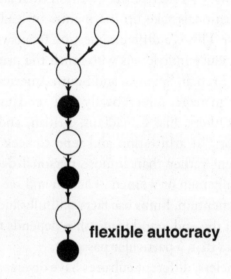

Figure 4.1   Leadership style: Italy

Italian leadership is fundamentally autocratic, but shows more flexibility than some other Latin styles, as managers mingle easily with staff and intersperse themselves at many levels. There are many "clan" and group interests in the southern half of the country and loyalty to the leader is automatic and mandatory. In Milan, Turin, and Genoa, there is a growing tendency to select managers on merit. In the north in general, professional competence is valued, though connections remain important. Essentially, Italians are comfortable in a hierarchy skillfully led by those of noble birth or from traditionally eminent or wealthy families. The patronage system is well established in the southern part of the country, especially in Sicily.

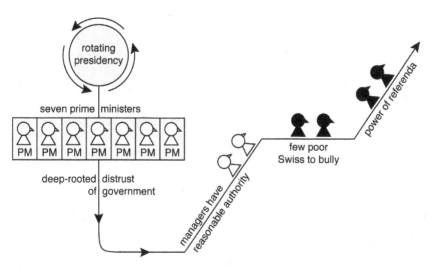

Figure 4.2 Leadership style: Switzerland

As in the US, there is a deep-rooted distrust of government in Switzerland and the system of rule resembles the American in its intricate and delicate array of checks and balances. The President has some powers, but only one year to exercise them, and is closely bound by the Federal Council of Seven and frequent referenda.

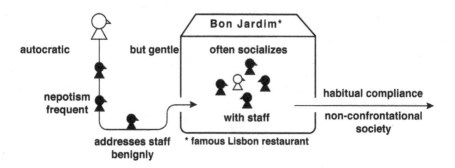

Figure 4.3 Leadership style: Portugal

Portugal is becoming a meritocracy, but business leaders and many political figures still come from the leading families. Portuguese senior executives make personal decisions, often in a family business context. Staff are generally obedient and deferential.

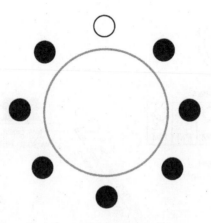

boss is in the circle

Figure 4.4   Leadership style: Belgium (Flemish)

Bosses in Flemish Belgium are relaxed and low key and it is generally accepted that decision making will be consensual. Responsibility is delegated downward to a considerable degree. The similarity with Sweden is striking.

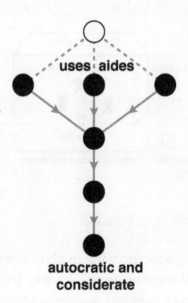

uses aides

autocratic and considerate

Figure 4.5   Leadership style: Belgium (Walloon)

Among Walloons leadership is exercised in a manner close to the French, where all final decisions rest with the boss. There is normally a general airing of ideas among staff, but this is more a fact-finding exercise than a referendum-style discussion.

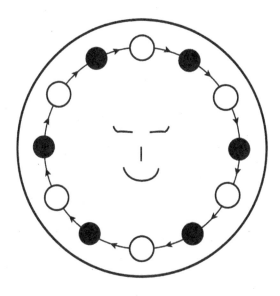

cosy *(hygge)* all round

Figure 4.6 Leadership style: Denmark

Danish top executives and middle managers are not always clearly distinguishable for non-Danes. Managers at all levels mingle for decision making and democratic procedures are mandatory. Danes are skillful in maintaining a decidedly congenial atmosphere in discussion. Horizontal communication is widespread and generally successful. Basic Danish assumptions are generally in line with their essentially democratic stance and Protestant fine tuning. Leadership is by achievement and demonstration of technical competence. Leaders are expected to be low profile, benign, consulting colleagues for opinions. Status is based on qualifications, competence, and results, yet materialism is downplayed. There is a focus on welfare.

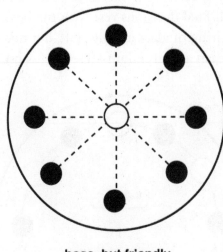

boss, but friendly

Figure 4.7   Leadership style: Norway

In democratic Norway, bosses are very much in the center of things and staff enjoy access to them at most times. Middle managers' opinions are heard and acted on in egalitarian fashion, but top executives rarely abandon responsibility and accountability.

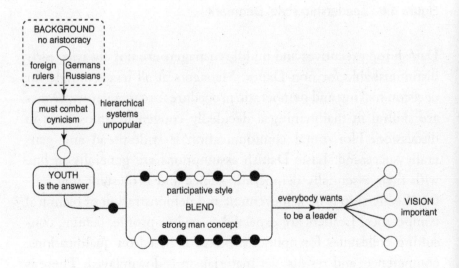

Figure 4.8   Leadership style: Estonia

Estonians are very individualistic. Everyone is a leader and no one likes being led. Estonia does not have a hierarchical system. It has never had its own aristocracy, only foreign occupiers (mainly Germans and Russians). Today Estonians have a cynical attitude toward authority, though their behavior is always well mannered. Expectations of leaders are at present a mix of Scandinavian participative management style and a more paternalistic approach, where the leader has to show clear vision and make all the important decisions. Estonia is a transition country where some managers might be very young. A 35–40-year-old person might start their second career as an entrepreneur after they have retired from the management board of, for example, a bank.

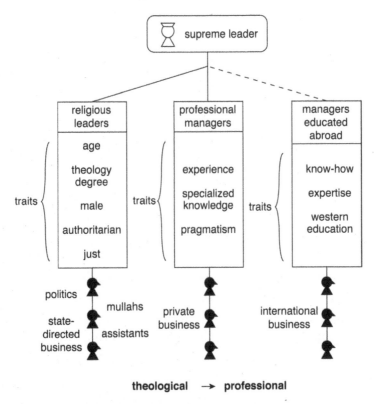

Figure 4.9 Leadership style: Iran

In general terms, in Iran spiritual leadership is dominant. When the spiritual leader Ayatollah Khomeini decided it was time for the Shah to step down, support for the move was massive and immediate (over 98 percent). In business, the leader may be identified as the last person to enter the room at a meeting, and he (and it will be a "he") will sit in the middle. Alternatively, he may show his hospitality by greeting the visitors at the entrance to the room. Academic achievement is of high importance. In government the Iranian leader must be a fully qualified theologian, selected by "experts." In business, education and specialized knowledge give managers status. They may have been educated in the West as well as Iran.

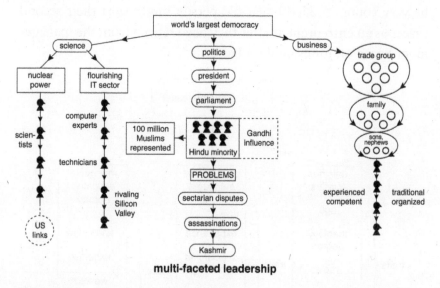

multi-faceted leadership

Figure 4.10   Leadership style: India

Indians accept a hierarchical system with its obligations and duties. The boss must be humanistic and initiate promotion for subordinates. In family business the elder son rarely decides what he wants to be – he is born to carry on the trade of the father. The father is expected to groom him for the job. First, a good education will be provided. The son must study hard, then the next step will be indicated. In the political sphere, India is the world's largest democracy. Leadership involves both the President and Parliament, but sectarian disputes are frequent. The Muslim minority (circa 160 million) are properly represented in Parliament, however.

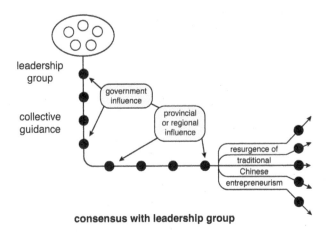

Figure 4.11 Leadership style: China

Consensus is generally highly valued in China, but in companies controlled by the state a leadership group (often invisible) will decide policy. In the developing expansion of capitalist-style companies, leaders are emerging with reputations of competence, and locally elected officials (such as mayors) are also becoming influential in the business sphere and may have only loose ties with Beijing. In Chinese family businesses (and there are many) the senior male is the patriarch and the usual nepotic structure is observable.

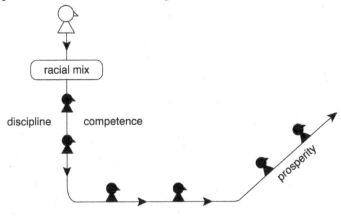

Figure 4.12 Leadership style: Singapore

Thirty years of skillful leadership by the "benevolent despot" Lee Kuan Yew converted the disputatious, multiracial community of Singapore into a disciplined, prosperous state of 4 million people with a per capita GDP of over $50,000 (2011). Lee had a firm hand, leading autocratically with an agenda of law and order, strict discipline, health and sanitation controls, hard work, and elimination of corruption. Managers continue largely in his image and there are few dissenters. One can set up a business in six days. The country is still multiracial, but the Chinese community dominates and observes basically Confucian tenets, spiced up a little with linear-active western concepts.

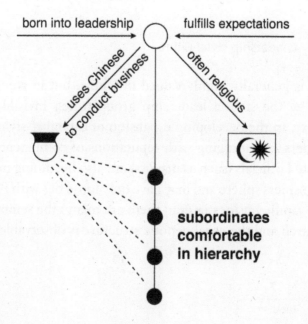

Figure 4.13 Leadership style: Malaysia

Malaysian people born into high positions are expected to demonstrate leadership capabilities. A good leader is religiously devout, sincere, humble, and tactful. Status is inherited, not earned, confirmed by demonstrating leadership and a caring attitude. Malays feel comfortable in a hierarchical structure in which they have a definite role. Work and idleness are not clearly delineated in Malay culture and language. Work is only one of many activities pursued. Deepening of relationships and time spent with the elderly may be seen as idle pursuits by westerners, not by Malays. They are modest and rarely request promotion; they expect it to be accorded by a caring senior when the time is ripe.

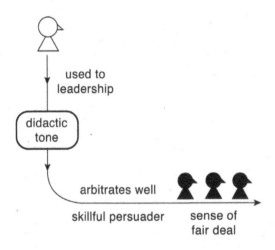

Figure 4.14 Leadership style: South Africa (white British)

The British South African community possesses business and political leaders of considerable perspicacity. Cultural sensitivity is generally a strong point and in this respect they compare well with Europeans. They often show a good grasp of human nature and are comfortable in managerial situations. They are usually excellent arbitrators, employing gentle persuasion to achieve their goals.

Using Nelson Mandela as a model, black African leaders (Figure 4.15) find him a hard act to follow, in view of his unique skills in leading from the front (even in jail), disarming manner, and all-encompassing perspective. Current leadership is often beset by factional problems. The flock is by no means docile or unified. So far democratic methods have enjoyed success and irremedial confrontation with the whites has been avoided. The gradual emergence of a sizable black middle class has facilitated steadiness and continuity.

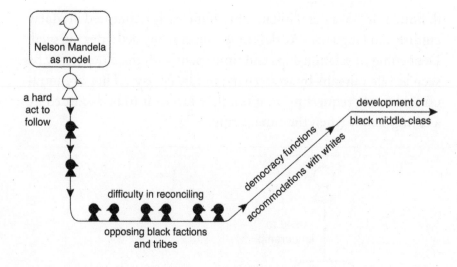

Figure 4.15 Leadership style: South Africa (black)

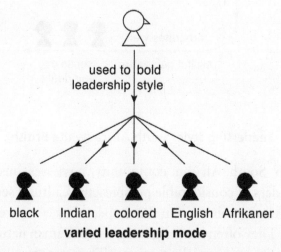

Figure 4.16 Leadership style: South Africa (white Dutch)

Afrikaner business and political leaders are characterized by their boldness and directness. Cultural sensitivity is generally a strong point and in this respect they compare well with Europeans. In conformity with their history, Afrikaners relish commanding and assume responsibility with gusto. They are clever in varying their leadership style according to which cultural group their staff belong to.

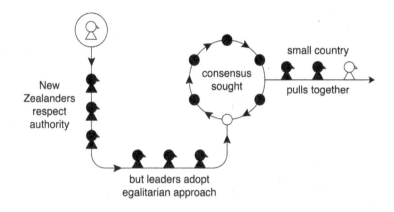

Figure 4.17   Leadership style: New Zealand

Most New Zealanders are brought up to respect authority and managers have a relatively easy task as long as they function in a calm, egalitarian, and reasoning manner. Consensus is generally sought before important decisions are made and if things go wrong, leaders are rarely made scapegoats. New Zealand is a very small country with economic disadvantages due to its isolation and "pulling together" is seen as advisable.

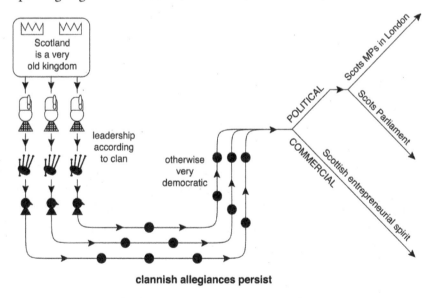

Figure 4.18   Leadership style: Scotland

Throughout history, Scots have remained fiercely loyal to their clan and these leanings, though less obvious in modern commercial enterprises, are often in the background. Apart from questions of clan hierarchy, power distance is low and leadership is very democratic. Many Scots seem to be "born leaders," inasmuch as they have figured conspicuously as inspirational people in British politics and the Civil Service. Their leadership qualities were frequently evidenced in the days of empire, where Scots gained fame as explorers, generals, and high-ranking administrators.

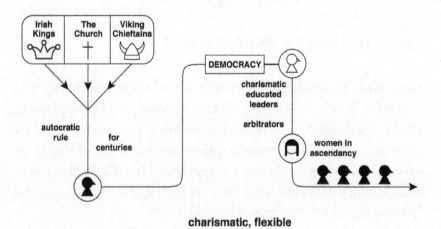

Figure 4.19 Leadership style: Ireland

The church has exercised enormous influence over Irish life for many centuries. Leadership has tended to be autocratic and centralized in the Latin manner. Irish kings, Viking chieftains, and ecclesiastical luminaries have all enjoyed considerable status *vis-à-vis* a rural and somewhat cowed populace. Since the establishment of democracy, Irish leaders have generally emerged as charismatic people with an educated background. As politics are often stormy, those who get on with different factions and have the ability to persuade and arbitrate are most likely to rise to the top. Women are in the ascendancy.

Leading the meeting

One of the tasks of the chair of a meeting or the leader of an international team is to establish or adopt a procedural or communicative style that will be acceptable to, even welcomed by, the team's members. There will be preconceptions in this regard, depending on where one comes from. Britons and Americans see a meeting as an opportunity to make decisions and get things done. The French see it as a forum where a briefing can be delivered to cover all aspects of a problem; they hunger for elegant processes. Germans, more concerned with precision and exactness, expect to gain compliance. Italians use meetings to evaluate how much support there is for their plans. Japanese regard the first few sessions as occasions where one establishes status and trust and finds out what possible sources of discord need to be eliminated from the outset. All these objectives may be seen as worthy by everyone, but the priorities will vary. A skillful chair must be sensitive to these expectations and be quick to create linkages that cut across traditional boundaries and define a mutually shared aim or purpose that transcends cultural differences.

A light hand and an open mind, laced with some humor, are essential. New teams should have a free discussion about taboos and recognize differences. Never mind who is right or wrong, how can we help or complement each other? Let's profile what we want and what we fear. Let's acknowledge and respect cultural differences and agendas, but let's not be paralyzed by them. If we are too democratic, little will be achieved.

The leader must know when to move things forward, albeit diplomatically and easily. Their strategy will include asking open-ended questions, paraphrasing when necessary, making acute observations and summaries, but also knowing the value of silences. They must keep in the forefront of their mind that there is no absolute truth. Germans often feel that there is, Chinese and most Orientals assert that there is not. The leader must look both critically and constructively at colleagues' proposals. They must balance challenge and support. If one can show team members the value of diversity in their own culture, the international team will grow in confidence about creating fruitful synergy. The leader must show them that they can shift perspective frequently without abandoning position. In this way they can loosen themselves from a restricting identity and move and think more freely. Women are often better at this than men. In the future, it is likely that companies and organizations will include far more women in international teams, following the Scandinavians' example.

Managing the priorities

Perhaps the biggest challenge normally facing the leader of an international team is how to prioritize matters for discussion with a view to achieving the maximum amount of progress in a very limited time. Most project teams, for instance, meet for one or two days, possibly three. Often some of the members are jetlagged. One of the chief qualities required of such a team leader is agility. However, by virtue of their previous experience as manager of a monocultural team, their day will follow a habitual routine common in their particular culture.

Research among managers from different cultural groups indicates that priorities can be very different, depending on accepted managerial style and staff expectations in the particular culture. Employees in some cultures require much more verbal attention than others. Indeed, one or two nationalities almost shun verbal activity once the task has been set. There is also considerable variance in how much praise and encouragement are expected by staff. In some cultures praise can be counter-productive. Other elements such as humor and brainstorming sessions have widely diverging degrees of acceptability.

Figures 4.20–4.26 show how managers from six different cultural backgrounds divide their time.

Nordic and Asian managers often think in silence, planning their day quietly. When they speak they are generally consultative.

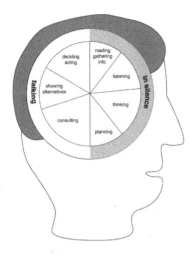

Figure 4.20 The Nordic manager's day

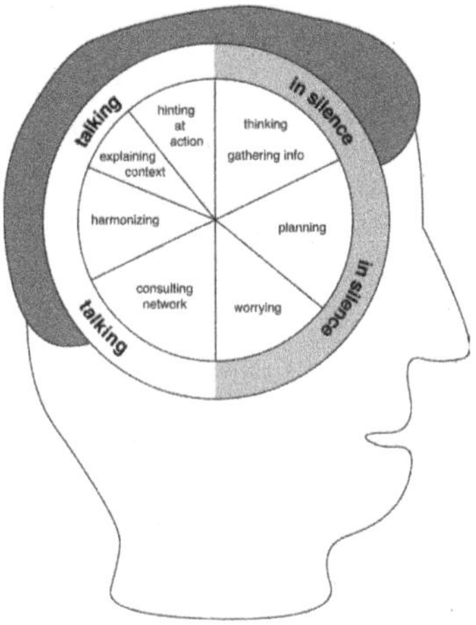

Figure 4.21 The Asian manager's day

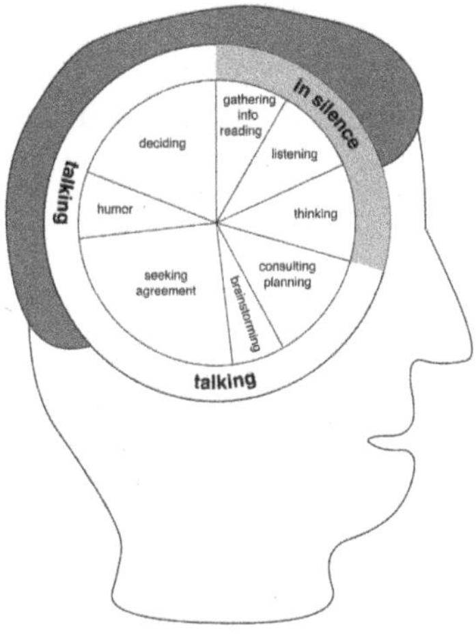

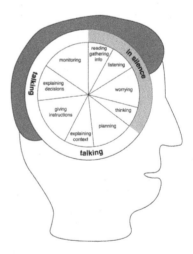

Figure 4.22 The British manager's day

Figure 4.23 The German manager's day

British and German managers often think aloud while motivating or instructing their colleagues. They are good at giving context.

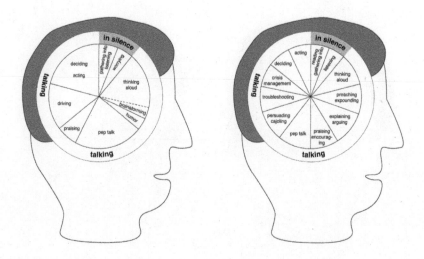

Figure 4.24 The American
manager's day

Figure 4.25 The Latin
manager's day

American and Latin managers – normally loquacious – are rarely
silent, the former brainstorming with his staff and giving frequent
pep talks, the latter praising and encouraging, often preaching and
persuading.

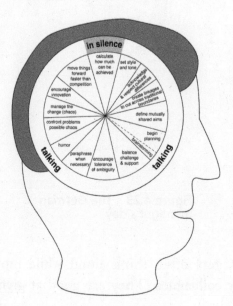

Figure 4.26
The multicultural manager

Managers of multinational teams can afford little silence, since they must be readily accessible to all, setting the tone and style of the session, challenging and supporting the team – playing the role of the multicultural extrovert and adapting rapidly to the diverse reactions of colleagues.

The oriental concept of "face" features strongly in many international relationships. In my previous work, *When Cultures Collide*, I discuss the question of "multiple face," which Chinese, Japanese, and Koreans have to show according to the precepts of Confucianism. Their different social obligations force them to be many things to many people. For instance, the face displayed to parents will be that indicating filial piety. That shown to a wife will be one of dominance plus kindness. To younger people it will indicate superiority but also guidance.

The leader of an international team has a similar problem. When facing a mixed-nationality group, empathy must be sprayed around in all directions, but it is variable empathy depending on what the recipient craves. Warmth for the Spaniard or Italian, courtesy for the Japanese, punch for the American – and all at the same time, at a turn of the head! It is not easy, but there are thousands of charismatic individuals who carry this off every day around the globe. It comes naturally to the willing multiculturalist, and to most good linguists. Unfortunately, there may not be more than one or two available per company. Individuals can also be trained to develop multifaceted empathy, but it takes time and application. The pay-off is significant, though. Figure 4.27 overleaf gives some guidance about what empathy means to some nationalities.

Leaders' self-image

Europeans, Americans, Asians, and others have different concepts of leadership and how a leader should behave. Effective leaders must have self-belief. This is often linked to self-image, which is surprisingly consistent within a given nationality. Thus, most English team leaders see themselves as good arbitrators, French as

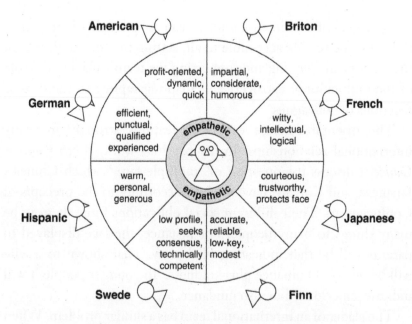

variable, simultaneous empathy

Figure 4.27   Face and the international team leader

effective orators, and Belgians as intelligent compromisers. Often one can trace the historical background to such self-evaluation (British colonial experience and so on).

England	Judge, arbitrator
German	Thorough, maintains order
France	Orator, logician
Spain	Romantic humanist
Italy	Communicator
Portugal	Negotiator
Greece	Wheeler and dealer
Ireland	Cosy, humorist
Denmark	Pleasant
Sweden	Consensus maker
Belgium	Compromiser
Netherlands	Honest but clever
Luxembourg	EU busybody
Austria	Sophisticated Germans
Finland	Champion of common sense

Table 4.1   Europeans' self-image

As a consequence of such thinking, an international team, though it will develop its own style and momentum, is likely to be led at least initially in a certain manner according to the provenance of the chair. Rare is the Irish person who will miss an opportunity to inject a shaft of Gaelic humor; even rarer the American who fails to push for a decision or action.

Among Anglo-Saxons, self-image is linked to action orientation. This is, however, arrived at in different ways and at different speeds.

America	People of action
Canada	Low-key dynamo
Australia	Open-minded, quick thinker
New Zealand	Solid, reliable
South Africa	Multiculturally experienced

Table 4.2   Anglo-Saxons' self-image

The Asian concept of leadership

The growing participation of Asians in international teams suggests that team managers should have increasing awareness of Asian concepts of leadership. Already many Japanese, Indians, Koreans, Malaysians, Singaporeans, Hong Kongers, and other overseas Chinese are international team members or chairs.

The following description of the tenets of Asian leadership is Confucian based, but most of the principles apply also to Indians, Malaysians, Indonesians, Thais, and Filipinos.

✧ In contrast with western liberal democracies, society is based on unequal relationships. It is organized in a strict hierarchy with a strong leader or leadership group at the top. In theory, the leadership consists of wise men (even scholars) who are eminently capable of leading and possessing vision.

✧ Orders from a superior are to be obeyed without question. There are strong obligations both top down and bottom up in the hierarchy. Subordinates owe allegiance, superiors owe guidance and protection.

✧ In theory, if leaders abuse their power (fail to protect) they may be overthrown. It is up to intellectuals (possibly students) to expose such abuse and to act to remove abusers.

✧ Except in communist régimes, leadership is gained through birthright (traditional upper-class families, wealth, and so on). Such leaders are expected to rise to the aspirations and expectations of those who are to be led.

✧ Subordinates are generally satisfied with their rung in the hierarchy. Suggestions for promotion are expected to come from above. Promotion is granted more in reward for loyalty and seniority than for brilliance or achievement.

✧ The leader is seen as the father of a big family, where everyone thinks collectively. They should place the welfare of employees before or on a par with the creation of profit.

✧ Asian leaders are situation-accepting managers rather than decision makers. When making decisions, they look for best precedents in the past.

✧ Most decisions are made through consensus. Leaders should achieve unanimity through soft persuasion.

✧ Though leaders must display paternalism, power distance remains great.

Changing notions of leadership

In the twenty-first century, with multinationals and conglomerates expanding their global reach, corporate governance and international teams will learn a lot about leading multicultural enterprises and workforces. The new impetus provided by fresh managers from Asia, as well as others from Latin America and Africa, will change notions of leadership. The traditional western managerial style is set to change soon. It could well be that international teams will herald the modifications. And more and more women – already prominent in politics – will enter the equation.

CASE STUDY

When Land Rover decided to cut the number of its overseas sales areas from 14 to 6, it needed strong leaders who would demonstrate a close affinity to the cultural traits of the area to which they were assigned. This matching had to be carefully examined.

Land Rover

In the early 1990s, Land Rover's overseas sales structure lent itself to unnecessary duplication of responsibilities in some cases (for example Germany, Scandinavia, Netherlands; Mexico, Central America, South America). The company came to the conclusion that six top-ranking area directors would ensure better results than fourteen good, mediocre, and weak ones. There was naturally intense competition among the incumbent area directors to finish in the top six.

The consolidated divisions were:

✧ China and the Far East
✧ North America
✧ South America
✧ Northern Europe
✧ Southern Europe
✧ Middle East and Africa

Around this time we had just finalized a Cultural Profile Assessment system to enable companies to identify the cultural traits of their employees and to give HR departments guidance on which employees (especially managers) would be suitable for which locations. Our assessment method involved 250–300 questions on candidates' worldview, attitudes, core beliefs, and communication qualities, which, when answered, would give us strong clues as to which affinities suited them to cultural areas where they might be expected to operate. Sticklers for punctuality are rarely comfortable in Mexico, slow decision makers are at a disadvantage in the United States, blunt advocates of facts and scientific truth are regarded as dangerous by the Japanese, and so on.

Our penetrative questions (on paper, later on the web) were supplemented by a 30-minute interview with the purpose of ascertaining the personalities, opinions, convictions, basic traits, and worldview of each manager. Such interviews served to confirm or clarify the views and statements made in writing. The confirmation of the written replies and the oral reaction to our (probing) questions generally made us feel that we ended up with a reasonably accurate profile.

We spent two days at Land Rover HQ administering the test and carrying out the interviews. It was an interesting experience, inasmuch as several of the managers had proven records of success, knew what they wanted next, and answered many of our queries with a fair amount of confidence. They also revealed considerable ignorance of cultures in which they had not worked. Many of them covered these gaps in their knowledge with an implicit assumption that "the British way works in the end." Among the British-born managers there was little evidence of humility. Other nationalities were more cautious (and understanding).

Initially, we were slightly cautious in our own judgments. While we trusted our assessment method, based on 15,000 tests (now 37,000), we were well aware that our invitation to carry out this assessment involved 12 HR officers who showed no lack of international experience. They obviously knew the candidates well. What were their own evaluations?

The managers we interviewed, apart from one or two who gave occasional signs of flippancy (or cultural arrogance), answered the questions conscientiously and looked forward to our opinions. They really wanted a job in the top six.

We analyzed the results and carried out the interviews; the HR department kept out of our way. We short-listed six outstanding candidates, whom we can call A, B, C, D, E, and F. The most forceful candidate by far was A. He had an impeccable record in North

America (his current position) and he wanted China. B wanted South America; C North America; D Northern Europe; E Middle East and Africa; F North America. All had had success in their current positions, especially A and B.

We felt that if B, who was Lebanese, wanted South America, he was very likely to fit in well, as he demonstrated a whole array of multi-active characteristics that would endear him to the inhabitants of that continent. He also spoke six languages, including Spanish and Portuguese. C, who was British, was after the North American post and was essentially linear-active; he had a lively streak that would please Americans and wake up Canadians. D was an excitable Englishman who never stopped talking. He fancied Northern Europe, but we felt that his loquacity and charisma would irritate Scandinavians and probably Germans. He was essentially human and compassionate, clearly better suited to Southern Europe. E, an Italian, was confident that he would be effective in the Middle East and was willing to tackle Africa as part of the package. He certainly was the most suitable candidate for what promised to be a difficult post. F, a middle-aged Frenchman, wanted North America, but had shown himself antipathetic to many US habits; we also felt that he was past his best.

Our big problem was A, the Englishman who was hell-bent on China. He had a lot going for him. Aged 45, he was smart, well groomed, and exuded confidence and efficiency. He had twenty years in the company and five years' solid profit behind him. He was regarded throughout the firm as a top manager – a star. He was determined to get what he regarded as the up-and-coming top job, tackling the huge Chinese market for Land Rovers. He made no bones about his ambitions, both in the written test and in a lively interview where he showed his strength of will. We had the impression that he was interviewing us.

The problem was that he showed both in the self-assessment and in the interview that he had no affinity whatsoever with basic Chinese cultural traits. In fact, he was diametrically opposed to all of them. Not a man to beat about the bush, he was forthright in his opinions, which he imposed on colleagues from the start.

Blissfully unaware of the importance the Chinese attach to "face," the only face he protected was his own. Quick in his decisions, he implemented them with impatience; long-drawn-out meetings and protracted debate were for cissies. Americans had admired his speed to market and sense of urgency. He would build a fire under the lethargic Chinese. A camel was a horse designed by a committee; he did not like committees, particularly political ones. He did not like communists and admired Margaret Thatcher for the way she had defeated the unions. Overseas Chinese he had met in the USA and elsewhere were efficient business people whose pragmatism and profit orientation impressed him. He intended to collaborate with them in exploiting the Chinese market. He understood that Chinese qualities included courtesy, modesty, respect for the elderly, filial piety, thrift, asceticism, gentleness, purity, and pride, but felt that none of these traits had any place in business. He had heard of Confucius, but anyone who had lived in 1500 BC had to be old-fashioned.

It was quite clear to us that assigning A to China would be a tactical disaster for the company. Not only would he dismay the Chinese whom he would need to win over and command, but he would also send the wrong signals to his western assistants out there. He himself would be ultimately uncomfortable and frustrated in the Chinese environment. We knew from experience that sending a misfit westerner to Asia often results in a premature and costly repatriation. Once a manager has shown a "healthy" disregard for Asian sensitivities, there is no way back (except home). If he stays on he will be a kind of "lame duck" president for the rest of his term.

How could we tell this to the dozen HR managers who would steer A's future? We had the choice of "telling it the way it is" in true American style, or hinting at our reluctance to endorse A in well-tried, woolly British coded speech (certain areas of misgiving…, falling somewhat short of an ideal…, and so on).

We opted for telling them the way it was. There was a moment's silence before they all heaved a collective sigh of relief. They had been of the same opinion all along, but had to some extent been bulldozed by A's palpable success and shining reputation. Unable to find holes in his competence, but nevertheless suspecting that he was not right for the job he sought, they needed an outside opinion to corroborate their suspicions. A's weakness was shadowy and not easily explainable technically. It could be defined clearly in cultural terms, however.

Subsequently, A was dispatched to northern Europe, where he continued to impress the Germans and Scandinavians with his drive and decisiveness. The Lebanese, we heard, fitted in well in South America and, as far as we know, C went to the USA, D to Italy, and E to the Middle East. Only F remained temporarily unassigned. He certainly was not suitable for the Far East. None of the 14 candidates we interviewed stood out as being right for China. We advised the HR department to scour its ranks for managers who already had experience in the Far East. Swedes, Finns, Canadians, Singaporeans, and a certain type of Brit are among the nationalities that are often acceptable to the Chinese, who seek partners who are reserved, on the quiet side, tolerant, polite, and definitely not pushy. They look for what they term as "wisdom." Ultimately, suitability lies in the personality of the executive.

5

Team Members' Profiles

A number of team members' profiles are described in this chapter to give team leaders guidance on how people of different nationalities are likely to react to and perform within the team.

Although all members of a multicultural team may be characterized by a considerable degree of easy internationalism, tolerance, and cultural sensitivity, they will bring with them their own national values and core beliefs, taboos and prejudices, preferences, pet hates, perspectives – in short, their own worldview. Each presents to the team manager a different type of colleague, a different personality, proposition, task, psychological challenge – an individual to integrate and control in different ways.

Personal attributes define an individual's behavior more than their passport. However, owing to the great variety and nuances of human behavior, they cannot be forecasted. On the other hand, national characteristics can.

Determining national traits is treading a minefield of inaccurate assessment and surprising exceptions. In putting together these guidelines, I have made certain generalizations, which carry with them the risk of stereotyping as one describes the typical Spaniard, Chinese, and so on. It is evident that Americans differ greatly from one another and that no two Italians are completely alike. Nevertheless, my experience acquired during 40 years of living in many countries has led me to the conviction that the inhabitants of any land possess certain core beliefs and assumptions that will manifest themselves in their behavior. Cultural characteristics are remarkably consistent over long periods – a national culture changes at a glacial pace. There *is* such a thing as a national norm.

As Kate Fox points out in her excellent book *Watching the English*, there seems to be an assumption that a stereotype is by definition "not true" and that the truth lies "somewhere else" – wherever that may be. But a stereotype does not come out of thin air. We can get closer to reality not just by avoiding a stereotype, but by getting inside it. Though generalizations about the English regarding "reserve," "humor," "eccentricity," and so on are not untrue, they are subject to complex layers of rules and codes that are not entirely visible to the naked eye. By dissecting and scrutinizing such concepts, we find that while they take on different colors in different lights, they are in fact valuable keys to understanding the national character. Thus, "humor," with its undercurrents of understatement, irony, self-deprecation, and coded speech, is a valid description of an enduring English trait. Similarly, Japanese "politeness" must be evaluated against an intricate background of East Asian face protection, search for harmony, and the complex rules of Japanese society. German frankness and direct criticism may be seen as tactless, even brutal, but on examination can be more correctly defined as an honest attempt to improve another's performance.

The durability of culture

Individuals may and will vary in their interpretation of their own culture, but the culture and its implications do not disappear. Rather than say "a typical German," we should say "a representative of German culture" (but that sounds a little pompous).

A culture can be defined as the entire social heritage of a group, including mental and material features, learned actions and habits, shared artefacts and institutions, collective reactions, and psychological tendencies. Cultures exist as shared features of groups prior to the advent of any new members (children or immigrants, for example). In a sense, cultures are "lying in wait" for individuals to come along and experience cultural transmission from the group to the individual.

A culture has an existence outside any particular individual. Two arguments for its independent existence are first, that particular individuals come and go, but cultures remain more or less stable, in spite of a huge turnover in each generation. Thus, a culture does not depend on particular individuals for its continuity, but has a life of its own at the collective level of the group. Secondly, no simple individual knows or possesses all the cultural knowledge or traits of the group to which they belong. The culture as a whole is carried by the collectivity – it is beyond the grasp or capacity of any person to be familiar with all the community's laws, philosophies, political institutions, or economic structures.

Cultural phenomena are collective phenomena. Because they transcend the individual person, Alfred Kroeber termed them superorganic. However, the processes of cultural transmission and acculturation lead to the incorporation of features of culture as part of the individual, making these part of their psychological make-up. Culture is simultaneously outside and inside the individual, being both "out there" and "in here."

For instance, Herr Schmidt and Herr Meyer may exhibit different psychological tendencies, which causes people to say that there is no typical German, but in fact they are displaying variables of German cultural behavior that were lying in wait for them (for centuries) before they were born. It may not be permissible to say "Herr Schmidt will probably do this and that," but it *is* to say "*Germans* do this and that." We must avoid being judgmental and should not say "Italians talk too much," but if we assert that Italians talk more than Finns, we are describing a phenomenon that has been witnessed for hundreds of years.

In *From Nyet to Da*, Yale Richmond defends the concept of national characteristics and differences. He says:

> *A national may be unfairly stereotyped and there will always be exceptions to the rule. But who will not agree that Russians differ from Poles, Poles from Germans, and Germans from French, although these nations have lived side by side in Europe from time immemorial?*

French historian François Guizot also confirms the durability of national traits:

When nations have existed for a long and glorious time, they cannot break with their past, whatever they do; in the midst of the most glaring transformations, they remain fundamentally in character and destiny such as their history has formed them. Even the most daring and powerful revolutions cannot abolish national traditions of long duration. Therefore, it is more important, not only for the sake of intellectual curiosity but also for the good management of international relations, to know and to understand these traditions.

It will benefit managers of international teams to be aware of these traditions and norms, as it will enable them to be more familiar with the particular aspirations of an Italian or a Russian or a South American and adapt their leadership style accordingly. National types live in cultural habitats, which they carry around with them. What is a cultural habitat? It is a kind of "room" or "house" put together by a cultural group, inside which one holds a plethora of beliefs, attitudes, and assumptions. Within those walls one behaves in a prescribed manner, which overrules one's personal preferences. If the team manager can learn to enter that habitat and temporarily share and follow the "house rules," it will greatly facilitate the handling and leading of the team members.

This tactic is in effect the exercise of a temporary shared mindset. There is nothing immoral or untoward in doing this (in a chameleon-like manner) with different individuals. In fact, sharing a number of such perspectives contributes greatly to the competence and performance of the team leader.

The following national profiles apply to business people of the early part of the twenty-first century. With one or two exceptions, however, they hold good for the way people conducted themselves in the preceding century and, most likely, for a good part of the next. I apologize for presenting 23 of the 24 profiles in the male versions only. This is for the sake of uniformity and brevity. As I acknowledge in various parts of this book, women are increasingly playing important roles in international teams and often outshine their male colleagues in the areas of communication and perspicacity.

Australia: Leslie Perkins

Australians feature more and more as members in international teams, in Britain and Europe, in the USA, and increasingly in Asia. Leslie Perkins, from Sydney, is a huge asset to his team, as most of his fellow nationals are.

Roaming the world, Australians bring refreshingly new perspectives to multinational gatherings. Semi-Americanized, they are noted for quick thinking and rapid decisions (to which they add a creative cheekiness all of their own). Conversation is cheerful, always lively and unpredictable, as there is no manual for correct social or business behavior in Australia. Australian speech – a fascinating, inventive, adventurous variety of English – is characterized by humorous directness and absence of any inhibitions. It is informal and "matey," and has cute, Aussie words and expressions (digger, dingo, heart starter), all irresistible in a young, classless society. Leslie is generous and hospitable, essentially sociable, tolerant of others' ideas, and fond of compromise. Habitually a protector of the underdog (the "battler"), he eschews all forms of arrogance and wants a "fair go for all." He has the courage of his convictions and is unafraid of innovation or risk – Australians love to gamble.

Leslie lacks the international polish of a Dane or a Swede; he is better described as a rough diamond. As such, he is at his best when managed, since, as is the case with Americans, he is blind to some of the intricacies and subtleties of many European and Asian cultures. He is popular with other English speakers. Americans recognize in him their own traits of frankness and daring; Canadians sympathize with his half but not full Americanization; with the English, South Africans, and New Zealanders he has cricket and rugby to talk about. Germans, however, are shocked by his irreverence to authority. Leslie is polite to the team leader but says what he thinks. An Australian is often uncomfortable in hierarchical situations. A British or Nordic chair will give him a lot of rope; French or German team leaders may not know what to make of him. Leslie might contradict a colleague openly, then laugh about it and follow it with a vague Australianism: "No worries, she'll be all right in the end." This occasional laisser-faire attitude causes less of a problem than the "tall poppy syndrome," which is an Australian cultural black hole (more on this in Chapter 11). This enduring national trait harks back to the convict transports when to rise above your mates or associate with hierarchy would damn you in the eyes of your peers. Modern Australians will discard their normal congeniality at the drop of a hat if anyone on the team shows any sign of adopting a superior attitude or pulling rank. On such occasions Australian cynicism reveals itself markedly, sometimes accompanied by profanity. Swedish and Swiss colleagues – disciples of correctness – may be dismayed, though human-rights-obsessed Danes will approve entirely.

All in all, Australians are fun and add spice to a multinational group. The team leader must adopt a rough-and-ready approach, use first names, avoid big or obscure words, flowery speech, or innuendo, and call a spade a spade. Leslie dislikes too serious or complicated discourse – he hates unnecessary padding or pleasantries. Status symbols are out, pulling rank is out, and a personal touch is essential. Australians like leaders to cuss a bit (difficult for Swedes); it adds to the mateyness they crave. Their inborn sense of irony and perspicacity enable Australians to home in on cheating or false premises. In a land of many sheep, you cannot pull the wool over their eyes.

Belgium: Emile Bindels and Dirk Pienaar

Helge Lindberg is the Swedish manager of an international team consisting of two Swedes, two Belgians, one Englishman, one American, and one Frenchman. The team belongs to a large Swedish manufacturing company with good markets in the USA and northern Europe in general and the Low Countries in particular. The two Belgians – Emile Bindels and Dirk Pienaar – have been included in the team on account of their familiarity with the Belgian and Dutch markets, which show steady growth and satisfactory profits. The English, French, and American team members are experienced executives who have been in the (basically sales-oriented) team from the beginning. Lindberg can anticipate their opinions and works smoothly with them. On the other hand, he has not quite figured out the two Belgians, who are recent additions.

Both are hardworking members, as befits representatives of an economy that ranks 18th in the world, despite being 70th in population and half the size of Latvia in area. Pienaar and Bindels are punctual, alert, innovative, and competitive, flexible and far-sighted. When facing obstacles or dilemmas, they avoid hasty decisions and try to work out gradualist solutions. They show respect to the office of chair, make occasional proposals with the right degree of humility, and are generally cooperative on all matters.

However, Lindberg finds it hard to put his finger on the Belgian pulse, as each of them reacts in a different manner as issues arise. He feels that he understands Pienaar better, as his values and communication style seem to align fairly closely with Swedish behavior. In this respect, Pienaar clearly wants a consultative manager in order to join him in consensus (so beloved by Swedes). He is generally humble, obviously is uncomfortable with rhetoric or too much charisma, wants plenty of context, or knowledge of the strategy, and is quality conscious.

Bindels, on the other hand, want to know the facts well enough, but proceeds quickly to feelings (judgments and opinions). Though French speaking, he refrains from French-style rhetoric or peroration, but often indulges in a little charisma. He is not afraid to voice an opinion different from that of the team leader, whereas Pienaar hesitates to do this. Like Swedes, Pienaar pays little attention to status points such as titles or perks, whereas Bindels is clearly concerned with such matters, though to a moderate degree. Paradoxically, it is Bindels who expects Lindberg to make all final decisions, whereas Pienaar wants to be part of the decision-making process.

Lindberg noted that the two men had different negotiating techniques. Pienaar had little time for preambles and quickly proceeded to summarize bullet points to form the basis of discussion. He then embarked on the agenda and expected all to adhere to it strictly. Arguments could be frank and forceful, but restraint must be shown. Many options could be looked at and everyone was expected to speak. A consensus would be sought; little time would be wasted. If no solution was immediately available, doors would be left as open as possible at the end of his meeting.

Bindels, in contrast, employed a period of up to 30 minutes as small talk prior to getting down to business. He obviously attached more importance to setting the stage. He would then conduct and supervise a full discussion of all aspects of the negotiation. He works to a kind of agenda, but it is a flexible one with frequent digressions. Arguments will be elegant rather than frank, though not devious. All options are looked at, but Bindels controls the discussion – he speaks most. The negotiation style is win–win, but only just. Gradualist solutions are sought in case of disagreement; some impatience may creep in. Bindels is more concerned with face than Pienaar is.

Lindberg is aware of a certain tension between the two Belgians. Pienaar is Flemish, Bindels is Walloon. The two groups share a rivalry that has historical and commercial connotations. Internal affairs have been affected by disunity between the Flemish-speaking north and the French-speaking Walloons to the south. In the 1970s, the constitution recognized the two regions of Flanders and Wallonia. Increasing discontent became evident in 1991 when one million people voted for extremists and antipolitical parties in the general election. Separatist trends have continued. In the north, increased economic strength has encouraged Flemish nationalism. Meanwhile, the Walloons feel that they suffer from minority status – most government leaders are Flemish speakers.

Lindberg must of course be above such rivalries and disputes. He must emphasize tolerance as a team characteristic. He can behave like a Swede with Pienaar, but show more conservatism with Bindels. Neither Belgian likes too much dogma, so Lindberg must strike a balance between appearing easy-going and principled. In Belgium, compromise is the name of the game. The monarchy is popular with both sides, especially the late Queen Astrid, who, Lindberg notes, was a Swedish beauty.

Brazil: Paulo da Silva

A Brazilian on an international team is likely to be the most cheerful member, whether he has good reason to be or not. Paulo da Silva is no exception. Optimistic and future oriented, he works any hours; there is little that can dent his exuberance and joie de vivre. Like most of his fellow nationals he enjoys being Brazilian; he is fond of music, dancing, and of course football. In spite of his rather jolly manner, he does not lack perceptiveness.

Receptive to foreign ideas, he gets on well with Anglos (both British and American). Compared with Spanish-speaking South Americans, he demonstrates a comforting impartiality when judging non-Hispanic nationalities (he is sometimes a bit cool about Argentina). The violent history of Spanish American wars of liberation from the motherland led to 19 separate republics. Brazil, in contrast, achieved an amicable separation from Portugal and was able to keep its vast tracts of land and provinces intact within the borders of one settled nation. This successful nation birth, allied to the development of easy racial relations with black people, contributes to the easy-going spirit of tolerance that characterizes most Brazilians.

Paulo seeks friends quickly among his colleagues. He is flexible, agreeable, and imaginative, and rarely contradicts other team members. He is not touchy, is humorous (his self-image), and is generally charismatic. His strong point, apart from his agreeableness, is compassion. In the postwar years the Brazilian business community transformed itself from a heterogeneous collection of family enterprises into a more cohesive and somewhat dirigiste economy that is led by a large and experienced professional class. The national fiscal system is one of its strengths. Though relaxed in manner, Paulo is good at figures. In general, little escapes his attention.

Though not Hispanic, Brazilians are nevertheless Latins, therefore they possess certain characteristics that occasionally unsettle Anglos, northern Europeans, and other non-Latins. Naturally loquacious, Paulo delivers his opinion in a theatrical manner and often sounds over-emotional. He is not afraid to exaggerate to make a point and one wonders about the elasticity of his truth. It seems to be his habit to tell you what you want to hear; he does not like to be the bearer of bad news. Like most Brazilians, he dislikes unpleasantness and he avoids it whenever he can. He also avoids responsibility occasionally. He comes from a culture that is notoriously unpunctual, procrastinates, and pays late. He is, however, unlikely to allow himself such liberties in a team.

Paulo will be happy with the orderly manner by which northern Europeans run meetings. Brazilian meetings are somewhat unruly and several people speak at once. This often delays decision making. Another Brazilian weakness is lack of follow-up. Brazil is a country rich in resources, which enabled its inhabitants to prosper by exploiting one bonanza after another. Billions were made from a succession of commodities – coffee, sugar, soya beans. Instead of developing these industries to the limit, Brazilians tend to look for the next El Dorado. For this reason, Paulo will be rich in future-oriented ideas, but his degree of tenacity will have to be monitored.

From time to time the team manager may have to restrain Paulo's imagination and occasionally his loquacity. He must remember, however, that the lengthier the discourse between him and Paulo, the more cemented will be the Brazilian's loyalty. The team leader must always be cheerful and informal, accept a close distance of comfort, be relaxed about time, avoid unnecessary arguments, show affection for Brazil or football (or both), be cool about Argentina, show compassion at all times, and be paternalistic when appropriate.

Canada: Jim Patterson

Few nationalities enjoy such popularity in international teams as Canadians. Not only are they steady, reliable colleagues, but they often make good chairs or team leaders. Why should this be?

Jim Patterson, born in Calgary, works out of Vancouver. He dresses smartly but comfortably, is accommodating and laid-back, and has a folksy air about him. He has easy social graces, respects women highly, and excels at friendly small talk at cocktail parties.

In terms of his contribution to an international team, he is highly qualified. Canada is arguably the most multicultural country on earth. More than 40 percent of Canadians report having some ethnic origin other than English or French. The Canadian government is very active in protecting Canada's multicultural heritage; over 60 languages are spoken in 70 ethnocultural groups across the country. In Toronto alone there are more than 100 foreign-language newspapers and the local television station has programs in a large variety of languages. Canadians of all cultural origins have the opportunity to contribute to the common goals of equality, national unity, social harmony, and economic prosperity. Canada is the only nation to have taken part in all of the UN's major peace-keeping operations.

It is no wonder, then, that Jim Patterson is antiracist and possesses a keen sense of multicultural sensitivity. Consequently, he is impartial *vis-à-vis* all his team colleagues and is habitually tolerant, low key, uncomplicated, generous, and fair. In meetings he appears calm and reasonable, seeks compromise as a way to a win–win outcome, and prefers the soft sell to assertiveness. He is a good listener and looks at all options before proposing action. When a course has been decided, he is keen on quick implementation. In essence he is a man of action, but he requires plenty of context before launching an initiative. Canadian English has a pleasing sound to others' ears, being well articulated and lacking the nasal tones of some US accents. An attractive lilt enables Canadians to create a positive impression with people who hardly speak English. Jim's powers of soft persuasion are considerable.

There are few criticisms of Canadian behavior in a team atmosphere. Canadian affairs (and politics) are sometimes described as parochial, even dull. In some fields apathy is not unknown, and there is a certain prudishness about society. On the whole, however, Canadian low-key behavior engenders confidence rather than boredom. A certain amount of anti-Americanism exists, but it is intriguing rather than virulent. As Trudeau, one of the few well-known Canadian prime ministers, put it, "Living next to the US is like sleeping with an elephant – you lie awake waiting for him to turn over (and crush you)."

Patterson expects low-key leadership from a manager who shuns any form of ostentation or rhetoric and is truthful, trusting, egalitarian, and tolerant. The team leader can afford to impute the best motives, for Jim is a reliable ally guided by innate honesty and common sense. Canadian education teaches the young to question accepted wisdom and Jim may challenge his manager at any time. He needs plenty of context and loves debate. The team leader can benefit from such a give-and-take colleague. The leader should demonstrate cultural sensitivity and seek all-round agreement in the group before expecting Jim's approval.

It also pays to distinguish between Canadians and Americans, as in Table 5.1.

Americans	Canadians
self-centered	world awareness
pushy	low key
boastful	modest
prone to exaggeration	prone to understatement
jump to conclusions	methodical approach
individual is paramount	society counts too
nationalistic	moderate, even apathetic
don't respect cultural differences	multicultural
distrustful	trusting
superiority complex	occasional inferiority complex
reckless	moderate caution
restless	internal comfort
rushing	measured pace
expansionist	conservative, consolidating

Table 5.1 Americans and Canadians compared

China: Kong Dehai

Kong Dehai is a mainland Chinese who worked several years for IBM in China and has substantial experience of working with westerners and traveling abroad. Now a member of an international team belonging to a European company with extensive interests in China, he has secured his position by giving his team insights into the Chinese mentality and markets. A native of Shanghai, he is more free-wheeling in his thinking than Chinese from Beijing and the bureaucratic North, in the same way that Vietnamese from Saigon show more initiative than those from Hanoi. Though familiar with westerners, Kong cannot, however, be classified as a fully fledged "overseas Chinese" similar to those from Hong Kong or Singapore (who rank among the most impressive, all-round business people in the world).

Nevertheless, Kong is an impressive human being. His values, molded by an unbroken 5,000-year-old civilization, are multiple and resolute. His Confucian tenets define him as humble, modest, kind, considerate, dutiful, respectful, loyal, sincere, and courteous. Imbued by a sense of hierarchy, his respect extends to his team leader, colleagues, even subordinates and opponents. Thinking collectively, he readily exhibits the necessary ingredients for team working: punctuality, conscientiousness, work ethic, diligence, tenacity, stamina, and, when appropriate, self-sacrifice.

Like most Chinese of a certain age, Kong seems to evince a kind of ancient wisdom, displaying moderation, frugality, gentleness, huge reserves of patience and tolerance, quick generosity, as well as a refreshing proclivity for self-disparagement ("My immature opinion is..."). Britons and Finns often excel in self-deprecation (in the Finnish case self-effacement), but nobody can outdo the Chinese in this area. Humility, as prescribed by Confucius, is one of the cornerstones of Chinese behavior; any form of ostentation or boasting is an absolute taboo. The greater one's ability to demonstrate personal humility, the higher the esteem one will enjoy. Westerners, though they will never be able to plumb the depths of Chinese self-abnegation, would do well to try to achieve at least some degree of modesty if they wish to win respect from a Chinese colleague.

There is a story of an 80-year-old Chinese master carpenter who visited his son in the USA. The son introduced him to a prospective temporary employer (an American), who reportedly had the following conversation with the carpenter:

Employer: Have you done carpentry work before?

Carpenter: I don't dare say that I have. I have just been in a very modest way involved in the carpenter trade.

Employer: What are you skilled in, then?

Carpenter: I won't say "skilled." I have only a little experience in making tables.

Employer: Can you make something now and show us how good you are?

Carpenter: How dare I be so indiscreet as to demonstrate my crude skills in front of a master of the trade like you?

Kong, a good and careful listener during team discussions, follows the usual Chinese practice of asking others to speak first, just as he would when negotiating with opponents. This custom, shared conspicuously by Japanese and to a lesser extent by Koreans, denotes the Asian predilection to hear the other side's position before declaring one's own. By speaking second, they are able to modify the degree of variance between their opinion and that of the other side (a preliminary alignment of views might be available); at the very least a head-on collision can be averted. In this way Asians are fundamentally reactive, not in the sense of being passive (the opposite of proactive), but with the aim of avoiding possible pseudo-conflicts due to different degrees of self-assertion or pontification. Another advantage gained by this tactic is that it leaves one's options open for a little longer.

Kong's colleagues notice that by seeking their opinions in advance and seemingly accommodating their point of view, he invariably appears compliant and cooperative. His comments are occasionally ambiguous, though never discordant or antithetical. He seems adaptable but trustworthy. Modestly, he asks the team leader if he may speak, as opposed to barging in like German and French members do.

On the occasions when Kong is called on to negotiate on behalf of the team, his colleagues see quite a different side of his character. Whether dealing with fellow Chinese or other nationalities, Kong reveals himself as a canny, tough negotiator in the time-honored

Chinese tradition. To begin with, he avoids getting down to business with the other party, preferring to spend an inordinate amount of time chatting about anything but the deal in hand, socializing, eating and drinking with his adversary, getting to know them in a friendly, unhurried manner. When the business discussion eventually starts, Kong uses his incipient "friendship" (on the back of excessive entertaining) as a tool to ask for concessions, smiling all the while. If he makes little progress, he falls back on other tactics such as flattery, feigned anger, or indignation, mentioning competitors and threatening to take the business elsewhere, canny repackaging of conditions, faking indifference to success or failure, making a show of granting a series of concessions (in reality minor throwaways), using his opponents' own words against them, and generally, through patience and tenacity, tiring the other by attrition. Chinese are experts at making last-minute changes at moments that are most inconvenient to the other party, who may regret letting Kong know of any time constraints that affect their decision making. Kong's colleagues see that where other Chinese are concerned, any written contracts are meaningless compared to the personal commitments made by the negotiators.

In his own team circle, Kong is regarded somewhat warily by some colleagues. Mainland Chinese are less ubiquitous on international teams (and therefore less familiar) than Singaporeans and Hong Kongers. Kong seems westernized enough and certainly on side, but suspicion lurks in western minds, no less than it might in eastern ones. For one thing, he rarely seems to give straight answers to straight questions and, slightly annoyingly, he doesn't seem to ask straight questions, either. He is a master of the oblique, only hinting at positives and negatives and rarely coming down hard on either side. One often has the impression that what he has *not* said has considerable significance. And certainly, he frequently says what he thinks you want to hear. How do we know? Well, he smiles when he is nervous.

Kong's concept of the truth is not the same as ours. Chinese seem not to believe in the existence of absolute truth, only situational or contextual veracity. Of course, we all say sometimes "It all depends...," but Kong seems to inhabit a very dependent world indeed. Is he a free thinker, or is he in a sense being controlled? Sometimes he remains silent, then it is "Yes, but not easy...," or "I suppose anything is possible," or "That is a moot point." If we are not English we look up "moot" in our dictionaries, to discover that it means "discussable" or "debatable," which does not get us much further in the matter of what Kong really thinks.

He also flatters us a lot (which we can see through) and frequently sneaks us little gifts, which annoys us, as we don't know what to give back. We can't decline the little presents, as the manager says this would cause him to lose face and it has been drummed into us often enough that the dominant factor in an Asian's behavior is protecting everybody's face, so we do this diligently and go to great lengths not to upset or criticize Kong. This can be quite a strain in the long run, as we are not innately polite like he is. And he is so status conscious. He's certainly respectful to the manager, but always contrives to sit on his immediate right, which, as we are told, denotes him as the second most important personage in the room (or would in China, at any rate). We don't mind this too much, but he does have a tendency to moralize (to westerners) and often hints at the numerous Chinese virtues (we sometimes wonder about their modesty!).

Although we like direct questions and answers (and Kong often fails us in this regard), he lacks no directness when it comes to grilling us about personal details. In this respect, he appears just as inquisitive as Indians, who have no qualms about invading our privacy. "Are you married, Mr Lowe? No? Don't you ever feel lonely? Do you have any children? How old are you? What is your income? How much did the watch you are wearing cost? I hope you are in good health? Do you have any brothers or sisters? Are your parents well?" Of course, we impute the best motives for this curiosity, but Germans, Brits, Swiss, Norwegians, Swedes, and Finns are not comfortable with these incursions. French, Italians, and Americans don't seem to mind.

At the back of Kong's colleagues' minds is the question: How do the Chinese really look at us? What do they truly think of us?

Are we still the "foreign devils" of yore? In fact, Kong is more enlightened in this respect than one might think, but he certainly does not see westerners in the same light as they see themselves. Chinese recognize western technical competence, but consider both Europeans and Americans as inexperienced in business relations. European civilization is considered as of short duration. Chou-en-lai, when asked what he thought of the significance of the French Revolution, replied, "It's too early to tell." Chinese see American hegemony as shallow and short-lived. More than even the Japanese, French, and Italians, Chinese are convinced of their cultural superiority over all other nations. China – "Chung-kuo" or the Middle Kingdom – is, and has long been, the center of the world. Until recently, some 90 percent of Chinese had not only never seen the world outside China, but had never thought of it.

Of course, Kong has transcended this restrictive mentality, but he has a silent agenda that differs from western ones. China today has no deep conflicts of interest with Europe (as it has with Japan and the USA), but Kong's version of history differs wildly from that of the West. Not only does China boast the oldest civilization in the world (Yellow River, 5000 BC), but he is aware that for most of recorded history his country was the most populous, influential, inventive, and technically advanced nation in the world. Europe, in no uncertain terms, was a latecomer. Rome boasted about 350,000 inhabitants in 200 AD; China at the same time had a population of at least 60 million. But weight of numbers is only one thing. Most people know of China's early technological achievements and inventions – gunpowder, pottery, silk, canals, paper, block printing – but few realize that throughout history China always had the world's biggest economy, until it was overtaken by the USA in the 1890s. China's return to economic preeminence in the twenty-first century is no great surprise for Kong.

How should a team manager get the best out of a mainland Chinese colleague – valuable as an East–West bridge and still on a learning curve, but inherently complacent about his qualities compared to others? First of all, Kong, though incontestably Asian, undoubtedly has the interests and aims of the team at heart.

He may not have "changed sides," but he is more than anxious to bridge cultural gaps, liaise successfully between his paymaster and Chinese markets, and, like most Chinese, make money through commerce. He knows his place in the current hierarchy: his team leader must tell him what to do, as clearly as possible. The manager must combine courtesy and firmness, maintaining a deferential manner (dropping his eyes when giving orders), always keeping the correct power distance from subordinates. Kong does not like surprises or any form of pressurizing and expects his superior to protect his face at all times.

Team leaders will have no problem remembering this maxim and trust will consequently develop in due course. They must support the tenets of Confucianism – showing respect for order, consensus, and family – and avoid difficult subjects such as the Tiananmen Square protests, Communism, human rights, Taiwan, and Tibet. Kong will be gratified if he sees the manager's behavior as non-self-centered and respecting intuition as opposed to implacable logic. A Chinese team member needs to be given time to reach conclusions – he likes them to be long term – though he quickly reciprocates favors and sympathy. Kong rarely (or never) says "no," but his manager must read between the lines. Sexual jokes are taboo, those based on irony or sarcasm risky before the group. The number 4 is unlucky and Kong certainly believes in *feng shui*. It does no harm to refer to the millennia of China's cultural glory and an occasional Chinese meal together will do much to help bonding.

Denmark: Knud Rasmussen

Danes are often the most popular members of international teams. Knud Rasmussen, smart and well dressed, has an easy-going, laidback manner that is likely to disarm new acquaintances. His surface behavior seems impeccable: smiling from the outset, he is punctual, uninhibited, flexible, tolerant, and transparently humorous. One does not doubt his energy, work ethic, and ability to deliver.

He sells himself well as a representative of a modern, efficient yet caring society, whose commitment to egalitarianism and integrity is there for all to see.

When asked to contribute to team discussions, Knud is capable of giving a low-key presentation, characterized by its reasonableness but also by its business acumen. When challenged, he is readily accommodating and skilful at avoiding confrontation. He does not abandon his stance but subtly aligns it with others' views. Under pressure, he is well balanced. Team managers learn to appreciate his international smoothness and, frequently, his creative ideas.

Knud is a tolerant, careful listener, who rarely interrupts a colleague, preferring to create ideas silently while listening. His feedback is often productive and his questions are likely to be penetrating. He knows how to disagree in the most charming manner.

The question of Danish charm merits the close attention of the other members of the team, particularly the manager. The Danish word for charm is *hygge*, which signifies a kind of mild obsession to maintain a jolly atmosphere. Danes like things to be "cosy." They strive to chat in a cosy manner, their houses have to be cosy, storks' nests in Ribe are cosy, postmen's scarlet jackets are cosy, Copenhagen Town Hall's square is cosy, the Mermaid sits cosily on her cold slab in the harbor, the changing of the guard at Amalienborg Palace is cosy, the ultra-democratic royal family is cosy. *Hygge*, surely, is a good thing to have around.

Looked at in another way, Danes set great store by their ability to charm others. This is quite different from the face put on by other Nordics; Swedes, Norwegians, and Finns are much more concerned with giving a first impression of honesty and solidity. To southern Europeans a Dane looks honest and solid enough, but Norwegians and Swedes have described Danes as "slick," while Finns comment on their lack of follow-up. They seem to agree to all proposals well into the discussion or negotiation, but are skillful at modifying or repackaging items, sometimes after the meeting. While Latins are no strangers to this tactic, and the English in conflict-avoidance mode indulge in the same pastime, Germans, Norwegians, and Americans want to rein them in. Danes are not entirely happy at being "roped in," but maintain equanimity with an eye to future relations and business.

It would be churlish to deny congenial Knud such maneuvering room, but fellow Nordics are invariably keen on word–deed correlation, which is not his strong suit. There is no denying his honest intent, but hidden cynicism is a basic Danish trait that often prescribes a separate, silent agenda. Danes feel that no one can pull the wool over their eyes and spurn anyone who tries. This attitude is reflected in the Ten Danish Commandments I outline in *When Cultures Collide*, of which "You shall not think that you can teach us anything" is the final one. This trait is related to envy (*jantelove*), a sentiment that applies not only to comparisons of intelligence or success, but also to status symbols or any show of ostentation. The Danish preoccupation with the slightest instance of boasting or assuming a superior air is a kind of cultural black hole not dissimilar to the Australian tall poppy syndrome. The cherished egalitarianism is a notion that may not be threatened, any more than human rights may be impinged on. Many a forthright American or confident Frenchman enjoying a measure of individualism has fallen foul of Danish cynicism in this area.

The team manager who is aware of these Danish psychological undercurrents finds an excellent, capable ally in solving team tasks and problems. Knud's cynicism and ironic humor can be deployed to combat scheming opponents or cunning customers. Danes are clever at achieving good deals without making enemies. Knud will expect certain qualities from the team leader: a sense of humor, appropriate anecdotes, tolerance, modesty, and respect among them. In Denmark, bosses mingle with staff and talk to them in a confidential, almost conspiring manner. A hint of wisdom born of experience is not out of order. Danes seem to love food more than other Nordics and it is said that many an intractable problem has been solved over a good dinner in Copenhagen. The casual, laid-back stance typical of Danish managers does nothing to interfere with their drive toward prosperity, however. Knud must be monitored, for sure, but the trick is to do this in a friendly, informal manner while maintaining propriety and correctness.

The Netherlands: Dick Egberts

Dutch members of an international team do not take long to make their presence felt, as their salient qualities are energy and industriousness, openness and directness. Dick Egberts is no exception, exhibiting a roll-up-your-sleeves attitude to getting down to business. He will waste neither time nor money.

Dick's English is impressive; he can often pass for an Englishman when interacting with most nationalities – sometimes even English speakers are not sure. He cultivates a cosy kind of relationship with Anglos, especially the British and South Africans. He can even talk about cricket.

Dutch people have a keen international outlook, born of several centuries of exploration, colonization, and ubiquitous trading. They often outpunched their weight in naval encounters; their political and commercial influence had a wide geographical spread, in both the East and West Indies as well as South Africa. At the end of the colonial era, the Netherlands permitted the immigration of large numbers of former colonial subjects. Today more than 15 percent of people living in Holland are not of Dutch descent. This background of international experience, and the lessons learned from it, make Dick a team leader's useful ally where issues involving cultural sensitivity are concerned. He can be outspoken and tough, but he knows where to draw the line. Dutch-speaking South Africans seem to have the same quality. Besides being at home with English speakers, the Dutch enjoy a linguistic affinity with other Germanic-language speakers and enjoy easy relations with Danes, Swedes, Norwegians, Austrians, and Swiss. There is a certain rivalry *vis-à-vis* the Germans, but a common no-nonsense approach results in good business. For an English or American chair, a Dutch team member can often serve as a useful psychological bridge to reach out to these colleagues.

Dick readily demonstrates an impressive list of positive qualities that contribute to the team's progress. He is punctual, orderly, calm and rational, efficient, tenacious, consultative, egalitarian, often inventive. There is no doubt about his work ethic and enthusiasm.

He is not, however, as straightforward as he seems. The caveat is that the Dutch are arguably the most paradoxical people in Europe. "God made the world, but the Dutch made Holland," the saying goes. This sturdy streak of independence and righteous pride in their ecological and commercial achievements have engendered certain paradoxical values that match the geographical anomalies. The Dutch are entrepreneurial to be sure, but they can also be ultra-cautious. They are conservative, but they admire innovation and invent many things. They are ambitious, often daring in their ventures, but they don't "give the store away." They are willing to invest mightily, while being essentially frugal by nature. They are champions of tolerance, but often appear stonily dogmatic. When they think they are right they are stubborn and opinionated, though they preach consensuality. They are proud of their permissive society, but often appear puritanical. Their pragmatism frequently has a didactic tinge to it. They claim to be direct and open, though they guard their own privacy jealously. They decry inquisitiveness, but ask many questions of others. They are basically truthful, but indulge in occasional "window dressing." They are disarmingly informal, but are suspicious of too-early familiarity and expect you to respect their titles.

As long as they are aware of these paradoxes, team leaders have excellent material to work with. Colleagues may find that Dick goes on too long about human rights and his hatred of any form of pretentiousness, but these traits suit the Nordics anyway. Dick cannot be easily persuaded or influenced by other team members' views; he is by nature argumentative and skeptical, but at the same time he is adept at avoiding giving offense. In the Netherlands, an accepted principle of discussion is that ideas are objective and are independent of the person expressing them. A worthy colleague may come up with a bad idea and vice versa, but negating a proposal is not equivalent to negating the person. This enables Dutch business people to express controversial ideas freely, even in front of superiors who are likely to disagree with them. The team manager will know this and no doubt respect the concept. What Dick may not appreciate in full is that when a Dutch engineer questions the judgment of a Mexican company president (in public), this is an occasion when Dutch directness and forthrightness may be less than productive.

It is advisable for the team manager to know the nature of Dutch leadership. The concept of status varies considerably between modern firms on one side and older (often family-owned) ones on the other. In the older industries the Dutch have a rather strong centralized tradition of power, with steep hierarchies and organizational divisions. Relationships between different levels are often difficult. Modern firms are in the majority in today's Netherlands. In great contrast to traditional firms, hierarchies are usually flat and boundaries between functions are flexible.

Leadership is based on merit, competence, and achievement. Managers are vigorous and decisive, but consensus is ultimately mandatory, as there are many key players in the decision-making process. Long "Dutch debates" lead to action, taken at the top, but with constant reference to the "ranks." Ideas from low levels, often debated fiercely and at length, are allowed to filter upward through the hierarchy (and be ratified). Dick, as a member of an international team, will adhere to the principles of such companies.

Dick's team manager must allow him to express his ideas fully and debate them at length. If they are not in accord with the leader's own views, quick concessions should be avoided, as the Dutch respect firmness. Dick should be permitted to be competitive in relation to other team members, as long as this is done covertly (as in Britain). Transparency is mandatory, emotion and charisma are suspect. Dick likes an agenda to follow; items should be in meticulous order. Like Germans and Norwegians, Dutch people have a tendency to indulge in soul searching in the presence of a superior, and Dick should be allowed this luxury when he is in such a mood.

England: Robert Bradley

Robert Bradley has the potential to be an influential member of any international team. To begin with, his likely fluent command of English (probably the team language) gives him an immediate advantage, perhaps shared by Americans, Australians, and so on.

He has to be careful, however, about how he exercises this advantage. Some English people new to international teams fall into the trap of exhibiting a certain linguistic arrogance. They may equate lack of language skills on the part of a Spaniard, for instance, with a lack of fluency of ideas. Another problem – only too common – is that they speak too quickly or (worse) too colloquially or idiomatically for their European or Asian colleagues, assuming 100 percent comprehension when it may be as low as 60–70 percent. Asians, in particular, tend to feign comprehension when they don't understand, which only makes things worse. This situation is not likely to persist, however, as Robert, perceiving miscomprehension, soon learns to eliminate from his speech idiomatic expressions, colloquialisms, specific jargon, slang, puns, and all but the mildest forms of sarcasm, irony, and double entendre.

There is one source of miscommunication that he will find hard, if not impossible, to eradicate from his style of address: the phenomenon known as coded speech. Britons often use coded speech in international teams without being fully aware that they are doing so. This type of parlance – often vague, understated, or humorous – can easily be misunderstood by non-English speakers, especially those who tend to take everything literally (for example Germans or Japanese). There is more on coded speech in Chapter 7.

This habit should not be considered as particularly negative. It is, in fact, generally well meaning, as it is often used to avoid upsetting or embarrassing one's interlocutor. The main intent of English coded speech is to avoid direct criticism of one's partner or team member by eschewing remarks that might "rock the boat." Nevertheless, it is hard to decode British ways of criticizing, praising, suggesting, condemning, or abandoning. Understatement and irony often lead to the opposite being said to what is actually meant. For example:

✦ I'll call you = I won't call you
✦ Hmm… interesting idea = Forget it

❖ We'll certainly consider it = We won't do it
❖ I agree, up to a point = I disagree
❖ I say, that's not bad = It's excellent

The French, who are direct and precise communicators, initially find Robert Bradley unclear and may suspect that he is devious. They are not used to having their questions answered with such phrases as "I'll have to think about it," or "It's a moot point," or "I'm not quite with you on that one." They find such replies rather condescending, especially when Robert tells them funny stories to distract them. Both French and Germans are wary of the English habit of using first names at the first or second meeting, thinking that not enough respect is being shown. Nevertheless, in an international team context, surnames rarely survive two or three encounters, particularly when Americans, Canadians, or Australians are involved. One of Robert Bradley's strengths is that he endeavors to strike the golden mean between excessive formality (French and German tendencies) and premature familiarity (American and Australian traits).

Humor is one of the most effective weapons in Robert's arsenal. He uses it to break up tension in a situation that is developing intransigencies, to avoid deadlocks, or simply to raise morale. He often tells a joke on himself (self-deprecation) or to direct criticism toward a pompous colleague. He tends to be more ironic toward Latins and other emotional team members; he rarely criticizes Nordics. Americans, Canadians, and Anzacs are likely to appreciate his humor, while Germans and Japanese find it intrusive and barely tolerate it.

Robert Bradley normally makes several positive contributions to the team atmosphere. He is diplomatic, tactful, laid-back, reasonable, helpful, willing to compromise, and seeks to be fair. He tries to conduct business with grace, style, humor, and eloquence. He is fond of debate and regards meetings as occasions to seek agreement rather than controversy. He is purposefully casual, portraying business as a kind of game, which one plays in a spirit approaching fun, but which one nevertheless wants to win. When he introduces an important point, he is likely to precede it with "By the way…"

Beneath the Briton's veneer of friendliness and casual refinement is a hard streak of pragmatism and mercenary intent. It is disguised reasonably well by a willingness to debate and seek accord. English people are often inventive and think laterally. Originality is prized and the diverse ethnic strands of British society facilitate this quality. It is often a useful resource for the team leader.

A number of British companies have vast international experience – the Anglo-Dutch firms Unilever and Shell are good examples. Their executives excel as international team members. Other enterprises send delegates who fall considerably short of these standards. Insularity is often a problem, where British business people, perhaps having won the war of words, fail to understand or address seriously the psychology and cultural habits of Europeans and Asians. Often they take few notes and pay only casual attention to continental aspirations and characteristics.

Robert Bradley comes to meetings with a plan that, to all intents and purposes, is characterized by its reasonableness. He follows agendas religiously and maintains calmness throughout, even if others become agitated. He attempts progress through arguments that demonstrate compromise and common sense. He uses reserve and understatement to combat heavy arguments. He agrees with colleagues whenever possible (but might qualify the agreement). He avoids being rushed into decisions and stalls if necessary. He uses vagueness as a tactic to relax the meeting or to ridicule an inimical team member. He appears open and decisive, but does not play all his cards early on. He enjoys alliances, but keeps as much independence as possible. Like many Brits, he cultivates the self-image of an impartial arbitrator. He listens well and gives lively and productive feedback. He likes brainstorming.

Motivating or handling Robert Bradley is easier for a fellow Briton than for a non-English speaker, though it is always a somewhat complex procedure. English people usually accept career challenge as an incentive (as well as money). One can encourage them to be competitive, but they must not tread openly on others' toes. There are unwritten rules about fair play. The team leader's strongest weapon *vis-à-vis* a Brit is dry humor, supported by a cool, laid-back approach. Self-disparagement is probably the most effective of all. Neither should one be too serious about making money. One loses nothing by being casual about it. The English like a little leg pulling. They also like orders to be given in the form of suggestions or hints: "What do you think would happen if we tried this?" or "May I make a humble suggestion?" Team leaders are wise not to impose any strong opinions on Robert Bradley, who doesn't wish to jeopardize future compromise. Neither should they push logic; many English people pride themselves on their intuition.

Americans and some Europeans often complain about the English tendency toward conflict avoidance ("How the hell can we get things done in this time frame when he's so reluctant to confront?"). In fact, the problem is less likely to arise if the team leader involves Robert in planning from the beginning. Get each day's summary down in writing and mutually agreed. Don't see things as only black or white, right or wrong; Brits like to qualify all they can. If one emphasizes joint goals where he and the team leader depend on each other to achieve completion of the task, Robert will move forward. Hinting that one will be in trouble if he doesn't help out is most likely to be effective.

Finally, one must remember that there are many types of Brits. Robert Bradley is a typical southern Englishman, not unlike the prototype often shown in British films or by the BBC. People north of Birmingham, as well as Celtic Brits, tend to be more focused and hard-headed, show more openness and warmth, have less respect for class distinctions, resemble Nordics in many ways, and often get on well with Americans.

Finland: Tauno Tähtinen and Ritva Vaulamo

Finns are reserved, often introvert by nature, and may seem less than cheerful when joining an international team. Tauno Tähtinen, initially unsmiling, has a firm handshake but says little after being introduced and takes stock of his companions before revealing his views. He distrusts verbosity, enjoys silences, and is good at self-effacement. In due course he will venture his opinions, but will limit his words to what he considers necessary. Gossip and idle chat are alien to him; he has been taught not to pry or to impose his views on a listener. He has an independent streak and resists persuasion by others. One cannot twist Tauno's arm. He dislikes the hard sell; even charisma is suspect. He never gushes and frequently appears pessimistic. When left alone, he obviously enjoys his solitude. To sociable Italians and exuberant Spaniards he is enigmatic, opaque, and unfathomable.

In spite of his gruff exterior, Tauno has a heart of gold. He not only brings to the team efficiency and utter reliability, he is essentially a very modern individual, possessing the type of perspicacity and inventiveness that enabled Finns to transform their struggling, war-battered state in 1945 into one of the most developed countries in the world. The exponential rise of Nokia from tires and timber to leading the global telecommunications industry is indicative of the Finns and their characteristic business style. Tauno's colleagues may ask themselves: How did Finland become number one in global competitiveness? Why is it dominating the field of cellphones? How did it become the world leader in managing water resources? Why is it designated annually (along with Japan and Korea) top in educational standards? Why are Finns regarded as the ideal peace-keepers? Why does the country lead the world in environmental sustainability? Why has it won more Olympic medals per capita than any other nation?

Tauno probably knows the answers to many of these questions, but he is not likely to tell you. Finns are modest about their achievements and rarely mention them. They are, however, intensely proud of what they have done and have innate self-confidence (though that was not the case until the end of the twentieth century). In the postwar period they suffered from a periodic inferiority complex; it took them several decades of effort and struggle to convince themselves that they really were the best. Now they believe that they are more efficient than Germans and work faster than Americans, but that belief rarely escapes their lips. Suffice it to say that their standards of truth, honesty, and task orientation are irreproachable. Though jealous of their privacy and the right to dissent, they have a strong concept of service. Their tenacity (*sisu*) is legendary.

Tauno is a valuable ally to his team leader. Though decidedly reticent in discussions, he has a habit of delivering succinct summaries in the later stages of a meeting. His colleagues notice that though he speaks little, he is worth listening to when he does. His apparent pessimism (for he often makes gloomy pronouncements) turns out to be realism. Finns regard statements as promises; Tauno is careful not to forecast anything he cannot deliver. His fellow nationals have retained humility in the midst of their success. Any form of boasting is taboo in Finland; adherence to facts and accuracy is mandatory. One of the great advantages of having a Finn in the team is that he is always willing to discuss worst scenarios as well as best ones. This is a valuable resource for a chair who might feel that the group is getting carried away by American or Italian optimism.

Tauno is a good listener and hardly ever interrupts a colleague. If he disagrees, however, he will say so at the end. His directness is legendary and he is not afraid of confrontation, though he remains polite. The structure and thrust of the Finnish language do not calibrate too closely with Indo-European tongues, so occasionally he may sound brusque or too blunt for delicate listeners like Swedes or Japanese. Finns are in fact hardly ever impolite to the point of rudeness, but sometimes have to learn to soften their expressions as English people tend to ("That's an original thought" = "That won't work").

Team managers find that they can rely on Tauno's work ethic, diligence, decisiveness and courage, fidelity, straightforwardness, and dry humor. He has respect for authority; he considers that status is gained through achievement. He is of course democratic and classless. As a citizen of a young, vibrant nation, he is results and future oriented. His twin ideals are reliability and capability.

Tauno, though reticent, has transparent goals. The team leader can motivate him by being transparent himself: open, direct, and to the point. People managing Finns must remain low key at all times, and display modesty and understatement. Tauno is not terribly interested in small talk; one has a cup of coffee and then one starts. Importance is attached to accuracy: what is said is more important than who says it. Tauno likes clear instructions and then wants freedom to carry them out. A manager should never hover over a Finn, who needs both physical and mental space. Give a Finn a task and he will go away and do it, preferably alone. He will bring the results to you in due course. It does, however, pay a team leader to share planning early on with a Finn and ask for his ideas. If that doesn't happen, the Finn will proceed alone to an entrenched position from which it will be difficult to dislodge him later.

Tauno's pace is steady and consistent, but not overly hurried. The day should finish with an understanding of items agreed. Mutual agreements must be adhered to, and no debt of any kind must be left hanging. Protocol is minimal and lunches are quick. Almost any service or help can be extracted from a Finnish colleague by showing him that you are relying on him. The team leader should be willing to share Tauno's silences, learn a few words of Finnish, know the name of the Finnish President, and refrain from praising the Swedes or Russians too much.

Cultural traits attributed to Tauno Tähtinen, particularly with regard to communication, reflect attitudes of the Finnish male in social and business situations. Finnish women such as Ritva Vaulamo, while sharing many of the same characteristics, are nevertheless much more outgoing than the men, displaying few signs of uneasiness in the presence of foreigners. The Finnish woman could be described as strong-willed, adventurous, restless, often fearless, not without charm, and decidedly in love with life. Her level of education is second to no one and this gives her a feeling of self-confidence, making her a force to be reckoned with in international business.

As a communicator, Ritva outshines Tauno. She often commands three or four languages (speaking better English than many

British people). Unlike the Finnish male, she plays her full part in a two-way conversation, not missing her "turn" and shunning the reflective silences so popular with Finnish men. She has many of the communicative qualities they would dearly like to have. With foreigners she does not always find the right message, but usually she picks the right response.

The number of Finnish women participating in multinational teams is growing rapidly. Perhaps the most famous to date has been Sari Baldauf, former President of Nokia Cellular Systems. The trend for the future is quite clear. Given their ability to establish early rapport with non-Finns, Finnish women have been somewhat under-utilized. Ritva has much of the attractive, human-oriented magnetism that is required in an international group and has developed the psychological skills to enable her to interact successfully with ethnic cultures differing widely from her own.

France: Yves Martin

Yves Martin is a Parisian, with all the clear-sightedness and quick imagination typical of the people of that city. The team leader has to keep an eye on him, for French people believe in their uniqueness (just as Japanese and Chinese do), the difference being that in the case of the French they are not shy in telling you about it. Their vivacity is such that they often see others as somewhat wooden. They accept the authority of a chair, but are not afraid to be a maverick. As they tend to clarify their own thoughts through wordiness (ruminating aloud), this can cause meetings to over-run.

While a Frenchman may not be an ideal member of any international team that wants to run smoothly and harmoniously, he nevertheless has a lot of positives to contribute. His perceptive and quick mind will animate a team (on occasion he can set it on fire). Yves Martin is consistent; that is, though he is clearly opinionated and pushes his proposals forward with vigor, he does not desert logic. Rationality – indeed, Cartesian logic – is the cornerstone of French argumentation.

Cartesian logic is related to René Descartes, a seventeenth-century French philosopher and mathematician. Descartes' methods of deduction and intuition inform modern metaphysics. The theory is to doubt all one's impulsive ideas, but to find one indubitable truth or fact, then focus on it and proceed to build theories and propositions on it. This gives French people great confidence and momentum in pursuing an argument. Others, such as Japanese or Americans, may find fault with this approach, being guided perhaps by different cognitive processes (Asian) or simply fondness for hunches (American). They may also judge the "indubitable" truth as "dubious."

Yves Martin will display considerable determination using this type of logic. Like most Frenchmen, he would rather be right than popular. It is often said that French people regard theories as more important than truth and may ignore certain facts for this reason. An official of the British Statistics Board, working on an Anglo-French team, actually quoted his French counterpart, who had been clearly shown that a certain pump had functioned perfectly for 18 months, as saying: "Yes, it may work in practice, but does it work in theory?"

To be fair to Yves, he will cooperate with you readily if you defeat his logic. After that, he will be hospitable toward your suggestions and will remain your supporter and good friend for ever. As long as you remain rational, of course. He is human and considerate – he just sets great store by clarity of thought and vision and always has in mind the historical perspective. He can live in the present, also be futuristic, but fundamentally he is firmly past oriented. The past is not dead; in fact (as Faulkner said) it is not yet even past.

French executives in teams or at high-level international meetings (GATT, OECD, and so on) not infrequently conflict with colleagues, in big and small ways. During team projects they irritate Anglo-Saxons and others by digressing from the agenda at regular intervals. They do this more than any other nationality, except perhaps Italians. Their reasoning is this: all items leading to progress on the project are inter-related; one thing affects another. If you

fire M. Dupont unconditionally during item 2, you will be in des-
perate straits if he is the only staff member who can help you out
in a vital matter that comes up in item 6.

The French have a deep-rooted distrust of the Anglo-Saxon
habit of segmenting issues and finalizing solutions in sequence.
Discussion of the project should, in their view, be all-embracing,
considering actions and decisions from many different viewpoints,
before finalizing anything. Perhaps it is better not to decide today,
but to leave it till tomorrow, or even later. Anglo-Saxons habitually dislike leaving anything "hanging in the air." One English
chair, working together with his loquacious and digressive French
counterpart (on a Channel Tunnel committee I attended regularly),
used to take up his pencil at 4 pm every day (after hours of deliberations) and say wearily, "Mr Chairman, could we please both write
down any points we have agreed on?" The Englishman was not too
aware that French people regard conversation as an art, and consequently have no objection to prolonging it for its own sake.

Another recurrent problem is that posed by the French sense
of intellectual superiority. A Frenchman does not fully believe that
a Finn, American, Swede, Slovenian, or Bulgarian (among others)
can ever really tell him anything he does not know. Consequently,
he does not listen too carefully to Americans or "minor" nationalities and may often adopt a condescending or patronizing tone
when he addresses them. He shows a little more respect to opinions of the older, "established" nations – Germany, Britain, Spain,
and Italy – but even with them it is a close thing.

Yves Martin is likely to be criticized by his fellow colleagues
as being too verbose, too opinionated, too French-centered, anti-
American, or anti-Anglo-Saxon and lacking understanding of other
cultures. He is also too fond of long lunches!

How to control him? A good start is for the team leader to speak
good French – if he can, it will win him a lot of allegiance. He
should also mention La Belle France, as well as French history, culture, and brilliance at every opportunity. He should acknowledge
that the French resistance to American influence is partly consistent with playing the role of defender of European culture. A good

tactic to defend the team from French verbosity is to agree with Yves early on. One can always repackage later or confuse him with funny stories.

Yves will appreciate a chair who is well dressed, tries their hand at wit, and knows something about French wine and cheese. He enjoys fierce debate. The team leader should let him win; Yves is ready to compromise later if some small concessions are made. One should, however, avoid the word "compromise," as French correlate it with American wheeling and dealing.

Team leaders should show Yves their human side – mild emotion suits both. They should also display generosity when they can, as even hubristic Frenchmen respond well to and reciprocate generosity. They should try to ignore too much body language, extroversion, or cynicism, and tolerate over-inquisitiveness or finicky behavior. Long-windedness and French interruptions may also have to be permitted. Yves means well, but is used to perorating in a French environment. Also, when negotiating a point he may only reveal his hand at a late stage. Americans see this as devious. The chair should point out to Yves that all-embracing solutions are often difficult and slow to achieve, and that HQ has a tendency to encourage quick action. Above all, team leaders should be careful not to contradict themselves, should use self-deprecation as a tactic, and, when they can, should tell Yves something he doesn't know!

Germany: Hans Stollmeyer

It is natural that Hans Stollmeyer should be an ideal member in an international team. Since the formation of the European Community (now the EU), Germans have been dedicated and disciplined internationalists, preferring collective teamwork and cooperation to individualism and competition.

Hans thinks that he is among the most honest, straightforward, and reliable people on earth. He believes in scientific rather than contextual truth and conducts his private and professional life on this basis. He has great respect for facts and figures, the law, property, and hierarchical rank. He knows his place in the pecking order of the team (if there is one). His standards of cleanliness, orderliness, and punctuality are beyond reproach; his work ethic and efficiency are surpassed by none. He habitually stands by his commitments and keeps his word. Concepts such as fidelity, loyalty, and honor are very much alive in Hans' world.

His German communication style is serious, frank, and open. He is rarely, if ever, devious; he prefers to disagree openly rather than simulate compliance. He is not slow to criticize because he believes that constructive criticism is helpful and beneficial. If a team member makes a mistake (of calculation or judgment), Hans is most anxious to help him not to make the error again! American, Canadian, and Nordic colleagues usually take this well. French, Spaniards, Dutch, and Japanese, among others, are often less grateful.

During team meetings Hans is polite, but does not indulge in too much small talk, which he suspects is a waste of time. He drinks in facts and information and often makes notes. He likes instructions to be given clearly and repeated when necessary. He often seeks clarification from colleagues or the chair. He is a good listener and rarely interrupts another speaker. He believes that business is built on reliable procedures and processes and works hard to perfect these within the team context. He comes to meetings well prepared and often goes into great detail. He always tries to stick to logic; his strong points are adherence to quality, on-time delivery, and competitive prices or conditions.

The German concept of good leadership is interwoven with the notion of *Ordnung*, where everything and everyone has a place in a grand design calculated to produce maximum efficiency. It is difficult for the impulsive Spaniard, the improvising Portuguese, or the soulful Russian to conceive of German *Ordnung* in all its tidiness and symmetry. It is essentially a concept that goes further in its theoretical perfection than even the pragmatic and orderly intent of Americans, British, Dutch, and Scandinavians.

In the German business world, established, well-tried procedures have emerged from the long experience of their older companies, guided by the maturity of tested senior executives. In Germany, more than anywhere else, there is no substitute for experience. Senior employees pass on their knowledge to people immediately below them. There is a clear chain of command in each department and information and instructions are passed down from the top. Communication is vertical, not horizontal. Germans do not go across the company to chat with people at their level in other departments. Most business ideas are proposed either to one's immediate superior or one's immediate subordinate. Obviously, in an international team Hans will free himself of these restrictions. Team members gain most from speaking as equals, though Germans have a tendency to tread delicately with the team leader. Hans strives for consensus at all times, but in a different manner from Italians or other Latins. In his view, consensus is obtained by clarification and justification, not by persuasion or truly open discussion.

Hans' social behavior within the team is likely to be more formal than others', especially in the first meetings. He smiles less than Americans or Italians, but he is sincere. He shakes hands more frequently than Anglo-Saxons do. He is reluctant to use first names in the initial stages of a relationship and persists with surnames and titles until the team leader asks him not to. Subsequently, he is benign. German executives tend to come across as a bit heavy to some nationalities, especially when they evince impatience with the Anglo-Saxon habit of interjecting humor in the business discussion. They also dislike flippancy; Germans believe that a serious question deserves a serious answer. After a few meetings, however, Germans take pains to develop friendships with other team members, who discover that a German friendship is really worthwhile.

From their position of authority, team leaders have a relatively easy task in getting the best out of Hans Stollmeyer. Any instructions they issue should be firm and unambiguous – Germans hate misunderstandings. Even criticism should be direct. If Hans is criticized in a subtle (perhaps British) manner, it may not register with him at all. Cooperating with Germans means respecting *their* primary values – punctuality, orderliness, efficiency, persistence, work ethic, and sincerity – according to *their* standards.

The German obsession with completing action chains must be taken into account. Hans expects to be instructed, supervised, and monitored until the task is completed. He is admirably single-minded; too casual an approach will be misunderstood. A simple rule when addressing Hans is to say what you mean, as irony, sarcasm, or subtle undertones will fall on deaf ears. On the other hand, Germans dislike over-simplification. They often see Americans and some others as naïve. If you ask a German why he is fond of the complex and complicated, he replies by pointing out that life is not simple. Wisecracks, gimmicks, and slogans do not impress Hans. Once team leaders have established their status with him, they must live up to it and maintain an earnest, purposeful mien.

Remember to greet Hans fully whenever you meet him and to shake hands frequently.

Hong Kong: Andy Chen

International teams who do business with China or with Chinese business people in South-East Asia (Indonesia, Thailand, Malaysia, Singapore, the Philippines) are glad to have Andy Chen, a Hong Konger, as a colleague. To begin with, he seems more European than Chinese, or at least Anglo-centric, and often conveys the impression of looking at mainland Chinese as an outsider rather than being one of them. In fact, 99 percent of Hong Kongers are ethnic Chinese, so that Andy's mentality is basically Chinese and for this reason he is a valuable team member: he knows how "the other side" thinks.

The basic characteristics of Hong Kongers are similar to those of mainland Chinese, but they are not the same. In the first place, their ancestors came almost exclusively from the Guangdong province, which means that they speak not Mandarin, but Cantonese. People from Hong Kong and Beijing have difficulty understanding each other orally, though they can do so in writing. In the world at large, language determines thinking rather than the other way round: people who speak different languages or dialects think in different ways. In the brain our thoughts are channeled along Anglo-Saxon grooves, neo-Latin grooves, Japanese or Chinese grooves, and so on. Regional speech determines regional thought, so that Canadian and Louisiana speakers of English think differently, as do Yorkshire people and cockneys and, moreover, speakers of Mandarin and Cantonese. People from Shanghai, speaking and thinking in Shanghainese, act differently (and in a freer way) than inhabitants of Beijing. Andy, who has been brought up speaking Cantonese and who was partly educated in English, is closer in mentality to Anglos than are mainland Chinese or most other Asians.

If we look at some of the differences in the psychological attitudes between Hong Kongers and mainlanders, it is fairly clear why there is ample compatibility between the British and the inhabitants of the former colony. This compatibility also extends to other English speakers who are familiar with British traits. How much do Hong Kongers and mainlanders diverge? In the first place, Andy is no stranger to English history and traditions. Hong Kong, founded in the 1840s by the British for the sole purpose of trade, is by any standards one of the world's leading business centers and the preeminent focal point for trade in East Asia. Comparable to New York, London, and Tokyo in commerce, development, and wealth, it is the meeting place of two great cultural traditions: East and West. Andy is versed in Hong Kong law, which is based on the British legal system, and not only has he conducted business according to British principles and practices, he knows all about Ascot, Wimbledon, Oxford, Cambridge, Harrods, soccer, cricket, fair play, and parliamentary rule. His familiarity with British institutions is therefore the chief difference between him and continental Chinese. There are also numerous differences in behavior.

In business, mainlanders are slow and methodical, Andy is brisk and speedy; mainlanders are by necessity bureaucratic, Andy cannot stand red tape; mainlanders are patient, Andy is impatient; on the mainland delays are common, in Hong Kong they are avoided; mainlanders often have complex commercial aims, Andy is single-minded (profit); mainland China brings eastern wisdom, Hong Kong combines eastern and western strengths; mainlanders may not lose face doing business, Hong Kongers are pragmatic; ortho-dox Chinese habitually resist change, Andy is adaptable; mainland-ers make concessions slowly, Hong Kongers act quickly to secure business; mainlanders focus on process, Hong Kongers on the bot-tom line.

Mainland Chinese are hard-working and diligent, but in Hong Kong the pace is different. Energy levels may be comparable, but in Hong Kong energy is concentrated on speedy decisions and oppor-tunist action. Mainlanders doing business may be slowed down by government control or the necessity for numerous lateral clear-ances. In Hong Kong, where most of the business is carried out by small families, entrepreneurship has free rein (American style). Mainlanders strive for the collective good, Hong Kongers think more individually (about the family good). On the mainland people are generally statically employed, in Hong Kong job mobility is an important factor – that is why Andy is on an international team.

His negotiation abilities are similar in character to those of Kong Dehai. He combines tenacity and canniness with surface courtesy and amiability; he can, however, be more openly rude to over-cautious opponents and often interrupts them (which mainland-ers rarely do). Though he observes a certain amount of preamble and small talk with opposing parties, he often barely tolerates this procedure and betrays his anxiety to get down to business without undue delay. In Hong Kong grass does not grow under the natives' feet!

Andy's team manager knows how valuable he can be when the team has to engage with any party east of Kathmandu. He is not difficult to manage, since he is familiar with British mentality and knows a lot about westerners in general. His Sinic traits of work ethic, calm, and a sense of order and hierarchy make him a com-pliant recipient of instructions and discipline, while at the same time his entrepreneurial spirit, relish for speedy action, and lurking sense of humor lead to frequent displays of initiative and endeavor. He could almost be described as the ideal team player, especially when looking East.

India: Sachin Dravid

Sachin Dravid is a go-getting Indian who feels that the numerous positive factors in India's recent development make him a valuable member in any international team. His country is the largest recognized democracy in the world with relative political stability, has a reputation as a neutral, long business experience with Africa, South-East Asia, and Europe (especially the UK and Portugal), and serves as a geographical, cultural, and psychological bridge between East and West. India has a fast-expanding pool of skilled, educated manpower with a good command of English, familiarity with market economics, and 10,000 listed companies with large capitalization. Its strong historical ties with Britain – commonalities include parliamentary rule, a large civil service, army traditions, tea, cricket, tennis, an Oxbridge-educated élite, admiration for English literature, a class system, and titles for nobility – facilitate an easy working relationship with British and most English-speaking team colleagues.

Sachin shines as a warm, generous, courteous, and moral personality with human, family values and ample resources of patience, tolerance, and humility. His language skills (eloquent, sometimes Victorian English) are matched by his interpersonal skills. He is difficult to dislike, being readily accommodating, quick to praise, and reluctant to disagree or criticize. He is a good listener, who rarely interrupts other people and tries to align his views with those presented to him. He never deserts respect, shows professional loyalty (to team, company, or group), and sees himself as a reliable arbitrator when the occasion presents itself. His own negotiating skills equip him admirably for this. He is quick and perceptive and focuses on reasonableness and fair play. He abhors brute force or any form of abrasiveness.

Indians have a good work ethic, are capable of working long hours, and almost never watch the clock. Experienced in and skilled at business, they are frequent risk takers and make bold decisions once they have thought a matter through. Chaos is not uncommon in Indian business, though they are good at handling it. This is often effected through a characteristic DIY mentality (Indian variety) known as *Jugaad*. This can be described as a sort of hurried collective resourcefulness to get a job done against all the odds, the rapid finding of an alternative, laterally thought-out solution to gain time before the proper means to carry out the job arrive; one may use one's connections or possibly bend some rules along the way. *Jugaad* people never say it cannot be done. It is the spirit of whatever-it-takes. It is the spirit of India.

Sachin's go-getting manner notwithstanding, his team colleagues may sometimes find him less than perfect. He can be unpunctual and now and again seem disorganized. Not always calm, he can be judged verbose and even over-emotional. He has the habit of giving ambiguous answers to straight questions and one suspects he has a flexible sense of truth or perhaps window dresses. Is his regular compliance only surface amiability? His skill at "repackaging" issues is well known. Too much charisma? Indian charisma is hard to pin down, as it is always infused with courtesy and humility. What about his fatalism? To what extent is he involved with the Indian rigid class system, abusive treatment of women, and rampant nepotism in business? Are his everyday decisions affected by his Hindu religious tenets?

As a modern, well-educated, enlightened, and internationally minded team member, it is more than likely that Sachin rises above all these suspicions. Team managers have excellent material to work with. They must respect Sachin's sterling qualities, show sympathy with Indian circumstances, avoid being judgmental, and save face at all times. They must communicate clearly and often; Indians love follow-up and a close relationship can develop quickly. Sachin accepts hierarchy completely; he also expects empathy and paternalism. His team leader must look at things from an Indian point of view (if he can); one can learn a lot from them! Courtesy is always mandatory – one must avoid sarcasm or irony; even jokes are risky as Indians take remarks seriously and often literally. It is also better to tread carefully when mentioning the caste system or the current relationships with Pakistan or Bangladesh. On no account should one discuss Hindu–Muslim disputes (180 million Indians are Muslims). The team manager has everything to gain by learning something about Indian religions and by knowing and referring to some of the glories of the country's 4,000-year-old civilization.

Ireland: Ronald Morgan

Irish people often liven up an international team as they tend to be independent, unconventional, and resist too much structure or routine. Ronald Morgan, from Dublin, evinces immediate friend-liness and warmth. A romantic idealist, he is decidedly folksy. It is hard not to reciprocate his informality and what appears to be rustic simplicity. His sense of humor, obvious charm, and irony set him apart from the typical modern executive. He would not object to being seen as old-fashioned and his sense of poetry and philoso-phy suggests a strong affinity with literature, music, and the the-ater, none of which he would deny. One might ask oneself what his particular niche in international business is, if indeed he has one.

Only a few decades ago, Ireland had the reputation of being a poor, backward country with no industry to speak of, agriculture producing little other than flax and potatoes, a troubled political relationship with its neighbor Britain, and an archaic, "patriarchal, male-dominated Catholic church," as described by the country's first female president, Mary Robinson. Then suddenly everything changed. In 1973 Ireland joined the EC/EU. Mary Robinson was elected in 1990 and women went on to play meaningful roles in Irish politics and business. A peaceful settlement was achieved with Britain and heavy EU subsidies revitalized the country's economy. Industries sprang up, infrastructure was transformed, property values soared, and for ten years Ireland was the darling of the European Union.

Irish business people, previously considered by many as hardly progressive, now showed a wealth of inventiveness and business acumen and began to feature ubiquitously in international teams, acquisitions, and mergers. The country's recent economic problems have not dented its nationals' enthusiasm for business.

Ronald Morgan, speaking clear English with a delightful, disarming Irish accent and lilt, communicates successfully with English and non-English speakers alike. It is often said that the Irish are audacious in speech; certainly, they have good entertainment value. To their sense of poetry they add vision and imagination (perhaps sometimes too much of the latter). Though essentially engaging, they occasionally indulge in what they themselves call blarney. Blarney is not strictly untrue, but is embroidered with gentle hyperbole (understood and accepted by listeners who are familiar with Irish manners). Germans, Swiss, and Swedes have to be told about it, of course, but Australians, Canadians, and Americans normally love it.

Having said that, Ronald is perspicacious and creative. Unlike the English, he is a good linguist and understands Latins much better than Anglo-Saxons or Nordics do. He is likely to be popular (*sympathique*, *simpático*) with French, Spaniards, and Italians. Like the French, he considers ideas more important than facts, while his occasional forays into deviousness and ambiguity entertain Italians and Spaniards. He is a great raconteur and knows and tells innumerable stories, most of them with great humor. He is clever at self-deprecation, disarming would-be critics who are perturbed by his frequent digressions from the agenda and occasional tendencies to procrastination.

Ronald, with his spontaneous wit and meandering creativity, must be managed more carefully than most. His team leader would do well to reciprocate his warmth, folksiness, and humor and match his stories if he can. One needs to accept his irony and gentle philosophies, allow him digression and freedom of expression, recognize his creative talent, and, with the right words, keep him on track.

Italy: Franco Tonelli

Franco Tonelli brings to an international team much of the charisma and exuberance of a successful Italian executive. He is a charming and excellent communicator, outgoing and friendly, quick and opportunistic. He possesses ultra-keen perceptiveness and ever-present flexibility, and exudes immediate warmth and humanity.

Linear-active people, such as Germans, readily associate Italians with poor time-keeping, late payments, low legal consciousness, clannishness, an inadequate degree of commitment, and being subject to backroom influence.

Franco would have you dispense with such notions of what might be seen as the fragility of Italian cultural baggage. These characteristics are background – a kind of Mediterranean scenery. More importantly, other attractions are on offer. These include ready accommodation, physical and mental closeness, a sharing of emotions, help in difficulty, willingness to share conspiracy and to use the influence of friends, and free interpretation of the rule book if it is in your interest.

A team with northern European members may view this flexibility of interpretation as a form of dishonesty. Franco sees no harm in "bending" or "getting around" certain regulations, even laws. This is the way Italians do business and the team may very well be able to benefit from this "flexibility," particularly if operations are taking place in the Mediterranean area or anywhere east of Istanbul. Italians regard the Anglo-Saxon or northern European law-abiding approach as somewhat rigid, old-fashioned, short-sighted, or even blind. In this respect they consider they are closer to reality and less ideal bound. Italians do not consider their approach to be corrupt, immoral, or misleading. They will happily take you into their "conspiracy" and share the "benefits" with you if you accept. If you stick to the letter of the law, they will go on without you. There are many gray areas where shortcuts are, in Italian eyes, a matter of common sense.

During team discussions, Franco Tonelli is winningly persuasive without being aggressive in argument. Neither is he touchy (as are Spaniards and some French) when others criticize him. On the contrary, he accepts criticism with grace and humor. He is among the least chauvinistic of men, exhibiting a national modesty rivaled in Europe only by the Finns. His manners are charming and his innate people orientation guarantees his adherence to teamwork. He is a good and active listener. While you are talking, he is evaluating your personality and formulating his reply, trying to construct a relationship based on what you say and how you say it. Franco is anxious to gain your trust and draw you into his ingroup or inner circle. Once you qualify, he will be your most reliable ally through thick and thin.

Italians are less private than many nationalities and will share details of their personal lives, exchanging photographs and telling about their family, their aspirations and disappointments, where they were educated, where they go for their holidays and so on. Germans, Finns, and some others often react against such confiding behavior, seeing it as none of their business. Franco feels, however, like most Italians, that mental closeness contributes greatly to the cohesion of a team. Such revelations, including admission of personal weaknesses or deficiencies, indicate trust in the interlocutor. Italians do the same with customers, viewing interdependence positively. They are not averse to putting their feelings into words, seeing little advantage in vagueness or ambiguity.

Anglo-Saxons often decry Italian loquacity, opting for succinctness or economy of expression. But in Mediterranean countries, where words are cheap in the sunshine, conversation is not only an art and social enjoyment but an information-gathering and sharing mechanism, a valuable vehicle of communication for both social and business purposes. Even gossip – a word with nasty connotations to Nordic ears – has its place in business and teamwork. Italian *chiacchiera*, conducted by women on doorsteps and men in cafés, is a kind of social glue that aligns people's opinions and increases trust between them.

Franco Tonelli may respect an agenda, but he does not regard it as holy. He has a tendency to loop back to rediscuss points that Anglo-Saxons thought had been settled earlier. By doing this, he often discovers links that in fact need to be considered. French team members do the same. Franco often seems to look at matters from a personal or emotional angle, though he respects the views of others and accepts his place in the team hierarchy. Occasionally he speaks over someone else, but he shows he can listen and speak at the same time, which is difficult for Anglo-Saxons and Germans to do.

An experienced team leader can get a lot out of Franco Tonelli by handling him in the right way. This involves acknowledging the cultural debt that Europe owes Italy, by being explicitly human at all times, by frequently asking him for help and being unafraid to ask for advice. Italians respond well to praise and flattery and like discussing openly matters that some nationalities consider private, such as religion and political views. One should confide in an Italian, exposing a personal weakness for him to protect (this makes him trust you). One should also value the acquaintance of people he may introduce to you. One should enquire about the health of his relatives, share family details, and speak with a laugh in one's voice, all in an implied context that only Italians really understand what makes the world go round.

Italian team members often constitute the social glue that holds a team together.

Japan: Hiroshi Tanaka

Hiroshi Tanaka is likely to be the politest member of your international team. The Japanese, packed together in large numbers in big cities on overcrowded islands, have developed a social system that requires *ne plus ultra* standards of courtesy and conscientiousness. Hiroshi distrusts verbosity; he speaks little, compared with other members of the team. Even when he does speak, his communication is not always clear, as often the point he wishes to make may be lost in a fog of impeccable behavior. He is frequently ambiguous, avoiding confrontation with other opinions, but also leaving his options open. To colleagues he seems likable, but somewhat opaque.

In spite of this opacity, his sterling qualities shine through. He is punctual, immediately cooperative, and evinces stamina and a work ethic. His natural Japanese inclination toward teamwork causes him to be invariably modest, self-effacing, and ready for self-sacrifice. Any individual views he has he subordinates to the general interests and objectives of the team. His (perhaps secret) role is to promote harmony among his team members. He cannot lose face, but he also strives to avoid loss of face for others.

Hiroshi Tanaka is ultra-honest and always keeps his word (when you have found out what it is). The oral agreements he makes are as valid as written ones; he is a fairly solid character. By nature he is (like most Japanese) kind, thoughtful, and hospitable. He offers, and searches for, trust. Any form of personal debt is anathema to him. His self-image is one of a highly cultured individual with a keen aesthetic sense. He excels in considerate, delicate, and graceful behavior. He is the ally of the team leader.

If all this sounds good, that is because it *is* good, as most Japanese are more sincere and trustworthy than many westerners give them credit for. The rather fixed Japanese smile, which some people consider deceitful, normally does indicate pleasure, only rarely the opposite. After all, many Americans and Italians habitually flash smiles, so why pick on the Japanese? What the Japanese do not do (as many westerners might) is glare at colleagues who disagree with them.

There are, however, certain aspects of Japanese behavior that must be properly understood by colleagues if harmony is to prevail. Japanese believe that they are a unique people (Americans heartily agree with them!) and consequently they never fully accept that foreigners can understand them. This causes them to "shut off" occasionally when they think they are not getting through. They are basically uneasy with foreigners and are still, after centuries of isolation or hostility, finding their feet in terms of self-expression and cooperation. This may blind some westerners, put off by Japanese vagueness or minimal expressiveness, to their true values of earnestness and goodwill. It is said that the Japanese never say "no" and indicate agreement when in fact they disagree. This is true up to a point, but it is as a result of politeness rather than deceit. The English, with their coded speech ("We shall certainly consider it"), are no less devious; probably more so.

Hiroshi, with his mandatory preoccupation with face protection, may annoy colleagues with his platitudes and lack of directness. International team members are used to challenging each other and expediting decisions and actions. This is not Hiroshi's forte. He does not see issues in terms of opposites, right or wrong, black or white, true or untrue. Japanese see conflict resolution not as a victory by one side over the other, but as a gradual convergence of points of view that, when merging, extract the best elements from originally diverging standpoints. On account of this, Hiroshi may be seen as indecisive by his western colleagues.

Japanese "indecisiveness" and "slowness to act" are born of a traditional and unalterable belief that issues of importance – both commercial and social – should be resolved collectively. The individual is alone and vulnerable; within a group one is supported, advised, and strengthened. The American, faced with a Japanese delegation, fixes on one of the leaders and asks: "What is your proposal, Mr. Tanaka?" The Japanese, even though possessing authority to speak, will immediately look sideways at his colleagues and prevaricate. From birth, Japanese are conditioned not to make decisions alone, especially if they involve the fate of other people. The American sees indecisiveness and hesitancy, rather than laudable consensus seeking and prudent caution. Within an international team a Japanese cannot consult other Japanese, but will still steer clear of giving instant opinions. Hiroshi may in fact gain sympathy from Swedes, Swiss, and some German and English colleagues.

Another Japanese characteristic that tends to discomfit some westerners is their over-sensitivity to hierarchy. Hiroshi will never contradict the chair or argue too strongly with team colleagues. French, Dutch, and some other nationalities thrive on vigorous debate. Hiroshi is not ready for this give-and-take. Staying on the sidelines during most of the debate, he may, however, surprise people with a short, penetrating summary at the end of the discussion.

Finns, also, are good at this. Japanese and Finns usually get on well together as they share several traits, including distrust of verbosity and overt body language; they are good listeners, modest and self-effacing (never pushy), and they excel in succinctness and economy of expression.

With Japanese, one must always consider the language question. It is probable that Hiroshi, like most twenty-first-century mobile Japanese, will speak fluent English. His comprehension of quick, idiomatic English, however, may be only 90 percent or less. The problem is, he will not admit it. In Japan, to ask one's interlocutor to repeat something is to suggest that the message was poorly delivered. There is also the question that Japanese thought is conducted along different channels from that of English speakers, which results in occasional misunderstandings about aims, priorities, and emphases. For example, in Japanese one does not use reported speech, so that Hiroshi would be reluctant to discuss information he has received from third parties, even though it might have some value for the team. There is a basic difference in cognitive processes between East and West. Asians analyze phenomena in a different manner from Europeans, because they are using different analytical and cognitive tools. When they focus on objects, things, or people, they do so holistically; that is, they refuse (or are unable) to separate them from their context or environment. They see people and things as parts of a whole that cannot be manipulated or controlled piece by piece.

Holistic thinking takes time and is not carried out aloud. The contemplative nature of Japanese leads them to remain silent for lengthy periods. Some westerners, for instance French, Italians, and Americans, cannot stand much silence; in fact, they can be unnerved by it. Finns and Swedes, on the other hand, quite enjoy Asian quietness. Hiroshi invariably remains amiable, though colleagues are uneasy when he gives them presents they have not earned, and apologizes for mistakes he has not made or for rudeness he has not shown.

How to handle this unique team member? How does one get the best out of him? To begin at the beginning, the team leader must make sure that he is properly introduced to all members of the team. Full exchange of business cards (tenderly) is the first step. If you do not exchange calling cards in Japan, it is like meeting each other with no clothes on. Hiroshi will shake hands, but don't expect him to do it twice a day in the French or Belgian manner. The team leader must be well dressed, appear modest, speak to Hiroshi in a deferential tone, and always take pains to protect his face. Flattery is acceptable (to give and receive). Hiroshi likes to be addressed in a quiet voice and not to be rushed. The content of the manager's exchange with him is less important than the manner in which it is delivered. In Japan, what is said is often insignificant or irrelevant. What is crucial is how it is said, when it is said, why it is said, and who says it.

Japanese are rarely completely informal, even within a team. It is best to observe certain formalities with them, such as asking permission to use first names (almost unheard of in business meetings in Japan). The manager should maintain only weak eye contact, restrict body language, and apologize for misunderstandings before Hiroshi does. One must remember that he takes remarks literally, therefore types of humor such as irony will have no effect. Instructions must be given clearly and in detail. One word of warning: Japanese managers often hint to other Japanese at what they want done. In the near-telepathic atmosphere of a routine Japanese *kaisha*, a timely, gentle hint constitutes an order! If, therefore, you were to ask Hiroshi "What do you think would happen if we were to try this?" he will not tell you, but is likely to go ahead and do it.

It is often difficult to extract clear opinions from Hiroshi. He does not like brainstorming – an exercise infrequently used in Japan. In essence, differences of opinion are not aired in public among Japanese, who are almost strangers to abstract debate. How to get Hiroshi's opinion? Either the manager can ask him in private (outside the team meeting) or, even better, in writing. This may sound strange to Europeans or Americans, but it works. Another method is to pair the Japanese with a Nordic (not a Latin) in team exercises. This causes them to open up, as they love sharing.

It is obviously beneficial for the team leader to take advantage of Hiroshi's strong points: reliability, sound methodology, and long-term perspective. For instance, Japanese are normally more interested in market share as opposed to quick profits. If a current arrangement or contract does not work, they are skillful at renegotiating it. Hiroshi's judgment should be trusted, but it is not advisable to put him in charge of a subgroup, especially if they are charged with quick decisions. Japanese are often accused of slow decision making. They reply that Americans are used to making a lot of small decisions during a day, and that Japanese are capable of doing the same. However, big decisions take time.

Finally, Hiroshi's manager must remember that when he closes his eyes during a meeting, he is not sleeping, he is concentrating! Above all, never mention the war. It was all a big mistake.

Norway: Terje Riise

Terje Riise is a tall, middle-aged, energetic Norwegian who brings a "fresh air" style to the international team to which he belongs. A manager in his own right, he lends invaluable support to his team leader, who recognizes his rough-and-ready straightforwardness and transparent reliability. A Norwegian executive sees himself as a man of action, combining prudence and foresight and making firm decisions, fairly quickly, based on common sense. He is not overly aggressive or dominating (indeed, a certain shyness is part of the Norwegian character), but once he has analyzed a situation and familiarized himself with the full context, he proceeds to act with confidence and conviction. His values are clear: honesty, pragmatism, thrift, self-determinism, and an unswerving belief in his own integrity.

It is not surprising that such a vigorous approach occasionally causes unease among certain other nationals. His directness, bordering on extreme bluntness, can lead some to think that he lacks sophistication. Swedes, Italians, French, and others detect stubbornness in his communication style and would like him to debate issues in a more delicate fashion. If Norwegians are not enticed into debate at an early stage, they tend to adopt entrenched positions from which it is difficult to dislodge them later. Moreover, they often display a Norway-centeredness that implies a certain sense of superiority over other nationals. Terje, asked for his opinion on human diversity, replied, "There are only two types of human beings – Norwegians and those who wish they were Norwegians." He was of course being humorous, yet few Norwegians are deprecatory about their nationality. It is said that their stubbornness originates from their use of long boats in Viking times. The sails were square, so they could not sail against the wind; they had to row. Some of them rowed all the way to America a few hundred years before Columbus. You can imagine the obstinacy and tenacity that such a feat engendered.

A Norwegian in an international team is good company. Though jovially stubborn, he makes up for his obstinacy with personal soul searching. He is happy to do battle with his own feelings. Like a Dutch person, he wishes to be seen as a progressive, tolerant, modern individual, but is reluctant to demolish the traditional pillars of a rather strait-laced society. Humor accompanies this procedure. Norwegian humor, ironic and very dry, is much appreciated by the British, Finns, and Australians. Moreover, Norwegian team members are popular on account of their modernity, courage, word–deed correlation, and stamina, as well as their utter egalitarianism. Norwegian senior executives, though never pushovers, are nearly always accessible.

In general, there are fewer Norwegians in international teams than there are Swedes, Danes, and even Finns. The main reason for this is their renowned Norway-centeredness. Tom Colbjörnsen, a Professor at the Norwegian Business School, conducted a survey of over 3,000 Norwegians in leading positions. The survey pinpointed complacency as a prominent feature of Norwegian managerial makeup. Norwegian CEOs and senior managers appraised themselves as among the best in Europe. Managers from other countries could learn a lot from their Norwegian colleagues, though they often fail to do so, as the Norwegians saw many of them as lazy and unprofessional. Corruption is a daily problem abroad and Norwegian managers are not particularly keen to go and work there. They prefer to work in Norway, as domestic issues are considered more important. Salaries are high in Norway, where most families enjoy two incomes and social welfare is guaranteed. Many Norwegians consider foreign countries as holiday destinations and believe that they have little to learn from non-Norwegian managers. According to the survey, only 10 percent of Norwegians believe that it is necessary to get more information about other countries and their cultures, and only 20 percent want to have more international experience. As a result of this belief, only 6 percent of Norwegian managers had been given a job offer from abroad during the two years preceding this survey.

Lack of international experience causes Norwegians to suffer a certain degree of blindness to context (for instance when interacting with excitable, rhetorical Latins or Arabs) and to find it difficult to deal with various forms of bribery and corruption. Other criticisms leveled at those Norwegians who do work in more southerly locations are that they are too factual and product oriented, lack interpersonal skills, are too blunt, too egalitarian (do not respect hierarchy), work short hours, fail to benefit from intertwining business and social life, eat too fast and drink too much, are too rule bound, are not compassionate enough, and are spoiled by the welfare state.

If these views enjoy some currency among southern Europeans and some Asians, they are hardly valid among Anglo-Saxons, Nordics, and Americans. Norwegians, who have extremely close relations with Britain, consider themselves in a sense part of the Anglo-Saxon world. Terje Riise's team leader need only be straightforward and decisive (never devious), give clear instructions, and show a certain acceptance of Norwegian entrenched positions, and the team will benefit from Norwegian colleagues' efficiency, resilience, clean dealing, ever-present humor, and unfailing support.

Russia: Vladimir Kosov

Vladimir Kosov is a Russian member of an international team set up by a western industrial conglomerate with extensive interests in eastern Europe. Initially shy and unsmiling, his regular contact with colleagues from an assortment of countries has resulted in his shedding much of his traditional reserve and caution. After taking part in half a dozen meetings of the team, he has begun to display a benign, almost jovial attitude to joint activities.

Warmth, big-heartedness, and innate friendliness are indeed typical Russian characteristics, once a Russian feels that he is being accepted by other nationals. Kosov quickly became popular among his colleagues, showing his love of children and family, of literature and the arts, and displaying spontaneous generosity and hospitality whenever the occasion arises. He has a strong people orientation and a keen sense of humanity; he is refreshingly blunt and direct in his remarks, but is unquestionably well mannered. He is not afraid to think big and is also willing to take risks ("If you are afraid of wolves, don't go into the forest"). He is a poetic and eloquent communicator, though somewhat rambling and roundabout. He conveys feeling well, but is not high on clarity. In western eyes he lacks succinctness and fails to summarize adequately, but he is consistently perspicacious and anticipates colleagues' reactions. Like a good chess player he can plan several moves ahead, but sometimes loses his listener in doing so. His chair is grateful for his obvious respect for authority and his positive attitude toward teamwork.

Vladimir Kosov is a clear-sighted and adaptable, modern individual who is in the process of shedding certain inherent Russian traits that not so long ago hampered successful interaction with westerners. During most of their history, 90 percent of Russians were peasants and more than 50 percent still are. Rural traits such as secretiveness, suspicion of authority and foreigners, caution, apathy, pessimism, aversion to change, and expectation of coercion are still persistent features of Russian behavior. Of more concern to a team leader is the low legal consciousness of Russian

colleagues. Vladimir is learning fast, but the concept of entrepreneurial activities for many Russians borders on the illegitimate.
Russians do not see the law in the same light as western Europeans
or Americans do. In Russia laws were passed to protect the state,
not the individual. The changes they introduced were invariably
disadvantageous to citizens, hence the Russian aversion to change
and innovation. Neither do Russians define truth as westerners do.
After centuries of domination by the Orthodox Church and the
Tsarist police, followed by 70 years of Communism, official statements were seen inevitably as lies; personal views, gossip, and even
rumor, on the other hand, heralded truth. It is natural for Vladimir
to seek personal views from team members, to discuss openly his
own feelings, and to conspire with others to "beat the system."
This tendency can have both positive and negative outcomes, but
the team leader can monitor these.

A certain understanding of the Russian character is advisable.
Why are Russians initially unsmiling? Because they traditionally do not smile at strangers. Smiling recognizes a cheerful or
happy event. Similarly, laughter with no reason signifies foolish-
ness. A person who remains serious in discussion creates a good
impression in Russia, though humor is important, when it is seen
as appropriate. Russians do not have the tradition of turning up
early in the morning for work. They are neither punctual nor out-
rageously unpunctual; 10 am is a good time to start a meeting.
Unpunctuality or failing to turn up at all does not imply rudeness,
though westerners find this difficult to believe. Another problem
is the Russian use of *vranyo*, the acceptable untruth. This is used
ubiquitously in Russia, though not necessarily with the purpose
of deceiving someone. It is actually close to the English concept
of coded speech, where one avoids a strict truth if it is likely to
embarrass somebody. Hence, a Russian who turns up two hours
late to a party (because he overslept) will tell his host he had a
puncture on the way there. His host will accept his excuse even
though he knows his friend does not have a car.

A team leader with a fair understanding of the Russian character
will be able to mold Vladimir into a valuable, energetic, original,

and respected member of the team. The keen Russian sense of collectivism and self-sacrifice will guarantee a cooperative and sustained team spirit. Vladimir is very proud, in a patriotic sense, and occasionally he may appear over-sensitive or tetchy. The manager must recognize his sense of vulnerability and counter this with a personal touch and frequent praise. Vladimir, like most Russians, is eager for recognition and respect. He listens best to a person who presents an opportunity, shares his fate, and "conspires" with him to achieve joint goals. He respects hierarchy, but expects close personal attention and, if necessary, sympathy.

To share woes with a Russian is to become their friend. If Vladimir's subjectivity is prioritized he will become his manager's closest ally. As such, he can solve all kinds of problems for the team leader. As Stalin said, "Everything depends on the personnel." In Russia, if one has the right contact, the latter can prove extremely versatile and one can stop worrying about many things. Vladimir wishes to focus on his boss for instructions and opinions. Russians are uneasy with western pluralism (too many voices) and like a close association with the "key" person. Such a relationship is more important to them than material success (they have an aversion to excess profits). The team leader must acknowledge an element of schizophrenia in Russians. The Tartar invasion of 1234 to 1480 did not make Asians of them, but it prevented them from being fully European (mixed blood – Slavic, Finnish, Tartar).

Further insight into the Russian character can be gained by observing some of their proverbs:

✧ "If all laws perished, the people would live in truth and justice."
✧ "It's easy to steal when seven others are stealing."
✧ "The slower you go, the further you'll get."
✧ "A person without friends is like a tree without roots."
✧ "At home do as you wish, but in public do as you are told."
✧ "In Russia, even honest men can lie."
✧ "Russians do not fear death because every day is a struggle. It is a pity to die and a pity not to die."

The following quotations also provide useful information about Vladimir Kosov's background:

✧ "I have never met anyone who understood Russians." (Grand Duke Aleksandr Mikhailovich)

✧ "A man who was not Orthodox could not be Russian." (Fyodor Dostoyevsky, *The Possessed*)

✧ "All civilizations are to some extent the product of geographical factors but history provides no clearer example of the profound influence of geography upon a culture than in the historical development of the Russian people." (George Vernadsky, *A History of Russia*)

✧ "Among our Russian intellectual classes the very existence of a non-liar is an impossibility, the reason being that in Russia even honest men can lie... I am convinced that in other nations, for the great majority, it is only scoundrels who lie; they lie for practical advantage, that is, with directly criminal aims." (Fyodor Dostoyevsky, *A Word or Two About Vranyo*)

✧ "Yes, the Russian is incapable of telling downright lies; but seems equally incapable of telling the truth. The intermediate phenomenon for which he feels the utmost love and tenderness resembles neither truth nor *lozh* (lie). It is *vranyo*. Like our native aspen, it pops up uninvited everywhere, choking other varieties; like the aspen it is no use for firewood or carpentry; and again, like the aspen, it is sometimes beautiful." (Leonid Andreyev, *Pan-Russian Vranyo*)

✧ "Contradiction is... the essence of Russia. West and East, Pacific and Atlantic, Arctic and Tropics, extreme cold and extreme heat, prolonged sloth and sudden feats of energy, exaggerated cruelty and exaggerated kindness, ostentatious wealth and dismal squalor, violent xenophobia and uncontrollable yearning for contact with the foreign world, vast power and the most abject slavery, simultaneous love and hate for the same objects... The Russian does not reject these contradictions. He has learned to live with them, and in them. To him, they are the spice of life."
{George F Kennan, *Memoirs*)

❖ "To the Russians, a commitment is binding as long as it is historically valid, so to speak. And its historic validity depends on the degree to which that commitment is either self-enforcing or still mutually advantageous. If it ceases to be self-enforcing or mutually advantageous, it obviously has lapsed." (Sbigniew Brzezinksi)

❖ "Russians maintain their integrity in a way that conforms to their inner notion of what a human being should be, in a manner they consider proper, and with an honesty and decency that I have seldom seen anywhere else in the world. Above all, they have an appreciation for *tselnost* (wholeness, complete commitment) and faith, no matter what that faith may be related to. To be a real human being, one must maintain that full commitment and respect it in other people as well. In this sense, it makes no difference to them whether the other person is a Marxist or a reactionary." (Irwin Weil)

❖ "Russians are more emotional, more likely to strike deep friendships, less superficially gregarious. They make great sacrifices for those within their trusted circle, and they expect real sacrifices in return. Their willingness, indeed their eagerness, to engage at a personal level makes private life in Russia both enormously rich and incredibly entangling. Close emotional bonds are part of Russia's enchantment and also its complexity." (Hedrick Smith, *The New Russians*)

❖ "Logical categories are inapplicable to the soul. But Russian sensitivity, permeating the whole culture, doesn't want to use logic – logic is seen as dry and evil, logic comes from the devil – the most important thing is sensation, smell, emotion, tears, mist, dreams and enigma." (Tatyana Tolstaya, *Notes from Underground*)

❖ "The famous 'Russian soul' (dusha) was to no small extent the product of this agonizing uncertainty regarding Russia's proper geographical, social, and spiritual position in the world, the awareness of a national personality that was split between East and West." (Tibor Szamuely, *The Russian Tradition*)

❖ [*Dusha* is] "sensitivity, reverie, imagination, and inclination to tears, compassion, submission mingled with stubbornness,

patience that permits survival in what would seem to be unbear-
able circumstances, poetry, mysticism, fatalism, a penchant for
walking the dark, humid back streets of consciousness, intro-
spection, sudden, unmotivated cruelty, mistrust of rational
thought, fascination with the world – the list could go on and
on – all these qualities have frequently been attributed to the
'Slavic soul.'" (Tatyana Tolstaya, *Notes from Underground*)

✧ "On this continent – and not only on this one – we had since
time immemorial been rivals with the Americans. We are
now attempting, and not unsuccessfully, to interact." (Eduard
Schevardnadze, April 1990)

Singapore: Lee Huang

Lee Huang is a Chinese from Singapore, a multicultural city-state
where Malay, Indian, and Chinese traditions coexist beneath a
veneer of western cosmopolitan culture. Singapore rivals Hong
Kong as a major crossroads of international trade in South-East
Asia and Lee is used to dealing with people from all walks of life.
Singapore is one of the easier places in Asia for foreign business
people to work and a Singaporean in an international team imports
this compatibility into the team atmosphere. Like a Hong Konger,
his origins and experience are invaluable to a western team with
projects in Chinese communities; he also possesses considerable
insight into Indian and Malaysian mentality.

While his versatility equals, or even exceeds, that of Andy Chen
from Hong Kong, Lee's team behavior differs in many ways. He
grew up in Singapore in the years when it evolved from a loose,
heterogeneous collection of racial groups – Malay, Chinese, Indian
(largely Tamil), Europeans, and Eurasians – to a prosperous city-
state with a strong sense of national identity. This transformation
was effected in 31 years by the country's first prime minister, Lee
Kuan Yew, who, in the words of *The Economist*, "ran Singapore
like a well-run nursery." Lee Huang was brought up in a (sometimes harshly) disciplined manner where chewing gum, littering,

spitting, and long hair were taboo and failing to flush a public toilet incurred a heavy fine. The government censored the media and imposed strict political control, along with what some people considered excessive social controls. On the plus side, Lee Huang had thrust on him a good education and health system, a hygienic environment, job stability, cheap housing, and relative affluence. Lee Kuan Yew's citizens were going to be happy, whether they liked it or not.

Lee Huang's unquestioned work ethic is based largely on the Confucian principles of diligence and obedience to superiors. He is inherently disciplined and, like most Singaporeans, achievement oriented. He wants to make money, honestly if he can, but is in less of a hurry than his Hong Kong counterparts. Colleagues appreciate not only his all-round education and linguistic skills, but the courtesy and smoothness with which they are accompanied. He talks somewhat less than a Hong Konger, but is patently more articulate. He listens to others carefully and gives good feedback. Adaptable Hong Kongers often see him as rule bound, but Lee is comfortable with regulation. Hong Kongers, like Americans, are impatient and work at speed. Lee's pace is more British – less impatient, steady but not slow. His moderation and frugality earn him respect. He wastes neither time nor money. His respect for authority may cause some to see him as dull or excessively sober. Openly he does not show much initiative, but one suspects that he is savvy. Mainland Chinese are touchy about face protection; Hong Kongers more cynical and pragmatic; Lee adroitly avoids loss of face. In team discussion he is nimble and makes no enemies. In many ways he is an ideal team member, having experienced years of Singaporean welding of diverse cultures. Perhaps the greatest asset he brings to the team is his palpable multiculturalism. His unfailing tolerance serves as a good example to others.

It is normal for team managers to consider themselves fortunate to have a mature Singaporean in their team. Lee is easy to manage: dutiful, civic minded, tidy in mind and person. For his part he expects the team leader to issue clear directives, be essentially transparent in his motives, respect his educational and professional qualifications (including titles), praise Singapore's progress and achievements, and utilize his multicultural talents to the full.

South Africa: Arthur Rhodes

South Africans fit well into international teams and more often than not make a big impact. First, they were brought up in a multicultural society and feel at home dealing with people of other nationalities and worldviews. Secondly, both British and Dutch white South Africans are imbued with a pioneering spirit not unlike the frontier spirit of many Americans. They bring to a team an entrepreneurial attitude, combining a bold sense of adventure with opportunism, tenacity, a willingness to take risks, and a committed future orientation. They have a confident self-image: they once built a country that outshone all others on their continent. Their energy is undiminished and they are comfortable in managerial situations.

Arthur Rhodes, from Cape Town, is of British heritage. Like many English-speaking South Africans, he is well educated and expressive in speech, has good manners, and is generally rather reserved. He tends to be conflict avoiding, especially in comparison with Afrikaners, who relish directness and friendly confrontation. Arthur personifies the soft sell, is a good listener who reads between the lines, and can be gently persuasive when he feels it is appropriate. He seeks agreement at meetings rather than controversy.

Before the team meets, Arthur Rhodes does his homework and prepares his position well. After an initial period for friendly small talk, he is not slow to adopt a business-like attitude. After hearing or setting the context and background to the subject under discussion, he makes solid proposals. If anyone disagrees with him, he listens carefully to their rationale and will accommodate their views when he can. He normally progresses an issue through a disciplined procedure of argument and counter-argument. He is usually reasonable and accepts compromise when this is appropriate. He is not over-hurried in an American sense, but he prefers to conclude business within a reasonable timeframe. If he fails to do this, he likes to come out of the meeting on good terms with all concerned and leave the door open for future possibilities. He is not afraid to show his multicultural experience and is very clear about what is and what is not viable in a South African context.

South Africans are generally popular and quietly affable team colleagues. They are punctual, calm, and correct, and are good planners guided by cautious optimism. They are realistic about the different ways in which business is achieved around the world and are unafraid to discuss bribery and corruption. They themselves are completely reliable in their adherence to contracts and commitments. For future business, South Africans focus more on Europe as opposed to countries east or west of them.

A team manager can motivate Arthur Rhodes by maintaining a professional appearance and a keen, business-like attitude. South Africans are impressed by leaders who are audaciously entrepreneurial and leave no stone unturned to find business. All avenues should be explored and all opportunities exploited. It is advisable to know South African history and be aware of African conditions. Managers are expected to be pragmatic, factual, and accurate and to have a sense of humor.

Spain: Luis Rueda

Luis Rueda does not speak English with grammatical perfection and he tends to leave final consonants unpronounced, both in English and Spanish, but he is an exuberant communicator in any company, projecting warmth, friendliness, and humanity in a voluble manner enhanced by luminous facial expressions and elaborate body language.

Spaniards on international teams, used to hierarchical structures at home, recognize the authority of the team leader, whom they expect to make all the important decisions. Having said that, they like to discuss issues at length and are not afraid to interrupt colleagues, or even the leader, when they have a point to make.

On such occasions they tend to deliver their opinions emphatically
(though not aggressively) and sometimes in a roundabout manner.
It is better for his colleagues to let Luis deliver his full message, as
Spaniards are not fond of being interrupted when they are in full
flow. Because of their circumlocutory style, it is also hard for listeners to know whether they have made their main point or not. When
one lets Spaniards conclude their remarks, they develop a fondness for their listener, to whom they will extend favors later. (This
point has been noticed by Finns and Swedes in EU committees in
Brussels, whose silences have won support from Spanish delegates
who had been frequently interrupted by French participants.)

Luis Rueda's national characteristics, both in terms of communication style and core beliefs, differ considerably from those of
Anglo-Saxon people and colleagues from northern Europe in general, not to mention Americans. Team members from these areas
may judge him as being overly verbose, hyperbolic, emotional,
weak on details, and less than accurate with facts and figures. This
does not stop him from being popular, since his liveliness, enthusiasm, and affability add spice to certain meetings that run the risk
of being boring.

Luis has vision, flair, and imagination; whether his vision cor-
responds with those of his colleagues may be debatable, however.
There is also the question of veracity. Nationals such as French,
Italians, Russians, and Romanians may indulge in "flexibility" of
truth and indeed (as mentioned in some Asian profiles in this book),
others such as Chinese do not recognize the concept of absolute
truth. Spaniards are enigmatic in their use of "double truth." This
can be seen in the way they look at time. On the one hand there
is the immediate reality of terms of contracts, deadlines, appointments, and schedules. On the other is the "poetic whole" of ideal-
ized relationships where the unnecessary distractions of the clock
or dates are far in the background. Preferring the "poetic whole,"
the Spaniard's actions are not so limited by precise timings, because
in the bigger picture fixed schedules have very little significance. In
the Hispanic world life is organized not around the clock – a mere
machine – but around a succession of encounters and relationships

that are qualified and quantified not in linear fashion, but in terms of personal involvement, excitement, opportunity, or caprice. Human transactions must be satisfactorily completed, not interrupted by a knock on the door, the ringing of a bell, or an impending appointment. Relationships take precedence over schedules. Spaniards often turn up late for meetings or miss them entirely, for good reasons of their own. Luis is unlikely to do these things in the context of an international team, but his concept of "double truth" will persist. When a German says "we can deliver this component on July 13th," he means July 13th. Luis saying exactly the same thing considers that the real delivery date will be determined by the (good) relationship he has with the recipient.

The concept of double truth is not unrelated to the *mañana* phenomenon. This behavior, strongly associated with the Hispanic world, is normally interpreted by Anglo-Saxons and Scandinavians as synonymous with laziness or bad organization. Often it is a case of late deliveries or tardy payments, accompanied by a paucity of communication. But Spaniards and Mexicans are neither lazy nor dishonest (they cannot afford to be!). Delays are more likely to be caused by the Hispanic partner having to juggle options or assets due to a lack of resources, or simply because he is not ready to make his move yet. One of the services that Luis can provide for his team is to explain these aspects of the Hispanic mentality when such problems arise.

Spaniards are, in the main, not dedicated listeners. They read less than any other people in Europe and do not pay great attention to the content of presentations. They do, however, watch interlocutors very carefully and sum them up by observing mannerisms, style of delivery, and degree of sincerity. This is an area where Spanish intuition can be very helpful to the team, particularly when dealing with Latins or other Mediterranean people.

Conformist Swiss and Swedish team colleagues may find Luis too individualistic in a team where consensus is being pursued; he also frequently shows something approaching scorn for laws and regulations. When he delivers his views in theatrical or declamatory style, they suspect that his opinions have an air of irreversibility about them. Can they refute his ideas without offending him? This brings us to the delicate part of dealing with a Spanish colleague, how to get round his touchiness. Spaniards and Italians speak with equal volubility, but Italians have innate flexibility – when stopped in their tracks they rarely take offense or lose face, and a seemingly heated argument can be transformed in a flash by a switch of direction and a rueful smile. Luis is different. A sense of personal honor (*pundonor*) is a living reality in Spain (and Mexico), as is *la dignidad del hombre* (the dignity of man). One must be careful, when admonishing a Spaniard, not to impinge on his credibility or integrity with the wrong choice of words. It is all tied up with the concept of machismo.

These sensitivities notwithstanding, Luis's contributions to team activity can be numerous and valuable. His knowledge of the workings of Latin/Mediterranean minds can be put to good use. At team meetings he is habitually energetic, cheerful, inventive, and humorous; Spanish humor is often earthy. When won over by colleagues' ideas, he will crusade for the team's objectives, approach decisions with courage, protect underdogs, roguishly despise materialism, and show great loyalty to both leader and team members. He projects an image of romanticism, generosity, tolerance, and reliability. His team manager must manage him cleverly, giving him full rein to express his ideas, impute the best motives, protect his face at all times (never pressurize him), persuade him to do things through personal appeal, rather than logic or rules, accept physical closeness, maintain at all times strong eye contact (a Spanish feature), and above all give him a faith or a vision to live by.

Swedish: Lars Svensson

On first appearances a Swede would seem to make an ideal team member. Swedes, more than any other Europeans, are consensus minded. Their preference for collective decisions equals that of the Japanese. Swedes in teams – even managers – wish to hear the opinions of all those present and are reluctant to move forward if there is not unanimity. There have been outstanding leaders in Swedish business history (Barnevik, Wennergren, Gyllenhammer, Carstedt), but a Swede sees individualism as the personal contribution he makes toward the group effort. Lars is patient, even cautious, never overbearing. He wishes to avoid confrontation with other team members if at all possible and will rarely, if ever, contradict another's view.

This desire for harmony and willingness to postpone controversial decisions can seriously slow things down. This trait plus a tendency toward over-analysis often invites criticism by more action-minded colleagues, such as Americans, Finnish, and Dutch, but in general Lars cannot be rushed. Hofstede and others have described Swedish society as the most feminine in the western world, a culture that places a premium on quality of life, nurturance, rendering service, and interpersonal aspects. Swedes see power, wealth, and assets as less important than nonmaterial benefits.

If Lars is a member of a team consisting largely of westerners, his feminine tendencies will frequently be apparent. What do we mean by the terms masculinity and femininity in describing the nature of a culture? Femininity means that Lars will consistently prefer cooperation to competition, feelings to facts, intuition to logic, development to growth, subtlety to boldness, thought to action, timeliness to speed, right decisions to quick decisions, reputation to profits. He thinks of results as solutions, considers collective comfort more important than individual careers, a sense of proportion trumps personal honor, and social progress is better than material progress. Relationships pave the way for the sale of products rather than the other way around.

Lars' communication style is gently persuasive, always considerate. Swedes like to sound kind and caring, and they never *köra över någon* (meaning run over or bulldoze someone). Absolute egalitarianism is mandatory at all times. Swedish companies are run in a very democratic manner, are almost completely horizontal, and power distance is low. Lars respects his team leader absolutely, but discusses matters with the leader as an equal.

The good qualities of a Swedish team member are likely to be much in evidence. Swedes have impressive language skills (especially in English and German), are smart and modern in outlook, and are usually well informed and well prepared. They are usually efficient and reliable, very conscientious, and there is no problem with their work ethic. They are habitually punctual and believe in delivering on time.

Lars is careful about his behavior at meetings. He is polite, correct, and proper. Formal at first, he soon uses first names, like other Scandinavians, though he is slightly more distant than Danes, Norwegians, or Finns. He has a stock of good stories and anecdotes and makes well-prepared after-dinner speeches, but is actually rather poor at small talk. He discusses work topics well and accurately, especially technical points. He is strong on defining processes and carrying out detailed planning. He monitors well, but he needs lots of context and background information before committing himself. In general, he carries himself off well in front of an international audience (Sweden has many large international companies such as Volvo, Saab, Electrolux, SAS, and SKF), but is sometimes nervous when giving opinions in front of other Swedes, fearing that there may not be a consensus. However, he does trust fellow Swedes more than other nationalities and can be quite smug about his country's collective achievements. He has no doubt that the Swedish way is best (the EU joined Sweden, not the other way around). Other Nordics often find his complacency irritating.

Lars gets on very well with most nationalities, though he fails to read between the lines when French, Italians, and others speak in a rhetorical manner. He is more comfortable with low-key team members, especially Britons, Canadians, other Nordics, Swiss, and even Japanese. When it is his turn, he entertains lavishly, with good food and more than adequate supplies of alcohol and generous toasts. On such occasions he socializes jovially, but the next day he sticks to regular procedures if fellow socializers approach him for concessions.

Team managers will get the best out of Lars by consulting him regularly, being diplomatic rather than frank, promoting harmony over cold truth, portraying business as beneficial to society, compromising on most issues, seeking consensus and agreement, not pressurizing him, and never attacking cherished Swedish institutions.

Switzerland: Robert Ziegler

It could be said that the Swiss are made to order for international teams. Some may argue that there is no such thing as a Swiss; one writer described them as a collection of sedated Germans, overfussy French, and starched Italians, all square like their national flag. Yet, it is a brave people that attempts to weld together these three disparate cultures, with a sprinkling of Roumansh speakers thrown in for good measure. The odds against such a union surviving must have looked huge indeed in 1291, when the first three-cantonal alliance materialized, but the Swiss are more united than ever in the twenty-first century, showing an aptitude for multiculturalism unrivaled elsewhere.

Robert Ziegler is a German-speaking Swiss, but he speaks fluent French and English and understands Italian. He can be described as a clean-cut executive. He is polite, proper, correct, formal, and tidy. His punctuality and frugality are legendary. Disciplined and hard working, he sets great store by diligent preparation and he cuts an efficient figure at international meetings. Essentially linear-active, he works well in tandem with Germans, Dutch, Nordics, Canadians, Americans, Australians, and Britons. Neither are French speakers strangers to him and he can handle Italians with ease (about 100,000 Italian guest workers cross the Swiss border every day).

Robert's positive qualities do not stop there. He is honest and law-abiding and is strong on confidentiality, respecting personal privacy (as well as that of Swiss financial institutions). A natural conservative, he is prudent in business and social matters and is steadfastly pro-quality. When negotiating, he calmly resists bargaining, considering that you get what you pay for. The Swiss do not come cheap. Robert has a knack of extracting the best deal from opponents without ever appearing aggressive or exigent.

The Swiss mentality does not suit all other nationalities or psychologies. Team members who have an impulsive or impetuous streak, or who see themselves as essentially action minded or visionary, may experience occasional irritation when Robert plods on methodically. He is hardly mercurial. To some colleagues he often appears over-serious, even dull. His desire for plentiful context and willingness to be rule bound suggest that he is a perfectionist. He is not humorless, but tends to accept humor rather than supply it and treads warily when he does so. He rarely uses irony or sarcasm and does not like having his leg pulled (by Americans or French). The Swiss are obsessed with security in all its aspects, therefore they do not trust foreigners completely, though they disguise this well. They employ many non-Swiss and treat them fairly, but expect them to leave "at the end of the season." Because of the country's rugged mountain-and-valley geography, the Swiss often appear parochial.

All nationalities do not, however, share these reservations. Swedes, for instance, look kindly on Swiss circumspection and trudge along with them happily. I have attended numerous ABB meetings where the team composition was heavily Swiss and Swedish with a sprinkling of British and Americans. These project team get-togethers were among the most effective I have ever seen. They had, of course, been assembled under the influence of Percy Barnevik, whose maxim was "Every man or woman in the right place."

There is no doubt that Robert Ziegler is a great asset to his chair. Skillful team leaders learn to mirror colleagues' qualities when handling them. With Robert one begins by being invariably polite and correct, settling down to his pace, style, and viewpoints. The leader is less concerned with vision or spontaneity, prioritizing solidity, pragmatism, and common sense.

Punctuality, maintenance of administrative neatness, and command of technical details are, naturally, expected by the Swiss. Robert will appreciate the odd humorous shaft from the chair, but flippancy must be avoided at all times. Invasion of privacy is also taboo, as is eccentric behavior. The Swiss, in spite of their cantonal characteristics, like to appear conformist. Robert expects his team leader to be in command of all financial arrangements and to demonstrate frugality as the occasion allows. Swiss like to waste neither time nor money.

Bombast, the hard sell, or any form of over-emotional behavior should not appear in the chair's repertoire. Leaders should be logical at all times and take care never to contradict themselves. Robert likes taking notes.

USA: Jack Lowe

Jack Lowe hails from California and is endowed with many of the attributes admired in his state: energy, love of innovation and change, future orientation, and an unabashed competitive drive. He is a regular member of a sales and marketing team of a big American multinational company with branches in nearly all European countries. Though Jack is based at HQ in San Francisco, one of his functions is to strengthen the European sales division and act as a link between it and headquarters. The team meets in London, Paris, and Geneva and consists of seven Europeans and a British chair. Jack, who comes over the pond as often as ten times a year, sees himself as the action man of the team, which recently has had considerable success.

Many international teams contain Americans, whether HQ is in the USA or not. In general, American members make important contributions to team activity. One reason is that they think in an American way, which differs strikingly from the European. Whereas a European group combines a variety of approaches to problems – British, German, French, Italian, Nordic, and so on – and takes pains to synthesize or harmonize its deliberations, Jack arrives with a less complicated program, since he knows what he wants. Americans like to simplify issues, define clear goals and targets, and pursue them with vigor. In this type of team they are manifestly connected with growth and profits. In the USA, Jack knows the routes to growth and a profitable operation. Many Americans feel at home in commercial pursuits, since "the business of America is business." Of course, failure is not unknown in the USA, but those companies that are successful (and they are numerous) tend to breed executives who believe that American principles for doing business are universal and can be applied, perhaps with slight modifications, to any situation or environment. If the USA achieved the status of a commercial superpower in the last half of the twentieth century, doesn't that prove something? Isn't the American way best, even on foreign soil? Look at the proliferation of US corporations all the way round the globe. Who else, apart from perhaps the Japanese, was able to establish such a global presence?

These are strong arguments that Jack, though he may not state them explicitly, might hint at from time to time within the team. Kick-started by Marshall Aid in the early postwar years, American methods, supported by the vast majority of business literature and courses written in the USA, dominated commercial activity both in Europe and Asia. For two or three decades the US experienced few setbacks in world commerce and politics. Then came Vietnam, the emergence of Japan in the 1970s as a commercial superpower, the German miracle, the four Asian Tigers, and a growing awareness of the existence of acceptable alternatives to US ways of doing business. A successful Japanese model was copied by several Asian nations such as Korea, Malaysia, and Thailand. Other valid models appeared in Singapore, Hong Kong, Germany, Sweden, Finland, and, ultimately, Britain and France. It may still be difficult to define a European model, but closer cooperation between the EU countries will eventually produce one. This is one of the functions of international teams active in Europe, and is the new environment that Jack and other Americans enter at the present time. Given globalization and the plethora of information available on the internet, the American business model no longer enjoys the hegemony that it once did. Skillful team leaders seek to extract maximum benefit from both old- and new-world values and experiences.

Jack has many new-world qualities and attributes. Living up to his self-image as an action man, he is dynamic, courageous, competent, and optimistic. He is not afraid to think big and is prepared to take risks if the chair proposes them. His work ethic is unquestioned and he likes to do things at speed. In the USA it is important to "get there" first. Jack always wants to move things along ("What's the next step?"). He is frank and direct – his cards are on the table. Friendly, smiling, and humorous, he is good at small talk and makes friends quickly. Champion of democracy and free trade, he is essentially egalitarian and does not understand snobbery or class distinction. He is entrepreneurial and cheerfully pragmatic ("If life hands you lemons, make lemonade"). His business principles are simplified and clear: get up early, work hard (long hours and few holidays), don't waste time, dispense with red tape, define one's goals, contracts are binding, anything is possible (in the USA).

Such an admirably simple and straightforward American model runs into difficulties in the changing economic order, political linkages, new players, and added complexities of international commerce. Table 5.2 shows that many qualities that Americans consider positive may be viewed negatively in other cultures.

American qualities	Others' perceptions
democracy and equality	doesn't exist, impractical anyway (Asians)
individualism	lack of concern for others (Asians, Swedes)
competitiveness	aggressiveness (French)
speedy decisions	too rushed (Japanese, Chinese)
hard sell	over the top (Germans, Finns)
frank, direct	rude (Japanese, French)
optimism	lack of realism (Scandinavians)
charisma	charisma is suspect (Germans, Dutch)
seeks change and improvement	doesn't protect status quo (Saudi Arabians)
result oriented	lacks people orientation (Italians, Asians)
self-confidence	arrogance (South Americans, Arabs)
informal, smiling	lacks respect, insincere (Germans, French)
future orientation	lacks tradition (Chinese)
defends democracy and free trade	defends US interests (Russians, Arabs)

Table 5.2 American qualities, as seen by others

Even European members of an international team, while appreciating Jack's friendliness, energy, and drive, may feel somewhat uncomfortable with other aspects of his behavior. His broad smile appears too ready, his jocularity perhaps superficial. He offers and invites trust with people he hardly knows and though he makes friends easily, he does not engage in deep friendships. His humor, while amusing, often appears flippant. Germans, who expect serious answers to serious questions, are often disappointed. Nordics notice that Jack cannot stand silence and talks as much as the Latins. Even worse, he is fond of the hard sell and seems too preoccupied with the bottom line and quick profits. His thinking often seems short term; patience is not his strong suit. He is quick with his "Do we have a deal?" when often the deal may be months away. He listens in snatches and often interrupts others. His verve impresses Americans, but slightly irritates more conservative Europeans or Asians. No doubt he is egalitarian, but he observes dollar status.

American culture is different from any other, consequently Americans are unfamiliar with European and Asian cultural norms. They do not automatically realize this, however. Most Americans think that they understand other cultures, as they mix freely with the many subcultures in the United States. They are used to dealing with Italian-Americans, Hispanic-Americans, Polish-Americans, and all the others. They think that when they interact with an Italian-American they are dealing with an Italian. In fact, they are not. Italian-Americans are very different from Italians, just as German-Americans are very unlike Germans. Italian-Americans, German-Americans, and Polish-Americans, when they enter economic life, all join US mainstream culture. This is one where you turn up early for work smartly dressed; are frank, open, and speedy in your pursuit of targets; work overtime or miss out on holidays when there is a business boom or crisis; put your job before your private life; maintain optimism and keenness and think in terms of current deals, change and innovation, bottom-line focus, and quarterly forecasts. If you do not conform to these rules, you will not be employed for long. Mexican-Americans or Sicilian-Americans who behave like Mexicans or Sicilians will be fired.

When American drive and determination to succeed are combined with German caution, Nordic accuracy, British sense of proportion, French vision, or Italian imagination, the team leader may enjoy optimal results. It is up to the leader to harmonize these very different attributes skillfully. Some committee chairs show great adeptness at this. British, Canadian, Swiss, Swedish, and Finnish team leaders, who often prize impartiality, are suited to bridge the gap between American enthusiasm and European wisdom. Canadians, of course, are well placed to do this, as they understand their neighbors better than Europeans and Asians do. An experienced Canadian chair can be worth their weight in gold to a company that uses them adroitly.

Be that as it may, how does one best manage an American team member? The first step is to mirror some of Jack Lowe's qualities. The team leader, when dealing with him, must be informal, amicable, and essentially straightforward. As the Americans put it, the leader must "spell it out" and "tell it like it is." Any subtlety of expression runs the risk of appearing devious. The chair puts the team's cards on the table, shows confidence in results, exhibits a certain toughness, will undertake risks, and thinks big enough to win an American following. Leaders should not be afraid to talk about money and show the way to profit. Reticence will get them nowhere with Jack; better keep talking and thinking aloud. Good eye contact helps a lot. Leaders must envisage change and innovation and deal with any challenges that Jack may introduce. It is also the chair's job to explain the intricacies of different team members' cultures to Jack. Without this knowledge, Jack will continue to flounder. English-speaking chairs are better placed to do this, though Swiss and Swedes are often capable. And while he is perhaps amazed at different European mentalities, Jack may ultimately be trained. Avoid pulling rank at any time when dealing with an American.

CASE STUDIES

Team leaders who are thoroughly familiar with the individual cultural profiles of their team members will become adept at assigning suitable roles or tasks to their colleagues. The following mini-case studies give examples of such assignments that encountered varying degrees of success.

Social glue

In the 1990s a large British construction company was commissioned to erect a sewage plant in a desert location in Libya. A team of six engineers was assigned to the project, which took six months to complete. Two of the engineers were English, one was German, one was Dutch, one was American, and one was Italian. The Englishmen were constructors, the American was an electrical engineer, the Dutch a mechanical engineer, and the German a surveyor. These five men were highly qualified in their fields. Only the Italian, Moretti, seemed to have no specialism, though he used the title of Ingeniero.

The relative isolation of the site in desert surroundings offered few material comforts, apart from adequate air-conditioned accommodation for the six engineers. Long hours of work in blisteringly hot weather with limited access to alcohol, newspapers, and magazines, television programs, and other forms of entertainment or socializing resulted in increasing boredom for the group as the weeks went by. The company of women was out of the question under the prevailing regime, and fortnightly outings to Benghazi proved less than exciting.

On completion of the project, which over-ran by six weeks, the company did a post mortem on the outcome. The results were first class. The five specialists had performed well in spite of the inconveniences of the location. Technically all was perfect, though the management of the company was not quite sure if the barely qualified Italian had made any meaningful contribution.

On reading the completed questionnaires to which each engineer had replied, it seemed the unanimous opinion of the group that Moretti had been the key personality. Frustrations and difficulties had been numerous and some of the team members had been driven to distraction by the utter monotony and boredom of the task. Several of the men had quarreled with each other periodically and grudges were common. Only Moretti was above criticism. All the others agreed that he had been the social glue that held the group together. He had mediated in disputes, done menial jobs such as the dishes or cleaning, maintained a cheerful disposition at all times, run errands, distributed pills and medicine for minor ailments, got his hands on more liquor, organized transport, told funny stories, and cooked delicious spaghetti twice a week.

Ostracism

Peter Powis, one of Unilever's personnel directors, had assigned a 24-year-old Japanese, Ichiro Okada, to a London-based research group in the company's detergent division. Okada had obtained a good degree from Keio University, spoke English well, and was an extremely bright and sociable individual. His winning personality (unusually extrovert for a Japanese) made him the most popular member of his team and his original thinking led to frequent innovations and successful developments. After two years he emerged as the natural leader of the team, though most of his colleagues were ten or more years older than he was. He managed the team well for three more years.

At this point, Peter Powis decided to send Okada back to Tokyo, where his experience in the UK, especially at HQ, would enable him to inspire less-traveled Japanese staff, broaden their outlook on the world at large, and acquaint them fully with the aims and aspirations of head office in the Japanese market. As I had had frequent encounters with Okada in social situations, I was able to admire his all-roundedness, social graces, and obvious professional competence. It seemed clear to me that Peter Powis had done a good job for Unilever, completing the international training of a promising young man who would be a great overseas asset for the future. Okada suggested that I visit him on my next visit to Japan.

Six months later, I spent a week in Tokyo and phoned Okada, who invited me for lunch the following day. When we met I was immediately disconcerted by his appearance. His smile was forced, his body language negative and dejected. I asked him what was wrong. On his return to Tokyo he had been put in charge of a team of researchers in the field in which he specialized. They were a dozen men aged between 35 and 50. Okada, now 29, had been sullenly accepted as team leader and was experiencing considerable difficulties in engendering either cooperation or enthusiasm in his department. The lack of rapport manifested itself not only in the work at hand, but also in the social sphere. He rambled on in a resigned tone, enumerating the different instances of his rejection. Quite simply, this charismatic young man had been ostracized on account of his youth.

In retrospect, I realized that this was something both he and I could have forecast and should have perhaps mentioned to Peter Powis before he was selected for that particular position. There is no real solution to this problem on Japanese soil.

Peter Powis eventually transferred Okada back to the UK, where he once more blossomed and continued to excel.

Tall poppies

In 1993 I received a telephone call from the head office of BMW in Munich. The company had asked for my help in relation to its Australian subsidiary. As I had worked previously with BMW and was well aware of its excellent record in staff relations, I was happy to go to Munich and see if I could be of service.

It appeared that a few months earlier BMW had appointed one of its managers – a German who had been successful in the domestic market – to be its general manager in Australia. Based in Sydney where the staff numbered just over 100, he was also to oversee the sales activities of 40-odd dealers in various parts of the country. As manufacturing took place in Germany, the Australian subsidiary was basically a marketing and sales operation leading to distribution and delivery of the various models.

The company's problem was that there had been a sharp decline in sales a few weeks after the new manager's appointment. More seriously, dealers were leaving BMW and contracting with the competition. Evidently, the personality or method of the new manager was at odds with the Australian mentality. He had quickly become unpopular with his own staff and dealers around the country.

The manager was due to be recalled shortly and reassigned to Germany, where he functioned smoothly. The company had already identified and appointed a suitable successor – a 35 year old from Hamburg named Hartmann – whom they wished me to coach over two days in Munich before sending him to Australia. Hartmann was an alert and conscientious individual who was determined to make a success of the job that had defeated his predecessor. He knew something of the circumstances in which the previous manager had failed. Apparently, he had certain admirable German qualities that do not necessarily go down well in Australia. He was a disciplinarian who expected on-the-dot punctuality from his staff. His recipe for success was hard work. The company had well-tried processes that should be followed religiously. Originality was hardly required. Communication inside the firm was vertical rather than horizontal. Criticism of colleagues should be direct (and of course constructive). Management was top town – one took orders from one's immediate superior. One did not have the ear of the chair, unless of course one was vice-chair. Humor and flippant discussion were out of place in the office. One could enjoy a joke over a beer with colleagues outside working hours. Generally, one separated one's working life from one's social life. There was a time and a place for everything.

These principles were worthy ones; Germany has become a great and successful nation by observing most of them. However Hartmann, while respecting such traits, had begun to suspect that

Australia was organized in rather a different way. I confirmed his suspicions. Australians are indeed hard workers, but they are not 9 to 5 people and certainly not 9 to 6. Most Australians want to go to the beach at 4 o'clock – and there are many beaches in Australia. The early history and settlement of the Australian colony give many clues to why Australians show less reverence for authority than Germans do. Australians can be managed – and be perhaps as productive as Germans – but they have to be handled in a different manner. No one dares to be pompous in Australia. The tall poppy syndrome, where you are cut off close to the roots if you exhibit any form of self-importance, is ubiquitous and notorious. Australians must be led from the front, and modestly at that.

Hartmann, in spite of his name, quickly got a feel for Australian attitudes. Over and over again, I drummed into him the importance of humor and a touch of roguery when handling staff. Power over Australians is granted to those who appear reluctant to exercise it. Irony and cynicism abound, and must be met with a grin.

Hartmann insisted that he must prepare two opening speeches: one for his staff in Sydney and one for his first meeting with the dealers. I agreed with this, provided that they were the right type of speeches – laced with humor, of course.

"There is only one problem, Mr Lewis," said Hartmann, "I don't know any jokes." He took home with him the task of writing the speeches and showed them to me the next morning. They were earnest, sincere, and inspiring (or would have been to German ears). For Australians they were boring, dutiful, banal, and completely humorless. "I can't help it," wailed Hartmann, "I told you I don't know any jokes!" We agreed that I would write out for him 20 funny stories with which he could lace his two addresses. I did this and he practiced telling them all afternoon and evening. He was good at it – I suspect he would have been a humorist if he had been born in another country. We parted good friends, both satisfied with our progress. I asked him to send a report after three months on the job and he promised to do so.

The training took place in September and when in mid-December I had not received the promised letter, I rang BMW in

Munich to see how he was getting on. "We don't know for sure, he doesn't send regular reports like he used to," they replied. In January, I sailed halfway round the world and put in at Cape Town Royal Yacht Club in February. There a message waited for me: "Please ring BMW Munich." I spoke to the secretary in the personnel department, who said that she would send me a telegram on behalf of Mr. Hartmann. It arrived soon afterward: "PLEASE ASK MR LEWIS TO SEND ME TWENTY MORE FUNNY STORIES – URGENT. REGARDS, HARTMANN."

I sat down in the club library, wrote them out long hand, and telegraphed them to Munich for forwarding to Sydney. Hartmann was a success in his new posting. He was the right man in the right place with the right stories at the right time.

A compromise

A few years ago a major British conglomerate needed to appoint a senior marketing director for its ice-cream division in South America. Given the size and warm climate of this huge continent, not to mention the growing popularity of ice cream in the modern era, this was clearly a big job for the person who could lead the division to make handsome profits.

With this in mind, the company had spent two to three months trying to identify a suitable candidate, but had unfortunately met with little success. Candidates were plentiful, as the company had enormous personnel resources in five continents, and seven good candidates had been interviewed, all males in view of the macho characteristics of the area. But the company continually ran up against a recurring problem: Which language should the manager speak? It had proposed some good Brazilian men, but the Argentineans objected to a Portuguese speaker, as 19 of the 20 Latin American republics were Spanish speaking. Spanish candidates abounded, all the way from Argentina to Venezuela and Colombia, but in turn the Brazilians objected. "We are by far the biggest market," they pointed out.

It was unlikely that a manager would be appointed from one of the small countries like Bolivia or Paraguay, so the contest boiled down to an Argentinean or a Brazilian. However, given the often intense rivalry between these two countries, both sides remained adamant.

We interviewed half a dozen candidates for the company. We found what we thought was the perfect man. He was Indian. He had worked 20 years for the company, was 50 years old, and spoke excellent English, but not a word of Spanish or Portuguese. He was proposed to the South Americans, who raised no objections, provided that he could learn Spanish and Portuguese. We knew that he had good linguistic skills (besides English he spoke four Indian languages) and we promised to teach him Spanish in six weeks. This was achieved, after which we built on the back of the Spanish a reasonable facsimile of Brazilian Portuguese in the following four weeks.

He was packed off to South America, where he proved an outstanding success. The company appreciated our advice and training. Why had we been so sure he was the right man?

The secret of his success was twofold. First, the language problem had been solved, as an Indian was "neutral." Spanish speakers noted that his Spanish was not perfect, but they saw that he did not dominate Portuguese either, so that was OK. Secondly, and more importantly, he belonged to the same cultural category as Brazilians and Spanish Americans – Indians are firmly multi-active in character. Accordingly, he shared with them the same concepts of family closeness, compassion, emotion, and within-group trust. Like most South Americans, he was talkative, extrovert, persuasive, dialogue oriented, gregarious, and greatly concerned with maintenance or loss of face. In business he had a relaxed attitude toward time, he juggled facts, changed plans easily, pulled strings, sought and granted favors, prioritized relationships over products, and interwove his social and professional activities.

6

Speech Styles and Meeting Procedures

When international teams meet, their members have a chance to communicate – to use their speech skills to good effect. Speech is certainly a personal weapon, but different cultures use it in diverse ways.

Perhaps the most basic use of speech is to give and receive information. Germans, Finns, and the Dutch are good at conveying facts and figures quickly and efficiently. Other cultures think that speech can be a much more powerful weapon in terms of eloquence, fluency, and persuasion. Italians, particularly, believe that they can convince anyone of just about anything, provided that they gain sufficient personal access. The French, Spaniards, and South Americans use speech to great effect and at length, though Nordics and some Anglo-Saxons find it all too much at times.

Indians, Pakistanis, and Sri Lankans are very fond of flowery, Victorian-like speech to inspire people. Russians like to search their souls verbally. Confucian and South-East Asian cultures use speech as a give-and-receive-respect mechanism and establish relative status and rank in a few sentences. Americans often launch into speech with business or selling in mind. Arabs use it in a didactic or moralistic manner.

In some less democratic societies, speech may be used for coercion, propaganda, or deception. In some cultures, it can be deployed in such a vague way that it actually clouds issues rather than clarifies them. English and Japanese people can waffle and stall with ease, while Chinese and Polynesians excel in ambiguity.

Silence itself is a form of speech when applied at appropriate moments and should not be interrupted. Finns and Japanese are past masters at soothing or strategic silences.

Australians regard suitably broad speech as a mechanism for managers to show solidarity with their "mates."

Finally, some nationalities seem to love speech for the sake of speech itself, taking the stage to hear their own voice. French, Spanish, and Greek people often perorate in this manner. In this regard they may not be popular with Nordics and most Asians.

Managing speech styles

Good international team leaders will be well aware of the diverse speech skills of their team members and, using their interpersonal skills, will farm out "talking time" as equitably as possible and strive to defuse the tensions that are frequently engendered by opposing speech styles. Most problems of this type arise between down-to-earth linear-actives and loquacious Latins. Norwegians and Finns, particularly, develop an early contempt for superfluous speeches.

Another instance of conflict that I observed recently in a Belgian-led team was between a reasonably talkative Englishman and a much more reticent Frenchman. It was not in this case so much a question of loquacity as of style. The Englishman, who had a reporting requirement of his French colleague, phrased his questions in an open, exploratory, rather naïve manner. The Frenchman, high context and somewhat caustic by nature, replied in a taciturn and certainly caustic manner. He was actually showing his ability to summarize and paying his British colleague the compliment of not explaining everything piecemeal. The Englishman saw him as opaque and closed. The Belgian chair told the Englishman in private that the way to "open up" the French is to develop close personal relations, swapping information about families, holidays, hopes, aspirations, and so on. The reasonable Brit tried this and soon found his French colleague to be the sincerest of friends. The Belgian had a bicultural feel for the situation.

Toleration of styles

Just as the team will quickly settle for a mutually acceptable procedural style, they will also adopt a communicative style that will become their hallmark. It is in the area of communication that most misunderstandings occur. A Swede will never bubble over like an Italian, but it is essential that all team members, recognizing different uses of speech, tolerate styles that seem inappropriate at home. Germans regard speech as a vehicle for transmitting and receiving information; French see it as a means of expressing opinions or winning arguments; Japanese use it sparingly to create quiet harmony.

Table 6.1 lists the communicative features of linear-active, multi-active, and reactive cultures.

Linear-active	Multi-active	Reactive
Talks and listens in equal degrees	Talks most of the time	Listens most of the time
Rarely interrupts	Often interrupts	Never interrupts
Confronts with facts	Confronts emotionally	Never confronts
Frank, direct	Indirect, manipulative	Indirect, courteous
Truth before diplomacy	Diplomatic, creative truth	Diplomacy before truth
Cool	Excitable	Inscrutable
Partly conceals feelings	Displays feelings	Conceals feelings
Speech is for information	Speech is for opinions	Speech is to promote harmony
Defines problems and solves in quick sequence	Goes for all-embracing solutions	Prefers gradualist solutions
Admits own mistakes	Finds an excuse	Hides, covers up mistakes
Likes clarity and accuracy	Tolerates ambiguity	Likes ambiguity
Talks in turns	Often talks over the other	Takes turns slowly
Tolerates some silence	Cannot tolerate silence	Likes sharing silences

Table 6.1 Communicative features of linear-actives, multi-actives, and reactives

Quality of communication

International team members bring to the meeting their home-grown communication pattern, albeit modified or softened to accommodate the styles of others. In a sense, everyone is on their best linguistic behavior. Italians may restrict their volubility, Americans try to curb their impatience or bluntness, French go through the motions of agreeing with what someone has said, Germans inject some humor, Brits temporarily put to one side their coded speech (that is, actually say what they mean), and Finns have a crack at a little small talk. Teams normally do well in establishing a mutually accepted *modus loquendi*. Language imbalances must of course be corrected, but this is often not so great a problem as it seems, as the native English speakers may well be in a minority, so the "international English" speakers can bubble on merrily to a very complaisant audience.

Time constraints of course place a premium on quality of communication. It is noteworthy that "quality of communication" does not mean the same in every culture. At a seminar held under that title in Brussels, 135 delegates from 30 countries defined quality of communication as in Table 6.2.

USA	Spell it all out in a frank, open manner
Spain	Conveying feelings and human warmth
Russia	Chess moves/unburdening the soul
Finland	Say only what it is necessary to say
Italy	Verbose style for maximum communication
France	Visionary but logical
China	Speak collectively with humility
Korea	Protecting inner feelings
Japan	Polite formalisms to establish harmony
Germany	Be honest, whether pleasant or not
UK	Don't rock the boat
Sweden	Be as democratic as possible
Denmark	Be humorous and cosy (*hygglig*)
Portugal	Be conciliatory
Netherlands	Defend your opinion fearlessly
Belgium	Avoid dogma

Table 6.2   Quality of communication

National speech styles

Just as we have different notions of what quality communication is, national styles contrast sharply in terms of transparency, objectivity, and word–deed correlation. Figures 6.1–6.6 depict two relatively open, transparent communication patterns (Australia and Canada), two that might be described as somewhat devious (UK and Denmark), and two better described as complex (Korea and Brazil).

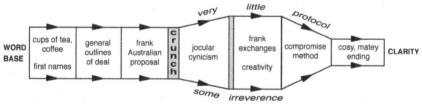

Figure 6.1 Communication pattern: Australia

Australian meetings are in the main relatively informal affairs, beginning with cups of tea and first names and ending in compromise where everyone feels that they have taken something away. In between, exchanges can be lively, blunt, cynical, even aggressive, though in general the participants are looking for solutions. With foreigners, Australians make efforts to curb their national irreverence for superiors and institutions.

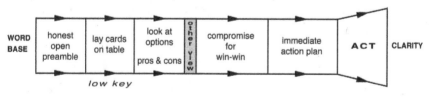

Figure 6.2 Communication pattern: Canada

Canadians are among the most reasonable people in the world to negotiate with and meetings are normally conducted in a pleasant, open manner aiming at a win–win result. They move quickly toward implementation and their lean style suits both action-oriented Americans and low-key Brits, Nordics, and Asians. Canadians make good chairs in international meetings.

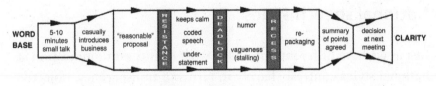

"don't rock the boat"

Figure 6.3   Communication pattern: UK

In the UK a meeting will probably be concluded successfully if no one rocks the boat. Humor, understatement, vagueness, stalling, repackaging, and a sprinkling of white lies are all weapons for keeping it all jolly nice, chaps.

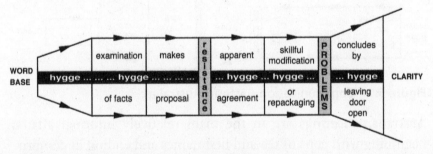

Figure 6.4   Communication pattern: Denmark

Danes believe that they can carry everybody (especially foreigners) by charm (*hygge*) and seem to agree to all proposals well into the negotiation. They are skillful at subtle repackaging and therefore have to be watched carefully. They are not happy at being "roped in," but maintain equanimity with an eye to future business.

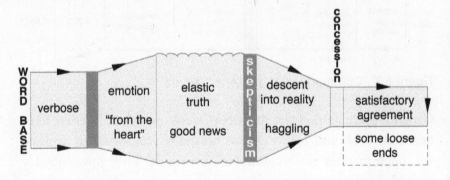

Figure 6.5   Communication pattern: Brazil

In Brazil, meetings are verbose and human feelings take precedence over close examination of the facts. Brazilians are rarely the bearers of bad news and a certain amount of healthy skepticism is advisable. Leisurely haggling often leads to satisfactory agreements, though it is as well to summarize carefully what all parties are supposed to do.

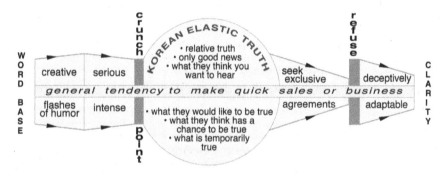

Figure 6.6 Communication pattern: Korea

Koreans believe that they can handle westerners better than other Orientals can and often try their hand at humor. They have a very elastic concept of truth and it is advisable to double-check anything that is promised. They often are looking for quick profits and one should be careful about granting exclusivity. It is better to judge their statements against past performance rather than future forecasts.

Team members and silence

It is frequently assumed that the more you talk, the better you communicate, though this is perhaps less true of the British than of the French, Italians, and Americans. Yet anyone who has done business in countries where words are used differently – in Asia and especially Japan – knows that a protracted pause can be as eloquent as speech. In Europe, Swedes and Finns can be similarly mute – the latter, in particular, excel at it.

The reason is perhaps partly geographical. Sandwiched for centuries between Swedish and Russian bosses in a cold climate, Finns had little incentive to open their mouth unless they were asked. Not only was it prudent to remain quiet, it suited the Finnish view of society. "Those who know, do not speak; those who speak, do not know" is an ancient Chinese proverb to which Finns, like the Japanese, adhere. Silence is not seen as a failure to communicate but as an integral part of interaction; what is *not* said is important. Silence means that you listen and learn; verbosity merely expresses cleverness, egoism, and arrogance. Silence also protects privacy and shows respect for others. In Finland and Japan it is considered impolite to force one's opinion on others.

In the Anglo-Saxon world and Latin and Middle Eastern countries, talking has another function. The British habit of discussing the weather with neighbors or even strangers shows both a preoccupation with climate and a desire to show solidarity and friendliness. Sociable discourse is even more evident in the USA, Canada, and Australia, where speech is a vital tool for establishing a relationship rapidly. Think of early pioneers bumping into each other in the outback. In France, fluency is an important social attribute; to the Finn the French may seem to babble – or be pushy and intruding – but to compatriots they appear intelligent and coherent. The American habit of thinking aloud, the French stage performance, the Italian baring of the soul, Arab rhetoric – all are attempts to gain the confidence of the listener and share ideas, which can then be discussed and modified. The Finns and the Japanese, meanwhile, listen to such outpourings with a kind of horror: in their countries a statement is a commitment to stand by, not to change, twist, or contradict in the very next breath.

It is a view of language that sets Finland and Japan apart. In both countries the whispers are the same: foreigners talk so fast; we are slow by comparison; we can't learn languages; our pronunciation is terrible; our own language is so difficult; foreigners are more experienced than us; they are cleverer and often deceive; they don't mean what they say; hence, we can't rely on them.

In Japan, what is actually said has no significance whatsoever. Language is used as a tool of communication, but the words and sentences themselves give little indication of what the speaker is saying. What they want and how they feel is conveyed by the way in which they address their conversation partner: smiles, pauses, sighs, grunts, nods, and eye movements convey everything. Japanese executives leave their fellow Japanese knowing perfectly well what has been agreed, no matter what was said. Foreigners leave the Japanese with a completely different idea. If they think all has gone well it is often only because the Japanese would never offend them by saying anything negative or unpleasant. Team leaders with Japanese, Finnish, Malaysian, or Swedish colleagues should be careful not to interpret their reticence as a sign of lack of involvement.

Procedural style and tone

The style of a meeting will depend a great deal on the personality of the team leader. They will set the tone and hint at the degree of formality or informality that might suit the team. The type and makeup of the group will also affect the meeting style. R&D teams or engineers in project groups like to deal in facts and figures. Sales and marketing groups are more excitable and perhaps exciting. Board members may retain a certain formality, while product launch teams ooze enthusiasm and dynamism.

After one or two meetings, the team will have adopted a style. The nationality mix will undoubtedly influence this. The manner of procedure (how fixed the agenda is, for example) will reflect the cultural habits of the majority. Are items to be segmented and dealt with point by point, or should an all-encompassing solution be explored?

CASE STUDY

Executives from different countries use varying speech styles for addressing meetings, in order to produce what they consider the optimal effect. Also, *how* a meeting is structured is seen to be vital. The airline alliance oneworld ran into problems in this regard.

oneworld

The various airline alliances lead to the natural creation of international teams. These meet several times a year, in different locations, to discuss structure and administration, sales and marketing techniques, financing the alliance, possible expansions and admittance of new partners, and a host of strategies to strengthen the organization. One such alliance is oneworld, whose members include British Airways, American Airlines, Finnair, Qantas, Aer Lingus, Cathay Pacific, Iberia, and LAN Chile. We were approached by oneworld to give advice on structuring meetings for a multicultural group.

At that time the alliance met four times a year, normally sending two representatives from each airline. The current chair was a Finn; the last two meetings had been held in the UK. There was disagreement about procedure, especially from Iberia and LAN Chile. The Finnish chair was anxious to find a formula for organizing meetings to everyone's satisfaction.

We noted that five of the airlines came from principally linear-active cultures (BA, Qantas, AA, Finnair, and Aer Lingus); two were from very multi-active cultures (Iberia and LAN Chile); and the two representatives from Cathay Pacific were both Chinese (therefore reactive in character), but heavily influenced by British culture, as they were from Hong Kong.

Previous meetings had been structured in classic linear fashion; that is, agendas were strictly followed, each item taken in turn and discussed until a solution had been found and noted to be included in the minutes. The meeting style was factual and progressive. Undue digression from the agenda was frowned on. Solutions were decided in sequence and decisions were expected to lead to prompt action. There was little time wasting. The Americans, particularly, pushed the pace. The minutes reflected the summary of items settled; the focus was on logic and rationality, order and discipline, action, implementation, and the bottom line.

The Cathay Pacific people went along with this style, although they might have preferred more discussion on consensus. The Finns liked the emphasis on quick decisions and action; the Irish frequently injected humor into the proceedings, but were happy to be carried along with the Anglo-American momentum. The Spanish and Chilean delegates were unhappy with the meeting formula.

In order to get the meeting off to a quick start, team members were presented on arrival, or possibly a little earlier, with six to eight bullet points that summarized the likely proceedings. The Latin delegates found these bullet points distasteful. How could the Americans present conclusions at the beginning of a meeting? The linear-active members replied that bullet points were not conclusions, they were simply useful guidelines on which an agenda could be based. "Rubbish," replied the Hispanics, "We are being manipulated."

The Finns backed the English speakers, though the Irish and Chinese were less happy with the bullet points' succinctness. "We have a ten-hour flight from Santiago," said the Chileans, "then you give us a five-minute cup of tea and get straight into the business with all your decisions lined up."

"Bullet points are only suggestions," replied the chair.

"They sound like conclusions to us," said one of the Spaniards. "Look at the first three."

◆ Advertising budget to be reduced by 20 percent
◆ Approach Japan Airlines to join the alliance
◆ Consider holding all meetings in Vancouver

"Just suggestions to give us a quick focus," replied the Americans.

One by one the Hispanics trotted out their objections to the way the meetings were organized. Five minutes' small talk was insufficient. No key issues should be discussed formally for the first two or three hours. Ideally, preliminary discussion (mostly small talk) should occupy the whole evening of the first day. It was time to get to know one's colleagues better and possibly spend time seeking support for some new ideas of one's own.

Cathay Pacific agreed, pointing out that in some cultures, like Thailand or Indonesia, one would spend at least a day socializing before business was mentioned.

"And this agenda thing," said the Spaniards. "You want to have a final solution on point 2 when sometimes you find it has a detrimental effect on points 5 and 6. We want to go back and reconsider point 2, but you won't let us!"

"We can't digress all day," said the Australians, "we'll never finish."

"But don't you see all these issues are closely inter-related? No decision should stand in isolation. First we need an all-embracing discussion to cover everything involved. We are looking at things from eight different cultural viewpoints. All aspects must be considered. Solutions must be linked to others."

The Finnish chair was perspicacious and understanding. He had the democratic and tolerant instincts of the typical Finn.

We analyzed at length for the team members the cultural characteristics of linear-active and reactive cultures, as well as the varying nuances in American, British, Finnish, Australian, Spanish, South American, Irish, and Hong Kong Chinese cultural habitats. It was agreed that a formula should be adopted that would take into account the exigencies of each cultural group. The Hispanics were allowed to organize the following meeting.

The results were good. Half a day's socializing was allowed for support seeking and several novel and creative ideas got a good airing. Bullet points were never mentioned; constructive small talk led to agreement on a rather loose agenda, which could be revisited at any time when some loophole was spotted. The Hispanic in-depth and somewhat verbose analyses were balanced by American factuality and Finnish economy of words. The British, Irish, and Australians were allowed their usual (frequent) injections of humor. The Chinese, given more to say, were able to make the point that clear distinctions cannot always be made between good and bad, right and wrong, true and untrue.

After several more meetings, the team morphed into an easy-going and successful unit. The personality of the rather benign Finnish chair greatly facilitated the creation of harmony, but all the nationalities involved were seen to make positive, even valuable contributions.

7

Communicating in English

Whatever the team member's national communication style may be – reticent or loquacious, open or closed, formal or informal – it is likely that they will have to project that style into the lingua franca or team language, which as we have seen is likely to be English. Even if they possess the linguistic competence, which is normally the case, other minefields lie ahead, particularly the differences between British and American English.

For speakers of other languages, the British are the harder to follow. This is not because their pronunciation is less clear, but on account of the hidden agendas in British speech.

Coded speech

Britons use coded speech without being fully aware that they are doing so. They rarely say exactly what they mean; they like to leave the interpretation of their remark to the listener, who is supposed to spot nuances, irony, and slight changes in tone of voice. Anything "woolly" or very indirect will usually have a second meaning, unclear to the foreigner, but obvious to most Brits.

It is not easy to fall into this way of speaking unless one has lived in the British Isles for at least several months, maybe years. The examples in Table 7.1 can, however, give a short cut to some of the more usual expressions and to the hidden agendas behind them.

What they say	What they mean
That's one way of putting it	What a stupid analysis
Let me make a suggestion	This is what I've decided to do
That's a good question	I don't know the answer
It has lots of future potential	It's failed

What they say	What they mean
It's too early to see how this one is going	It's failed
This is too vital to decide one way or the other at this very moment	It's my tea break
We'll certainly consider that	We won't do it
We must have a meeting about that	I refuse to talk about that now
You're always very systematic, I admit that	You haven't an original idea in your head
Remind me once more of your strategy	I wasn't listening last time
I hear what you say	It's old hat
We're challenging for leadership	We're fourth
You can take a six-week course in this, irrespective of cost	You cost us more when you're in the office
That's very perceptive	That's just what I've been saying for the last three years
I'll go the extra mile for you	I'm responsible anyway
It'll be a challenging three years there	We can't persuade anyone else to go to Kinshasa
Let's go and have a beer and talk about it tomorrow	Forget it
We must wait for a politically correct time to introduce this	Forget it
I'll call you	I won't call you
Let me play devil's advocate	You've got to see how stupid you're being
You're getting the picture	Finally you're beginning to see sense
It's enough to make the mind boggle	It's beyond my grasp
I haven't got a clue	I don't know
You haven't got a clue	You're a fool
She certainly communicates well	She gossips
She has interpersonal skills	She's computer illiterate
He has a strong oral culture	He can't read or write
She's a backup for us all	She makes the tea
He works intuitively	He's completely disorganized
He's nothing if not loyal	He's nothing
He's our best golfer	We keep him out of the office

What they say	What they mean
We'll have to review your position	You're going to be fired
At the end of the day remuneration must inevitably be results oriented	You're coming off the payroll
It's not bad	It's excellent
He can play a bit	He's the world's best player
I think it'll do the job	This product is exactly what you need
I'm not quite with you on that one	That is totally unacceptable
I suppose I could be seen with you	You look absolutely ravishing
Average	Fantastic shot!
Jack's finally managed to sell something	Jack's sales are incredibly good this month
It's low-cost housing	It's a slum
He frequently under-achieves	He's useless
That might just be a bit tricky	It's impossible
Hmm... that's an interesting idea	You can't really mean that
I think I've got the message	You don't have to tell me 10 times
With all due respect	What a mad idea
I've seen better	It was dreadful
I've seen worse	It was excellent
It's a bit thick	It's disgraceful
It's not on	It's disgraceful
You could be right	It's highly unlikely
There is some merit in that	I can't reject it outright
You could say that	I wouldn't
I agree, up to a point	I disagree
It's a bit dodgy	Nobody will take the responsibility
Jack might twitch a bit	The CEO will explode
The board might take a dim view of that	They'll crucify you
Could I have a word?	You had better listen to this
I don't want to make an issue of this	You had better fix it
It's not for me to influence you either way	This is what I strongly advise you to do

Table 7.1   British coded speech

A high-ranking Norwegian female executive at the World Bank discovered that it took a long time to decipher the way British people communicated with her and among themselves. On first meeting, she felt that Norwegians have a tendency to be either too cold or too friendly, whereas the Brits were more smooth and correct. They joked about their goals, but showed seriousness with other signals, usually coded. Norwegians find it hard at the outset to learn the code, which is a kind of verbal dance. They are not used to fencing with words and often appear clumsy to the British. When wishing to criticize, Norwegians attack directly, whereas the Brits attack in an oblique manner. Everything must always appear to be under control, even if it is not. A Scandinavian openly expressing their doubts is regarded as new to things. Negotiation without confrontation is the name of the game. Let's not ruin the atmosphere with Nordic pessimism or (worse) Latin emotion.

The executive found it hard to decode British ways of criticizing, praising, suggesting, condemning, and abandoning. Understatement and irony often led to the opposite being said to what was actually meant. She also noticed that different British groups used different coding systems. Various types of humor and critique were employed according to status and social class. The class system itself, so prevalent in England, is barely compatible with a Nordic mentality. She was astonished how elegantly patronizing English executives could be, often talking to their secretaries like they were servants, but no offense seemed to be intended or taken. It is a kind of theater where everyone knows their part and says the right lines. Not easy for a Nordic, who wisely should take up a neutral, outsider position when present during upper-middle–lower-class conflict situations.

The European or Asian team member hacking their way through this jungle of nuance will no doubt incorporate some coded speech into their own parlance in due course. The query may persist, however: if an English person says "interesting idea" to reject something, what do they say when they really find it interesting? It is, of course, a question of tone or lilt of voice, but nevertheless hard to spot.

American English

Americans pose a different problem, inasmuch as they are too direct to indulge in coded speech, but use a battery of expressions that are common in the USA but often unfamiliar to European ears. Some of these are listed in Table 7.2.

What they say	What they mean
He's on a roll	He's doing well
It bombed	It failed
Jack will blow his top	Our chair might tend to disagree
You're talking bullshit	I'm not quite with you on that one
You gotta be kidding	Hmm, that's an interesting idea
That's a beautiful scenario	We might find a way of making that work
You're going to get hurt	I'm not sure this is advantageous to you
Beancounters drive me mad	Accountants can be frustrating
It's the only game in town	I have no other choice
We sticker-shocked the consumers right off their feet	We over-priced the product
Go for broke	Stake everything on one venture
If they ever come back from the grave	If they are ever a force in business again
When you scramble, you scramble like a sonofabitch	Speed of action is advisable
I was full of piss and vinegar	I didn't have a leg to stand on
I want black ink on the bottom line	We must go for profit
I need it like yesterday	It's urgent
It just won't fly	It isn't viable
I can't fly it by the seat of my pants	I need more information
Don't make waves	Leave well alone
He never got to first base	He never got started
He's out in left field	He's way off the point
We're playing for all the marbles	It's a big deal
This is a whole new ball game	It's a different type of business
If you play ball	If you cooperate

Table 7.2 American expressions

Political correctness

Another feature of modern American speech is their preoccupation with what is or is not politically correct. This derives from the litigious nature of US society, where avoidance of sexual or racial discrimination has widened to include any type of disadvantaged individual. For instance, it is no longer permissible in American social or business circles to say "negro," "red Indian," "stupid," or "fat," particularly in the presence of the person concerned. It is hardly likely that European or Asian colleagues could master the full range of preferred expressions, but it is advisable to be familiar with some of those listed in Table 7.3.

Politically correct	Politically incorrect
Native American, indigenous peoples, First Nations	Red Indian
Cow hunter	Cowboy
Inuit	Eskimos
Afro-American	Negro
Asian-American	Oriental
Chicano	Mexican
Under-achiever	Failure
Heavily pigmented	Dark skinned
Melanin impoverished	Light skinned
Differently logical	Argumentative
Cerebrally challenged	Stupid
Motivationally deficient	Lazy
Charm free	Boring
Differently interesting	Boring
Incomplete success	Failure
Deficiency achievement	Failure
Nonpassing grades	Failed exam
Person of substance	Fat
Horizontally challenged	Fat
Vertically challenged	Short
Uncompromising natural aroma	Body odor
Ethically disoriented	Criminal

Politically correct	Politically incorrect
Nontraditional shopper	Shoplifter
Transfer of goods	Stealing
Chemically inconvenienced	Drunk, doped
Client of the correctional system	Convict
Cosmetically attractive	Good looking
Differently visaged	Ugly
Physically inconvenienced	Disabled
Emotionally different	Mad
Optically challenged	Blind
Achieve corporal terminality	Die
Negative patient-care outcome	Death in hospital
Pre-adult	Kid
Chronologically gifted	Old
Selective buying campaign	Boycott
Negative cash flow	Losses
Downsizing, streamlining	Firing
Involuntarily leisured	Sacked
Indefinitely idled	Sacked
Between career changes	Unemployed
Underprivileged	Poor
Fiscal under-achievers	Poor
Underclothed	Naked
Explicit language	Obscene
Revenue enhancement	Raising taxes
Aggressive defense	Attack
Friendly fire	Shoot your own troops
Destination advisers	Travel guides

Table 7.3   Politically correct language

Listening habits

Team leaders of any nationality addressing their colleagues in English must be aware that their remarks will not be interpreted in the same way all around the table.

Verbal communication appears on the surface to be a relatively simple operation requiring two basic components: a speaker and a listener. However, it is a more complex process than that. Even when two people with a similar cultural background are involved, there are several stages between delivery and comprehension. Words are spoken, but the actual message emerges only when the words are considered in context. What is said must be evaluated against the background of how it was said, when and where, who said it, and why. There is also the filter created by the speaker's personality and psychological makeup.

The listening process, too, is complicated. The listener has certain expectations that are or are not met. The filter of the listener's personality colors the speech that they hear. An interpretation is placed on the words, thus defining the message for the recipient. The intended message and the received one are rarely the same.

When the speaker and listener are from different cultures, the odds against an accurate interpretation of the message are great. Diverse backgrounds of history, customs, traditions, and taboos, as well as the accepted manners of communicating in different parts of the world, interfere with straight comprehension.

Captive audiences, like teams, generally appear to listen, but in fact they listen to different degrees and in different ways. There are good listeners and bad listeners. Others, such as Americans, listen carefully or indifferently, depending on the nature of their colleagues' remarks.

Although each nationality has its own specific style of listening, one can divide them into rough categories to which certain generalizations apply. For instance, Nordics (Danes, Finns, Norwegians, and Swedes) could readily be described as the best listeners, partly because their own natural reticence gives them no incentive to interrupt. Calm concentration is a strong point.

Germanic peoples are also good listeners. Both Germans and Dutch are hungry for the facts, though the latter wish to start a debate fairly soon. Disciplined Germans have perhaps the longest attention span of any nationality, diligently making notes as they listen.

As far as Anglo-Saxons are concerned, English and Canadians pay polite attention as long as the speaker is reasonably low key. Debate is required afterward. Australians are more cynical and can't take too much seriousness, but, like Americans, will listen well if technical information is being imparted. Americans, used to show business and encapsulated news items, tend to lose concentration if they are not entertained in some way.

In ex-Communist countries such as Russia, Poland, and the Baltic states, listening habits are directly and strongly affected by previous and recent political control (propaganda). Most eastern Europeans believe that all official statements are lies and that any changes introduced by the authorities (or companies) are for the worse. Speakers must therefore combat automatic skepticism in these cultures. This is compounded in Russia by an inherent suspicion of foreigners. Hungarians tend to be less apathetic than some of the others.

Team members who have had a colonial past – Indians, Malaysians, Indonesians – also listen with a certain amount of suspicion, though they can be won over by an eloquent and thoroughly respectful leader. Reaction is, however, deceptive, since listeners in these areas give feedback that they think will please. They also are reluctant to admit to gaps in comprehension.

As we go further east, the Confucian cultures of China, Japan, and Korea have language problems and are also reluctant to confess to noncomprehension. What they listen for principally is exaggerated respect from the speaker, so that nobody loses face. Chinese and Koreans are traditionally suspicious of westerners. The Japanese are more open to address, but so involved with politeness and vague expressions that messages often do not get across.

Latins are not very attentive listeners in principle, as they are normally anxious to speak themselves. A charismatic speaker may hold them for 30 minutes or more, but the French in particular do not believe that foreigners can teach them very much. Italians have busy minds and wander. Spaniards dislike monologues – they want to interject and argue vigorously. Latin Americans show interest in new ideas, but are somewhat skeptical about European caution and even more so about US exploitation.

All in all, it is advisable for team leaders to familiarize themselves as much as possible in advance with the traditional expectations of the audience that they are addressing. Both their style and
their content should be adapted accordingly.

Figures 7.1–7.10 give some indication of different listening
styles. Belgians, Bulgarians, Czechs, and Finns would have to be
ranked as good listeners, generally. Australians and Poles have to
be "hooked" to give their full attention. Italians and Brazilians are
always anxious to get a word in, or indeed take the stage. Americans
and Germans, though both fact hungry, have very different listening priorities.

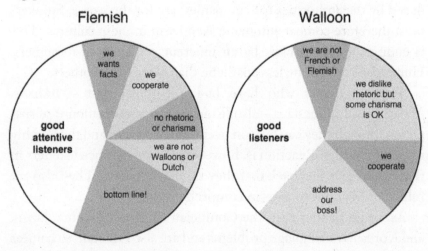

Figure 7.1 Listening habits: Belgium

Flemings listen to each other "in a circle." They are attentive, as
the end result is likely to be an amalgamation of all the ideas put
forward. Everyone should know the strategy.

To Walloons, meetings are for briefing, so that subordinates
tend to listen to superiors rather than the other way around. Staff
don't always know what the strategy is.

Bulgarians, with no urgent desire to dominate conversation, are
excellent listeners. They interrupt their compatriots rarely, foreigners hardly ever. Their attentiveness denotes their proclivity
toward sizing up the speaker and dispelling their own suspicions or
anxiety regarding motives. They want to impute laudable motives,

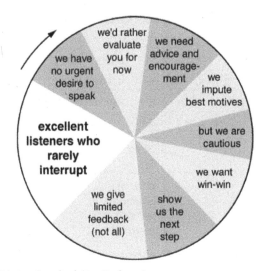

Figure 7.2 Listening habits: Bulgaria

but take this step cautiously. They are not used to western modes of discussion, so they learn as they go along. In general, they respect western opinions, though they do not always place the right connotation on what is said. They give a modicum of feedback a few minutes after absorbing a presentation or new idea. They do not reveal the full extent of their reaction, only a certain proportion. Their level of education and literacy is high, so they are capable of accurate evaluation and judgment. They can, however, be misled by western terminology.

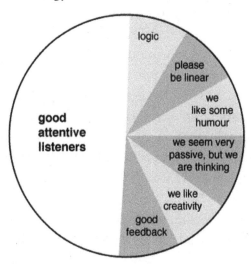

Figure 7.3 Listening habits: Czech Republic

The Czechs are dutiful listeners, always polite and courteous. They give little feedback. As they think in linear fashion, they are uncomfortable with roundabout or digressive discussions (Latins and some fellow Slavs) and have a low tolerance for ambiguity. Their response, if they are unhappy, can be ironic and contain veiled sarcasm. They don't like loudness.

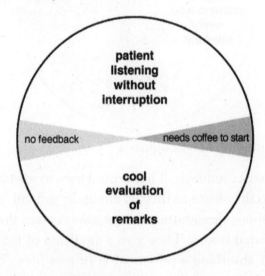

Figure 7.4 Listening habits: Finland

Finns are among the world's best listeners and are trained not to interrupt, to respect and value one another's remarks, and to give careful consideration to the opinions and proposals of others. Concentration levels are high. They may give little or no feedback to a business presentation. Among themselves, they often feel very little pressure to contribute actively to discussions. Active listening (showing interest and involvement in the conversation) is rare and this is often troubling to other nationalities meeting Finns.

It is fatal to talk posh or be in any way pompous in front of Australians, who have a healthy and enduring disrespect for anyone in a superior position or who seeks to promote themselves. It is also inadvisable to be too serious or complicated. Australians are fond of jokes and anecdotes, preferably delivered in broad speech. They make a friendly and lively audience once they have decided to like you.

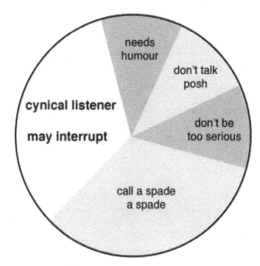

Figure 7.5 Listening habits: Australia

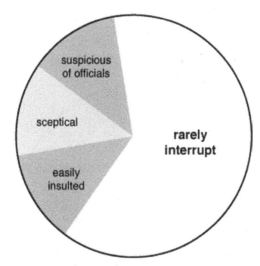

Figure 7.6 Listening habits: Poland

The Polish are courteous and rarely interrupt, but listen with calm skepticism and distrust to most official announcements. This last reaction is typical of the former communist regimes.

Italians are sympathetic listeners, but are often restless as they think ahead of the speaker. Politeness prevents them from frequently interrupting, but they only listen part of the time, because they are formulating their response for when the speaker has finished. They dislike careful instructions or explanations, as they

Figure 7.7 Listening habits: Italy

feel quite capable of understanding intuitively what messages are being conveyed. They are impatient to join the dialogue, which will define the relationship between the people involved.

Figure 7.8 Listening habits: Brazil

Owing to the exuberance of expression of Brazilians, their listening habits tend to be somewhat erratic, interrupting their interlocutor with ideas of their own, each individual wanting to make their personal contribution. They aim to form an in-depth impression of the speaker from watching their movements, gestures, and eye contact, rather than listening intently to what is being said. They have a relatively short attention span.

Among South Americans, Brazilians are perhaps the most receptive to foreign ideas, perhaps because their break with their colonial masters – Portugal – was amicable. The key to their attention is to talk enough about Brazil (even Brazilian football) and to be invariably cheerful, bordering on euphoric. They are not really recording efficiently what you actually say, but eagerly seeking *simpatísmo* to enable them to do business with someone they like.

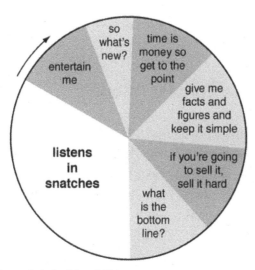

Figure 7.9 Listening habits: USA

Americans are keen on acquiring technical details, but, used to show business, their attention wanders if speakers are boring. They expect and appreciate a hard sell.

Germans, hungry for information and technical details, are among the world's best listeners. Price conscious and needing lots of context, they become suspicious if things sound too simple.

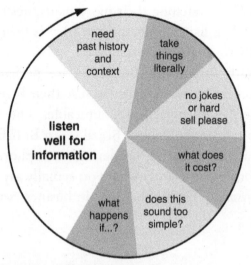

Figure 7.10   Listening habits: Germany

High- and low-context listeners

One of the frequent problems of communication among members of an international team is the difference in style between high-context and low-context speakers (and listeners). Anthropologist Edward Hall in *Beyond Culture* showed how cultures differ in the extent to which personal communication occurs explicitly via spoken words (low context) or implicitly (high context) through the context of particular situations, the relationship itself, and physical cues including nonverbal behavior. High-context cultures such as the Japanese and French rely on understanding through shared experience and history to give implicit messages, whereas low-context Americans feel that they have to "spell it all out."

There is a high correlation between linear-active cultures and low-context behavior. Most English-speaking cultures (American, Australian, New Zealand, Canadian) are both linear and low context. Britain, with some reactive tendencies and a strong sense of history, mixes high- and low-context communication. Multi-active and reactive cultures are typically high context (Latin, Arab, Asian). In high-context cultures the "rules," norms, and guidelines for various types of social encounters such as introductions, meetings, and pronouncements are unambiguous and widely known, according to Harry Irwin in *Communicating with Asia*. Fewer explanations are necessary and the listener is expected to read between the lines. In an international team environment, low-context Germans and Americans frequently exasperate high-context French or Italians by their painstaking emphasis on instructions, explanation, and clarification. Tell a Frenchman something twice and he is likely to reply, "*Je ne suis pas stupide.*"

The manager of an international team must also try to calculate how much different people deduce from the utterances of others. A high-context Italian will deduce much more from simple American messages than the American realizes. Italians "read between the lines" when perhaps they are not meant to!

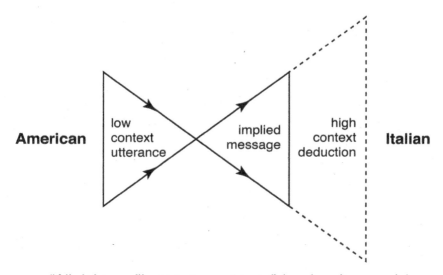

"All right, we'll accept your terms" (spoken brusquely)

Figure 7.11   A low-context American vs. a high-context Italian

For example, a sensitive Italian or French person might interpret a somewhat rough American manner of accepting terms as an actual indication of distaste for the terms, whereas the American meant simply what they said, and no more. By the same token, an American or Australian, expecting things to be "spelled out," may have a greatly reduced understanding of a Japanese or Mexican utterance highly charged with innuendo and *sous-entendu*.

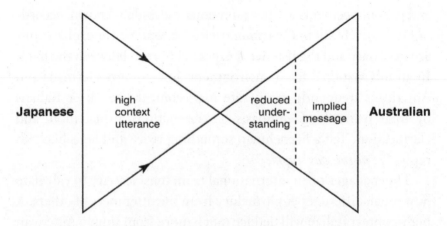

"We'll do our very best to deliver on time"

Figure 7.12   A high-context Japanese vs. a low-context Australian

In the latter case, the high-context speaker will assume that the entire message, with all its implications, has been fully understood. For instance, a Japanese may be quite satisfied that the physical cues they released in speaking manner and tone of voice indicated clearly that they are not in favor of a certain procedure, whereas the Australian has probably interpreted the politeness and apparent acquiescence of the Japanese as a sign of agreement.

Members of international teams get used to the varying degrees of context that colleagues employ and tend to adapt their communicative style accordingly. New members joining the team go through this learning curve, often helped by the team leader ("Don't worry, Jim is tactless, but you always know where you stand").

CASE STUDY

At BMW-Rover, language and communication difficulties hampered Germans who were trying to encourage increased clarity and productivity among somewhat parochial Midlands English people. The Bavarian executives battled gamely to "learn the language" of their British partners who, unfortunately, were seemingly unaware of German economic prowess and who never cleared the first hurdle presented by the German language.

BMW-Rover

When BMW took over Rover in the 1980s, several international teams came into being, consisting primarily, but not entirely, of German and British team members. We were given the task of facilitating several meetings of such teams. These workshop-style sessions were held in our training center at Riversdown House, Hampshire, where half a dozen teams discussed integration and other subjects. Each team had five English participants and five Bavarians sent over from Germany.

The top and middle executives of BMW were nearly all reasonably fluent in English, which was the teams' language. For good measure, the managers of the British company were advised to acquire a modicum of German to use in social situations. This was issued in the form of a directive. The result of this was that two years later none of the senior staff of the British firm had taken a single German lesson.

As far as the new-born teams were concerned, however, no German-language skills were expected at this stage, which made our facilitation task somewhat easier. Of the 30 Brits who attended the sessions, only one had a knowledge of German, though this was accompanied by a healthy disregard for case endings.

No momentous decisions were made or discussed at these workshops, which were designed primarily to get the Germans and British used to working with each other and to establish a common or at least mutually acceptable communication style that would set the tone for future meetings. German and British executives get across their views and messages in rather different ways. Germans want clarity and close, unambiguous instruction; codes of behavior within a British company equip staff to absorb and cope with a rather obscure management style reliant on tradition, class issues, and coded language. It is not surprising that Germans grope for meaning in such a context.

The seminars were significant on two counts. Most memorable was the contrast between the conscientiousness of the Germans and the frequent flippancy of the British. The Germans, though occasionally struggling with terminology, listened carefully to the remarks concerning British psychology and cultural habits and continually made notes. The British participants, with one or two notable exceptions, paid only casual attention to our description of German characteristics, took hardly any notes, and were unduly flippant about Germany's role in Europe. Even more astonishing was the ignorance displayed by the English of Germany's industrial performance. The English team considered that the GDPs of the two countries were roughly equal, though the senior executive on one team corrected their view, saying that the British economy, in total, was twice the size of the German! I had to admire the reticence of the German team members, who let the remark pass without interruption. When I asked the Englishman (in a private aside) what was the basis of his assertion, he replied that it was only natural, as the population of the British Isles was twice that of Germany. I was astounded and somewhat taken aback. Even the French know better than that.

Another, almost comical misunderstanding was revealed when one English group told me that the German team they were working with were all buyers. Thinking this rather strange, I checked. In fact, the Germans had told their British colleagues that they were all "Bayer" (Bavarians).

The second memorable feature of the sessions was the difference in attitude to protocol and formal procedures. It would have been our natural forecast that the British would find German formality, *Ordnung*, love of process, and established procedures somewhat rigid, perhaps tedious. We were prepared to tell the Germans that British casual attitudes, informality, not infrequent woolliness, and "muddling through" methods were actually a disguise for underlying toughness and not inconsiderable efficiency.

Things turned out to be quite the opposite. BMW had spent almost a decade scrapping unnecessary bureaucratic procedures, liberalizing individual capacity for action and decision making, and eliminating a lot of the red tape ubiquitous in so many Germany rule books. Rover, on the other hand, had tightened up procedures to an incredible degree, prohibiting individualism and unilateral decision making, implanting a strict hierarchy within each department, emphasizing discipline and consensus, and controlling expenditure so rigidly that the Germans described the submission of their expense accounts as "nightmarish"!

There was an explanation for all this. While BMW had studied the energetic, free-wheeling characteristics of some American companies, Rover had been merged for nearly two decades with Honda. Honda had organized Rover – formerly a typically traditional British institution with leisurely goals and little love of regimentation – along Japanese lines that mirrored the structure of the parent company in Nagoya. Individualism was taboo, discipline and regimentation were paramount, company goals were essentially collective, and all employees from the president down to the mechanics and cleaners were obliged to wear a drab, gray Japanese company uniform that resembled overalls with buttons. Rover foremen, who had slaved 15 years in overalls to be able to graduate to jacket, collar, and tie, fumed as they were re-uniformed. A Rover vice-president, sitting in the waiting room while visiting his opposite number in Rolls-Royce, was curtly told by a secretary to remove his lorry from the executive car park.

BMW's decision to put managers back in collars and ties was one of the early successes in the subsequent integration of BMW and Rover. Given the insularity and lack of productivity of the Britons, however, the merger eventually ran into trouble and was discontinued. Unlike Daimler (see the case study in Chapter 1), the Germans in this instance had tried hard to enter the (difficult) cultural habitat of Midlands English people, though the latters' frequent use of coded speech was a constant hindrance to good communication.

8

Team Humor

Humor, a human quality that exists to a greater or lesser degree in every culture, has always had its place in international dealings, both socially and in business. The use of humor between individuals of different nationalities generally has a beneficial influence on their interactions, though on occasion it can be detrimental on account of varying notions of what is funny or appropriate. We sometimes say "so-and-so has a strange sense of humor" or even "the [insert nationality, e.g., Japanese] have no sense of humor." However this may be, it is evident that not all national senses of humor are compatible.

In an international team, each member brings their own brand of humor to the meetings, some quick to try it out, others more cautious in approach. It is tempting to think that there is an international sense of humor, since certain jokes about restaurant waiters, elephants, and golf seem ready made for all, but these subjects are limited and belong to a golfing community or those business people who spend a lot of time in restaurants, rather than evidencing a worldview on what is amusing. Even in these areas, the national "rinse" appears. An Anglo-French joke such as:

"Waiter, have you got frogs' legs?"
"No sir, it's my rheumatism."

would fall flat in Tokyo.

International teams, with the chair in a key role, are well aware that judiciously injected humor will be a valuable tool for team building. In their first few meetings together, anecdotes are exchanged, gentle irony may be introduced, situational incongruity may be commented on. Various humorous strategies will gradually be accepted, rejected, or experimented with. In the course of a few months, a collective sense of humor will develop, which will be exclusive to the group and have its own cues, code words, and secrets. Outsiders or newcomers to the group have to find their feet. This collective sense of humor becomes a kind of social glue facilitating group cohesion. The level of shared humor within a group serves as a kind of barometer of team integration, according to Schneider and Barsoux.

Shared laughter is a concrete sign that a group is creating an identity for itself, and that the individuals are becoming a team. The team's independent existence is marked by the creation of its own jokes, jesters, and external "fools." Teams reinforce their norms and values by what they laugh at. Jokes based on shared experiences and setbacks are invented and become the exclusive property of the team.

Once developed and honed, team humor can be put to various uses. When discussions get bogged down, an ironic comment can introduce a new perspective and speed things up. The same type of intervention can dispense with excessive formality. Bureaucratic procedures or demands from head office can be attacked indirectly. Mysterious management priorities can be sidelined. Superiors can be criticized gently and in an oblique manner through team codes. Mostly the "rebellion" will go unnoticed or probably be "pardoned" in the spirit of fun.

In the early stages of team collaboration, humor can be used to break the ice. Later, it can break up intransigence. A cohesive team gains in confidence and regards nothing as sacred or holy. New, unusual ideas can be introduced humorously, so that the proposer loses no face if they are rebuffed. Wild ideas can be put on the table with impunity.

Chris Patten, former Governor of Hong Kong and later experienced committee chairman in the EU, continually disarmed his opponents with his quick wit and facility for self-deprecation. Make fun of yourself and it is difficult for others to criticize you. "Self-deprecating humor is exceptionally important for anybody with power," said Patten. "First, because it stops you becoming irredeemably pompous, and second, because it keeps you in touch with reality – keeps you sane." Chairs of international teams would concur. These strategies are used by all nationalities, though some are favored by different cultures. Self-deprecation is quite common in England, for example; oblique criticism of superiors frequent among Australians; wild, "trial balloon" ideas often introduced by Portuguese.

Most members of a team attempt to make a contribution to the team humor. According to lexicologist Samuel Johnson, there is no man who does not at some time cherish the belief that he shares the company of the world's greatest wits. The team's collective humor standard will, of course, depend on the combination of styles within the group:

- ✦ The French – masters of language – interlard their comments with clever puns and witticisms, though they are at a disadvantage when having to use English.
- ✦ Nordic humor is very dry, especially in Norway. Finnish humor is dry, too, and often mock rustic.
- ✦ Danish humor is cynical, cleverly contrived. Swedes try to be more sophisticated.
- ✦ Italians, no strangers to self-deprecation, are also fond of attacking their own institutions (government, Mafia, Roman Catholic Church).
- ✦ Spanish humor is frequently earthy; they can also be touchy when mocked themselves.
- ✦ Russians, less touchy, indulge in self-mockery.
- ✦ German humor is direct, less subtle, always managing to maintain the integrity of the speaker.
- ✦ There is no definitely identifiable Asian humor, as different Asian mindsets vary as much as European. Hong Kong and Singaporean team members often use British-style humor, if they feel they have to contribute. Japanese rarely make humorous forays in international company; they prefer to be on the receiving end.

English-speaking team members use humor most, regarding it as a necessary ingredient for smoothing business procedures.

Business meetings between Britons and Americans or Canadians and Australians are often characterized by frequent kidding or joking, often used as relief interludes to hard bargaining or making difficult decisions. Their styles vary – Australian friendliness cloaks cynicism; Brits are understated and love class jokes; Americans use quips and wisecracks and lean heavily on hyperbole; Canadians, rarely unkind, are great storytellers who usually have a "fall-back position" in case they offend.

When we speak of offense, we are reminded that humorous dialogue, while largely beneficial and stimulating, also has its dangers. The biggest offenders, often unwittingly, are the Anglos. This is not simply because English is likely to be the language of the team, but also on account of their inability to eliminate humor from discussion of business. Even when negotiating or when dealing with vital issues, they will continue to be jocular, debonair, waggish, hearty, or saucy, according to national custom and individual taste. Humor will gain them many points with Europeans and Asians, but not as many as they think. They had better be on their guard.

In an international team, the dangers are threefold:

❖ A representative of another culture may be offended or caused to lose face.
❖ Misunderstanding or miscomprehension may occur.
❖ Excessive humor may be seen as irrelevant or even boring.

Anglo-Saxons have no desire to offend any more than anyone else, but in their cultures they have a tendency to make "harmless" fun of local people, food, customs, and institutions. Humorous references to Hispanic *mañana* behavior, Italian loquacity, or Swiss stuffiness hardly delight the people concerned. The Koran and Allah are not to be trifled with; the King of Thailand is revered by all Thais; Koreans believe that they possess outstanding national characteristics besides being eaters of garlic and *kimshi*. Culture in all its forms should be respected; it is not an object of fun, any more than is a Goya painting or a symphony by Sibelius.

Miscomprehension and misunderstanding of humorous remarks often go unnoticed by Anglo-Saxons. This is partly because several cultures, especially Asian but also eastern European and South American, frown on the custom of interrupting to seek clarification. The nod and smile of the Japanese seem to indicate that they have understood and approved. This is by no means the case.

I once attended a team "kick-off" where the American chair told the following joke as an ice-breaker:

Billy the Kid and his sidekick, Jed, enter a Wild West saloon and survey the scene from by the door.
"You see that cowboy over there by the bar?" Billy asks Jed.
"Which one? There are six cowboys by the bar."
"The one with the sombrero."
"But they're all wearing sombreros."
"The one with the big nose, stupid!"
"They all have a big nose."
Now Billy gets impatient and shouts: "I mean the one smoking a cigarette!"
"They're all smoking," replies Jed.
"The one with blue eyes!"
"They've all got blue eyes."
"Idiot! I mean the one drinking a beer!"
"They're all drinking beer."
Now furious, Billy the Kid takes out his gun and shoots one-two-three-four-five cowboys. Five bodies slump to the floor of the saloon. The sixth cowboy keeps on drinking.
"Jed, now do you see that cowboy with the sombrero, big nose, and blue eyes, drinking a beer at the bar?"
"Yes," says Jed, "What about him?"
"I hate his guts."

Some laughter ensued, but the Japanese team member present stared at the chair like he was weak in the head. He was so astounded that he forgot to laugh – something that Japanese do out of sheer politeness when they fail to get a western joke. A Japanese will never fully understand this type of joke. The person in question asked me after the meeting, "But if he hated that one, why didn't he shoot him instead of killing all the others?" Logical, of course. The American would have great difficulty explaining why the story is funny. A whole background of Wild West lawlessness, American tough talk, imaginative hyperbole, and the final "twist" is missing in the Japanese mind.

Another international team went for their meeting to Atlantic City, where the US delegate greeted them with the words: "I'm sorry we have to hold this meeting in Atlantic City. This is such a boring place that when the tide went out last Wednesday night it didn't come back on Thursday morning." My Danish informant found this funny, but said that he could see the German delegate (an engineer) wrestling with the concept, while the Japanese team member wanted to know what was all this about tides.

Americans are by no means the only culprits. A British team leader asked me for help, complaining that his French and German colleagues continually failed to implement his directives delivered at bi-monthly meetings. He was somewhat annoyed, particularly since he always laid on a superb dinner in whatever location the meeting was held. He suggested that I go along with him to the next meeting, which happened to be in France.

The business meeting, in the afternoon, was fairly short and factual. The dinner was long, excellent, and entertaining. During and after the meal the English chair – an extremely humorous character – revealed his ideas and vision for the immediate and more distant future. The company was not doing very well, but his concepts were imaginative, bold, and compelling. He had a tongue-in-cheek style, a rich vocabulary, made striking comparisons and contrasts, and expounded his business philosophy in witticisms, anecdote, and parable. He was a joy to listen to. I had never heard a senior executive deliver his directives and instructions in such a clever, disarming, and literary manner. I liked the subtle way in which he disguised his orders in the form of clever suggestions.

The French people present heard no orders, instructions, or directives. They enjoyed the dinner, the evening, and the charming personality of their team leader. I – being English– knew exactly what he wanted them to do. They did not; there would be little implementation.

This was a striking example of lack of communication through the use of (fine) humor, but there are many others where miscomprehension results through English team leaders using an amusing turn of phrase that, because of jargon or idiom, is completely opaque to non-English speakers. One jovial Englishman broke off the morning session with the suggestion, "How about toddling off for a drop of mother's ruin at the watering hole?"

Highly idiomatic expressions such as this, as well as most types of jargon, should be avoided in international teams. If they are not, zero comprehension will be the result in most cases. Even more common idioms cause trouble. The French will understand "tolerate" but not "put up with." They comprehend "accommodate" but not "being put up for the night." "Turn up" and "turn down" are usually misconstrued by most Latins. Many English jokes contain a large number of words and expressions of Saxon origin that are opaque to speakers of Romance or Slavic languages, and not always correctly absorbed by Germans, Dutch, and Nordics, not to mention Asian delegates. Indians and South Africans know what "maiden overs" and "sticky wickets" are; Americans, Germans, Czechs, and Albanians do not.

The third risk incurred in exercising frequent humor is that some nationalities may find it excessive or even irrelevant to many business discussions. Nordics, Dutch, Spaniards, and Italians often display what is almost hunger for Anglo-Saxon humor, but with others the reaction may be different. The French only tolerate it to some degree; Germans prefer it compartmentalized, so that it does not interfere with progress; Swiss easily get confused by the English tendency to put a premium on casual remarks; Japanese hardly perceive it as necessary; among Asians only Koreans (who like to profess that they understand western humor) inject funny stories into their conversation.

The benefits of a humorous approach are evident to all, but in some cultures it has its limitations. Flippancy earns no medals east of Helsinki. Sarcasm causes Asians to lose face. The American addiction to humorous hyperbole makes Asians (and Germans and Swiss, too) believe that if they exaggerate mood and phraseology, they will also overstate quality and technical validity. Americans actually know when to draw the line, but how can Swiss or Turks perceive this? British humorous understatement can have the opposite effect. "I suppose it'll do the job" (describing a product) sounds very unconvincing in Asian, Germanic, and American ears.

A final word of warning to humorous Anglo-Saxon team leaders or persistent team wits: our more serious colleagues have learned to indulge us in what seems to be our favorite pastime. Asians are good at feigning amusement, but if they are amused at all it is more at our antics rather than at our irresistible wit. They have toler-ated (or suffered) jocund irrelevancies for decades, seeing it as the price for doing business with Anglo-Saxons. It is questionable if the communication gap is any narrower than it was in the days of Marco Polo. Nevertheless, if the commercial gains are sufficient, they will play along. The more serious Europeans will do some-thing similar.

If Anglos believe that Asians and Europeans are incapable of "humoring" us, they should think of other groups who do so in somewhat differing circumstances. Afro-Americans have long adopted "Uncle Tom" behavior when it suited them to hoodwink Whitey. Texans accentuate their cattleman traits when they go to Washington, New York, and other cities that aspire to sophistica-tion. Most Southerners in the USA put on the "reb" act from time to time. Lancashire and Yorkshire people do it to the southern English. The Scots and Irish have their own shows.

So, jargon is out, idioms are out, sarcasm and satire are out, flippancy and gentle irony have to be watched. Even proverbs (the encapsulation of human wisdom) are risky. An anglophile Swede, hoping to sharpen up his Mexican and Italian colleagues, told them: "The early bird catches the worm." The proverb might not translate into their languages, but who wants worms anyway?

Among the English-speaking peoples, Canadians, South Africans, and New Zealanders often come across well with multicultural teams, as they usually moderate their humor and emphasize correctness. Many Nordic, German, Italian, Dutch, and Swiss team leaders are outstanding in their leadership, knowing how to balance humor and serious progress. Not long ago I saw an excellent Belgian chair deal neatly with a serious error of calculation by a team member during open discussion. Quickly globalizing the incident he said, "There are only three types of human beings – those who can count and those who can't."

The Italian member chuckled gleefully. Everybody else missed it. I thought the Belgian deserved better.

CASE STUDY

Boots, a well-known international pharmacy, ran into a problem regarding internal staff tension in Thailand. Serious discussion and questioning failed to reveal the source of friction. Only when humor was introduced did things become clear.

Boots

In the last decade of the twentieth century the Nottingham-based international pharmacy Boots was beginning to enjoy significant expansion in Asia. Thailand was seen as a good market and I was asked to go to Nottingham to confer with the HR department at head office to discuss recent developments in that country. The brand had been established with some success and it was felt that the company was on track for developing considerable potential in various branches that were being opened in smaller towns and rural districts. Problems with customers were few; the arrival of Boots in the districts in which it operated had been generally welcomed.

Boots felt, however, that there was significant internal tension among its employees. Relations seemed strained between the Thailand HQ, the central depots, and the branch managers. An international development team had investigated this issue. The team consisted of two people from head office, one an HR specialist and the other an operations person; in Thailand the members were the HR director and two assistants. The team was all female.

They had tackled the issue of the less than cordial relations between the central depot and the branch retailers. Their own intervention as a team had been difficult. There were obviously problems in existence, but the Thai staff were unwilling to voice them. The British women were perceptive: they had set up brainstorming sessions to enable staff to voice their views and put forward solutions. These sessions produced little, if any, information, however. This is not unusual in most Asian countries, where courtesy and respect for elders virtually prohibit frank discussion. There was a divergence of method within the development team itself, with the Thai members only half-heartedly supporting the British women's investigative procedures.

I pointed out to the Nottingham international HR manager that brainstorming sessions in Asian countries were inevitably doomed to failure. Nobody would go out on a limb to speak out in front of superiors; nobody would voice open criticism of colleagues; nobody would take any step that might risk someone losing face. They knew where the problems lay, but how were the British members to find out the details? Certainly relations were strained around the organization, but why?

My advice coincided with the impressions of one of the British women stationed in Thailand. It is a well-known characteristic of the Thai people that they like work only when it is fun, or *sanuke*. Why not adopt a humorous approach to solving the problems? Role play was the answer. The British women set up training sessions where the staff had to act out various simulations. Each staff member assumed a role, a real functional one in the organization. Some people played managers, some depot directors, some branch managers, some shop assistants. Even drivers were included. Each person had a fictional name. All were assigned to different locations and functions and tasked with answering the question: How can we improve our organization?

Shielded by another person's name, without actual personal responsibility for their opinions, the staff were not slow to voice their grievances. The fictional branch managers, usually aged 40–50, screamed their vexation at having to buy supplies from a 28-year-old depot director. Their lives and prosperity were in the hands of a man 20 years younger than they were. What kind of hierarchy was that? And why was Mr. X in Chiang-mai so arrogant? Or Mr. Y in Phuket so stupid? Why had Miss Z been so rapidly promoted? The fictional company they created was attacked without reserve. They were not attacking Boots, of course, nor the real Mr. A, or Mr. B, or Miss C. It was only a role – a play after all. And it was fun.

The British team got the message all right. The problems had been pinpointed without hurting anyone personally. HQ was able to take steps in due course, based on the information the role play had provided. Other role plays were introduced and this became a feature of training in various Asian locations.

9

Decision Making

Decisions often have to be taken rather quickly in international teams, as time may be limited. Yet even what at first seem to be the most straightforward of discussions can run into dispute or deadlock. When such a situation occurs between nationals of one culture, the momentum can usually be regained through the use of a well-tried decision-making mechanism. However, the success of these varies among nationalities, and cultural difference can often mean that the nature of the deadlock is misconstrued by all parties.

Compromise

The mechanism classically favored by Anglo-Saxons in such circumstances is compromise, a form at which the British, with their supposedly innate sense of fair play, believe themselves to excel. The Scandinavians are very "British" in this respect, while the American willingness to compromise is seen in their frequent recourse to "horse trading" and give-and-take tactics. Yet, in any situation, intelligent, meaningful compromise is only possible when one side is able to see how the other sets out its priorities and understands how culturally affected notions of dignity, conciliation, and reasonableness come into play. In some cultures, for example, flexibility in negotiation is seen as a virtue. In others it is regarded as a weakness that inevitably leads to an erosion of one's position. An English dictionary typically defines "compromise" as the "settlement of a dispute by concessions on both or all sides." A second definition reads "an exposure of one's good name or reputation." Clearly, one has to tread carefully.

In some countries, accordingly, compromise is held in low esteem. To the French, for example, "give and take" is simply an

Anglo-Saxon euphemism for "wheel and deal," which they see as an inelegant tactic for chiseling away at their carefully constructed logic. "Yes, let's be reasonable," they say, "but what is irrational in what we have already said?" It is primarily this attitude that has led to the common perception of the French as obstinate negotiators. In reality, they see no reason to compromise if their well-formulated argument stands undefeated.

For Japanese, compromise is a departure from the company-backed consensus; woe betide the Japanese negotiator who concedes a point without authority. Here, adjournment is the least that they must ask for. The result is often long telephone calls back to superiors in search of directives. Again, the common assumption is that Japanese negotiators are unable to make decisions. Rather, the Japanese see meetings as occasions for presenting previously ratified decisions, not changing them.

Among Latins, attitudes toward compromise vary. Italians, though they respect logic almost as much as the French, pride themselves on flexibility. They are closely followed by the Portuguese who, in their long history of trading with the British, are quite familiar with Anglo-Saxon habits. The Spanish and South Americans, however, are horses of another color. Spaniards' obsession with dignity makes it hard for them to climb down without good reason. South Americans, similarly, see compromise as a threat to their *pundonor* (literally, position of honor). This is particularly acute among Argentineans, Mexicans, and Panamanians, who typically display obstinacy in conceding even the slightest point – especially to the arrogant, insensitive Americans, whose position of power and dominance they have long resented.

The nationality factor in decision making

As with humor, motivation, speech styles, and listening habits, each team member brings to the group their own culture's route to decision making. This will originate from the management style at home, which sets the background or context in which decisions

Linear-active preferences
Compromise
Take a vote (majority rules)
Debate vigorously and come to some conclusion
Use common sense
Let's decide today
Let implementation follow quickly
Avoid ambiguity
We dislike chopping and changing
Decisions are final

Multi-active preferences
No piecemeal decisions
Let's discuss everything comprehensively
Lateral relations must be considered
Majority rule has a fundamental weakness: the minority might be right
Matters need not all be decided today
Bosses make decisions: have we consulted them?
There is no such thing as international common sense
A good decision is better than a consensus or compromise
Relationships are more important than hard-and-fast decisions

Reactive preferences
There is nothing new under the sun
Decisions, therefore, should be based on best past precedents
Decisions are best if they are unanimous
One should not submit to the tyranny of the majority, but reason with all
until unanimity is achieved
A harmonious decision is better than an acrimonious one, however
convincing

Table 9.1   Routes to decision making according to category preferences

are formulated. The team leader will have to blend these diverse mechanisms into a style that suits the team. This varies from team to team according to its composition. When all or the great majority of members are from one cultural category, there will be little dissension about which style to adopt. A team consisting of an American, a Japanese, a French person, a Norwegian, and a Brazilian will present a greater challenge to the chair.

Besides the actual decision-making method (compromise, consensus, majority vote, and so on), other factors are important. One is the timeframe, which may be viewed quite differently according to country of origin. Americans are characterized by a sense of urgency – they want to get started and act soon. Germans will be much more cautious, looking carefully at the context within which they make decisions, as well as the period that preceded it. For them, as indeed for the French, the present grows out of the past and current decisions must pay homage to it. Asians like to make decisions at a much slower pace. Quick decisions for them are either bad ones or of relatively little importance. Swedes are not anxious to move forward until all opinions have been heard.

Another consideration is the finality factor. How final is the decision or agreement? Germans and Swedes are slow to decide, but are unlikely to chop and change once the decision is made. Latins are sometimes agile in deciding, but allow themselves the luxury of second thoughts. This can cause problems in teams that arrive at a decision, then disperse, then have some members who request modifications (by phone or email). Another factor is the speed of implementation. Asians defer big decisions for months, then want delivery or action within days. Japanese frequently exasperate American partners with this quirk. They themselves implement quickly (often having made semi-final preparations before an order was confirmed).

The combination of these factors constitutes the decision-making process, from initial ideas and vision through to final action and implementation. At company level the variance is great from culture to culture, as they deal and trade with each other. The international team, however, does not have the same latitude as the parent companies. A team that meets once every six weeks and fails to reach decisions to pressing issues would be viewed very dimly by head office. There must be a viable mechanism or method, there must be a reasonably quick timeframe, there must be assumed finality, there must be a route to implementation. That is why they all meet.

Most international teams rise to this challenge. It could well be that they give good lessons to head office, where bureaucracy might weigh heavily. In this respect one can see the importance of appointing perspicacious and effective team managers. The task is not easy: the American or Argentinean might be pushing hard for approval of a pet scheme; the Japanese, on the other hand, would be reluctant to propose even a sound idea if they were not sure whether it was already universally supported. The British might be making judgments according to unwritten rules that are of British origin and might be not at all clear to their colleagues. The French might argue at length, but really think that decisions lay only with the boss (as indeed in France they usually do).

Whatever the factors at play, the international team manager has to come up with a result and, while some deferment of decisions is acceptable, preparation for action takes priority. This consideration favors linear-active procedures and linear team members, but properly managed diversity remains the best formula.

Country	Management style	Decision-making method	Time factor	Finality factor	Implementation
Finland	Democratic but decisive	Survey of facts Best/worst scenarios discussed	Unhurried but no time wasting	Items agreed are binding	Swift
Sweden	Democratic Low-key managers	Consultative All opinions heard Consensus	Slow Several meetings	Normally binding	Moderately swift after double-checking
USA	Driving Bottom-line focus	Brainstorming Action oriented	Time is money	Normally binding	Swift
UK	Hierarchical but also consultative	Exchange of ideas Brainstorming Manager decides	Unhurried Calm	Binding but renegotiation permissible	Often slow–moderate
France	Autocratic	Top down after roundabout discussions	Slow, all aspects discussed	Often dubious Ambiguous	Moderate
Italy	Autocratic but flexible	Top down Long discussions	Slow to moderate	Decisions often changed	Slow in south Moderate in north
Spain	Autocratic but warm	Top down	Mañana factor, won't move until ready	Manager's decisions difficult to change	Often slow

Country	Management style	Decision-making method	Time factor	Finality factor	Implementation
Portugal	Autocratic Flexible	Top down after examination of all aspects Cautious	Often slow Risks should be limited	Written documentation final	Often slow
Germany	Autocratic with consensus	Survey of facts Adherence to proven processes	Slowish due to many lateral clearances	Binding when written	Moderate
Belgium	Walloon autocratic Flemish democratic	Pragmatic Compromise dominates	Reasonably quick	Renegotiation always possible	Moderate
South America	Autocratic	Combination of pragmatism and imagination	*Mañana* factor (Chile faster)	Conditions often unfulfilled	Unreliable, behind schedule
Asia	Collective	Collective after slow consensus taking	Unanimity required, therefore slow	Renegotiation common	Swift when everything is finalized

Table 9.2   National decision-making styles

Brainstorming

Under time constraints, it is only natural that international teams should consider brainstorming sessions as a useful mechanism for covering a lot of ground. This tactic is in fact often used, especially when Anglos, Dutch, Belgian, French, and Scandinavian team members preponderate. Brainstorming is not, however, universally popular, there being a variety of reasons why it does not appeal to some nationalities. It may be a question of power distance. In some cultures subordinates are unwilling to disagree with, contradict, or offend superiors (Indonesia, Brazil). Some cultures do not normally think aloud and actually dislike doing so (Finland, Japan, Sweden). Other nationalities just hate making mistakes or errors of judgment in public (Germans, Japanese). In some cases, political conditioning has undermined the concept (Russia, China, Indonesia). In other cases, the necessity for extreme courtesy and politeness will inhibit discussion (Japan, Indonesia, Malaysia, India). In some cultures women would practically be excluded from the process (Muslim, Korea, Japan). Some nationalities prefer to stick to established processes and proven theories (Germany, Japan). Over-concern with job security is an important factor in some countries (Mexico, Bolivia). In some cultures the tradition of instruction and passing on ideas is strictly top down (all Confucian societies – China, Japan, Korea, Vietnam). Finally, the existence of class or caste systems may prohibit joint or open discussion.

The brainstorming "league table" in Table 9.3 analyzes relative enthusiasms and hesitancies concerning the use of brainstorming sessions. Willingness to participate is indicated by 1–10 (10 = enthusiastic, 1 = unwilling).

USA	10	One of the chief ways of generating new ideas Freedom of speech taken for granted Americans think aloud
Canada	10	Debating and exchanging ideas encouraged early on in the education system
Netherlands	10	A clear separation is made between a person's opinions and their personality Right to speak guaranteed
Australia	10	Australians are always ready and happy to speak their mind Historically they resent any restrictions from above in this area
UK	9	Debating popular and freedom of speech historical In some companies, there would be a slight reticence in front of very senior persons Also the class question can interfere
France	8	Though French management is autocratic, few French people can resist the temptation to talk at length and show how clever they are
Finland	7	Absolutely democratic society where freedom of expression and independence of opinion are guaranteed Finns, however, do not normally think aloud – in fact, they dislike doing so.

Sweden	7	Long discussions and forming consensus are typical of Swedish meetings Their rather formal manner in exchanging ideas is, however, far removed from the American concept of brainstorming
Italy	7	Italians, like French, Spanish, and Portuguese, love to share visions They are full of ideas but there is a certain reluctance to offend superiors, especially in the south of Italy
Spain	7	Spaniards enter into brainstorming enthusiastically as they are great idealists and need a faith or vision to live by They are, however, unwilling to contradict strong managers
Brazil	6	Loquacious debaters who will examine all aspects of a project with gusto Power distance will, however, restrict how they phrase their opinion in front of superiors
India	6	Flowery speakers and keen on the debating tradition, which they inherited from the British They will be most reluctant to contradict superiors As Asians, they will be careful not to be impolite to anyone else Women are at a disadvantage
Hispanic America	5	Talkative people who think big and would like to brainstorm Another trait of most Hispanic Americans is, however, nervousness about offending superiors, especially evident in Mexico, Bolivia, Ecuador, and Venezuela
Germany	5	German society is vertical and few Germans wish to contradict superiors or disagree openly As they also wish to be honest, brainstorming presents a dilemma They prefer to work through established processes Brainstorming is possible if only younger people are present
Arabs	4	Most Arabs are too unfocused in discussion to contribute effectively to brainstorming sessions They would be very careful not to offend superiors They all tend to talk at once anyway Women play only a small part

Russia	3	Russians are extremely suspicious of public debate and would not often risk exposing their views in front of others However, when you get Russians "in the kitchen," they are very expressive and original
Korea	3	Koreans are more open and original than most Confucian Asians, but power distance will restrict their assertiveness More likely to brainstorm in front of foreigners than before other Koreans "Face" will always be a factor
China	1	Ideas in Chinese education and society are passed down, not discussed Confucius says that superiors are to be obeyed, not questioned Political matters also complicate discussion
Indonesia	1	Traditionally an obedient society where gentleness of expression does not sit well with brainstorming Freedom of speech is not taken for granted Differences of opinion are not normally aired in public
Japan	1	"Face" is all important and inhibits free discussion Society is extremely hierarchical People are very afraid to make mistakes in public Fundamentally, Japanese do not trust words

Table 9.3   Brainstorming league table

Disagreement

An element of disagreement will obviously be present in every meeting of an international team. Some cultures are not afraid of confrontation (Germany, USA) and make their disagreement known openly and bluntly. Their terminology is succinct:

✧ Germans: I disagree
✧ Americans: That is unacceptable
✧ Finns: I can't agree to that
✧ Dutch: I can't sell this to my board
✧ Norwegians: I have a different view

Other cultures, perhaps more tactful, are less open in their expression of disagreement:

- ✧ English: I agree, up to a point
- ✧ Canadians: Well, I don't see it exactly that way
- ✧ Swedes: I have to consult with my colleagues
- ✧ Italians: That is certainly a very original idea
- ✧ Spaniards: We'll do what we can
- ✧ Portuguese: I admit, everything is possible

Other cultures are more devious or ambiguous:

- ✧ Chinese: I agree and disagree at the same time
- ✧ Brazilians: You're the boss
- ✧ Russians: We'll find a way of making it work
- ✧ Thais: We would never have thought of that
- ✧ Japanese: I agree (faint voice)

It is the team leader's job to seek, reach, and cement agreement each time the team meets. The meetings are occasions for energetic debate, perhaps fierce argument, but conflict has to be resolved. As long as the chair is sensitive to nuances of expressions and manner when approval is sought, they will steer the group toward consensus. They must be aware that truth itself – scientific truth based on facts and figures – is a constant only for Nordics, Germanics, and some Anglo-Saxons. In Japan where no one must face exposure, truth is a dangerous concept. In Italy it is negotiable, in Brazil it will be intertwined with euphoria, in France it may be missed if it does not fit in with theory. Chinese, even overseas Chinese, distrust hard-and-fast precepts, preferring comfortable ambiguity. Many cultures reach for solutions intuitively rather than by rationality.

The good news is that after a few months of acquaintance with each other, international teams usually come to recognize colleagues' idiosyncrasies and find suitable antidotes to enable actions to progress without too frequent dissent.

CASE STUDIES

Pharmaceutical giants Upjohn (USA) and Pharmacia (Sweden) had an unhappy union for over a decade. When Pfizer took Upjohn's place, it determined to avoid the numerous conflicts that had arisen between the partners, particularly in the area of decision making.

The second case study, of INA/Cigna and AIG, illustrates the lack of understanding and the need for new perspectives in a large number of big companies when they undertake foreign operations. Instead of creating, from the outset, an international division, many of them try to organize and control overseas undertakings from the home base, initially assigning a handful of home-grown executives to handle foreign issues. In due course, an international department is set up, but it is too often an ad-hoc and little-understood procedure, after early mistakes have been made. US companies, particularly, fell into this trap in the expansive years following the Second World War, failing to take into account the cultural issues that were bound to arise from both European and Asian scenarios. Conservative insurance companies could hardly be expected to internationalize with the agility shown by Nokia, Michelin, or Unilever. The UK's Abbey National (now Santander) burnt its fingers in Europe through failing to set up an international division, though Allianz did much better, especially in its German business.

Pfizer–Upjohn-Pharmacia

In the 1990s it was well known that the union of Upjohn and Pharmacia was an uneasy one. We gave several seminars in Helsingborg to mixed Swedish–US teams without feeling that we were achieving very much. The "us and them" atmosphere was readily apparent. The workshops had in fact been arranged a few years too late: the damage had already been done in terms of working relationships and reputations. The remedial program was sporadic, actually spread out over three or four years.

In early 2003 the giant American pharmaceutical company Pfizer bought out Upjohn and took over Pharmacia. It was well aware of the cultural and operating difficulties that Upjohn had experienced and was anxious to avoid similar complications. It started out with the premise that Upjohn, operating in Sweden, had failed to come to terms with the Swedish cultural environment and had committed a series of gaffes not uncommon for an American company making new forays into European and Asian territory.

In the Pfizer HQ in Morris Plains, New Jersey, there happened to be a rather sophisticated and multinational team concerned with the takeover, led by Richard d'Souza and including members from Italy, South Africa, French Canada, and the UK. Aware of my knowledge of the Swedish operation, d'Souza asked us to hold a two-day seminar in Morris Plains to give his team of 25 a full briefing on the Swedish business environment. It was clearly quite different from the American one, not only because of wildly diverging national psychologies, but also due to dissimilar legislation and structures imposed by the Swedish state.

I was aided in my task by rather copious notes that the Swedish half of the Upjohn–Pharmacia teams had made in the months when the Upjohn exit was foreseen. Swedes, though generally nonconfrontational with partners and conscientious in listening to others' points of view, nevertheless do not abandon their own attitudes easily and like to have recourse to self-justification if their suggestions are set aside.

Frustration had been felt by both sides, though the list of Swedish complaints was the longer of the two. As I related them to Pfizer, they were as follows:

✦ In general they objected to the American managers' "hard-charging" style. Upjohn's "commanding captains" did not mesh well with the Swedish system of working in autonomous small groups.
✦ US managers were seen as brutally frank and direct. American frankness is almost unique. Only Germans and Finns accept it readily. Swedes certainly do not.

✧ The American managers often over-ruled Swedish top executives in public, causing them to lose face. Neither did they seem to realize they had done so.

✧ Upjohn required frequent reporting: monthly research reports, budgets, staffing updates, and so on. This type of monthly monitoring created extra process in Swedish eyes.

✧ Typically American quarterly rolling forecasts also annoyed the Swedes (traditionally uncomfortable with most forms of speculation).

✧ Monthly staffing updates seemed outright idiotic to Swedes. There is much less mobility in Swedish companies. Employees usually maintain a steady performance.

✧ Upjohn banned smoking and wine on company premises. Swedes felt that this interfered with personal liberty. They were further upset by and subsequently opposed alcohol and drug testing of workers.

✧ The US emphasis on personal accountability shocked the Swedes, who often take refuge in group responsibility.

✧ The Americans created an extra layer of management by setting up a London regional HQ. Swedes complained of having two bosses.

The American managers also found cause for complaint. Swedes normally take all of July as vacation. US executives scheduling meetings in July found that they were called off, as their partners were on the beach. American employees do not take time off when a major project is underway or at a time of business crisis. Swedes are sensitive about infringements on their leisure time. In American eyes they are quick to insist on their rights and often fail to focus on their corresponding duties. The power of the Swedish workers' unions irritated the Americans.

The blame for some problems lay at the feet of both sides. Often one side's computers did not relate to the other's. Product launches were delayed because of lack of communication between the teams. Nationalist overtones were observable on both sides.

The Swedes noted that Upjohn met with tough resistance in the Italian subsidiary. Problems concerned questions of hierarchy, impenetrable fiscal controls (Italian), and the struggles between company loyalty and family loyalty.

The Pfizer team discussed at length the sources of irritation between Upjohn and Pharmacia. It was a valuable learning experience. I stressed the key factors in motivating Swedish staff:

❖ Ask for everybody's opinion
❖ Attend meetings patiently (there are many of them)
❖ Wait for them to reach decisions by consensus
❖ Be part of this consensus
❖ Discuss technical points at length and in detail
❖ See business as beneficial to society rather than primarily profit oriented
❖ Always be consultative and understanding
❖ Never bulldoze them

I pointed out that while Swedes like to be considered internationally minded and impartial, they are not the easiest of people to deal with in multinational teams. Not only Americans, but other nationalities such as British, Finns, and Norwegians are often exasperated by Swedish complacency, slow decision making, and conviction that the Swedish way must be best.

Swedish business people have undoubted strengths in the international arena. They have a high level of education, technical competence, upstream industry based on science and technology, sound investment in research, absence of corruption, Lutheran ethics, and excellent linguistic skills. Their different political groups cooperate readily in promoting national business. This is the good news.

The bad news includes too many meetings (going round in circles), managers afraid of staff, over-cosseted employees who absent themselves at the slightest excuse (backed up legally), woolly directives given by low-key managers, obsessive admiration for the welfare state, and a tendency to over-analyze and to require too much context before acting. Some of these weaknesses do not sit easily with Americans.

The Pfizer executives digested this information. It was hard for them to visualize a twenty-first-century business person who did not share their driving work ethic, zest for results, and attachment to numbers and statistics. D'Souza saw clearly that they would have to adapt quickly to Swedish psychology if they were to make a success of their new venture. Compared to Upjohn, Pfizer would be low key, laid back (at least for a while), and demonstrate some humility in a new set of circumstances.

To a considerable degree, that is how it turned out. The new teams worked quietly and well. It was largely the Americans who adapted. They gave their Swedish colleagues what they considered to be an inordinate amount of time to reach decisions. They played to the welfare state and green mentalities and paid respects to the formal aspects of Swedish business, where correctness and harmony seem more important than results. Profit is one of the goals, but a distant last. Swedes are happy "traveling hopefully."

INA/CIGNA and AIG

While "cross-cultural" differences and mishaps might normally refer to the results of interaction between two distinct and different country cultures, there can also be "cross-cultural" problems arising between the domestic and international components of the same organization. Such problems can significantly affect the success of its international operations.

INA, through its major subsidiary, the Insurance Company of North America, was a leading player in the US insurance market and its international operations began very early. In 1930, it established an office in London, primarily to service marine insurance claims. In 1932, it set up an office in Shanghai, which, at that time, was a flourishing center of commercial activity, attracting considerable foreign investment. In contrast to the London marine claims office, the Shanghai office was "full service" (selling and administering insurance policies) and branches were later established in Hong Kong and Tientsin. At that time, the company was one of the very few US-based insurance companies to have operations overseas and, in doing so, displayed considerable vision.

Thus, an international mindset had been established relatively early in the company's history and, in the years immediately following the Second World War, its international network expanded dramatically; branches were established in Asia (Japan, the Philippines, and Singapore); in Europe (Germany, Italy, the Netherlands, and Spain); in Africa (South Africa, Kenya, Rhodesia); in Latin America (Brazil, Cuba, Colombia, Puerto Rico, Venezuela); and in Australia and New Zealand. Regional offices were considered necessary for proper management and control and were accordingly established in The Hague (Europe), Puerto Rico (Latin America), Hong Kong (Asia), and Johannesburg (Africa).

By the mid-1970s, after additional overseas development, INA was a multinational enterprise and, though the international business was a relatively small component of total revenues, its contribution to overall growth and profits was very important. For example, in 1974 the international business produced about 8 percent of total company revenue (relatively small), but approximately 50 percent of total profits. The international operations were consistently profitable, while domestic operations were subject to widely swinging profit cycles, the result of inflation and a difficult pricing environment.

With such a positive impact on overall results, it was not surprising to find that the management of INA Corporation began a concerted effort to expand international operations, in order to take better advantage of its international franchise and favorable operating conditions overseas. To direct this effort, INA hired a senior executive, John Cox, from American International Group (AIG). AIG was at the time one of the leading international insurers, with a longer history and broader operations, in terms of products and country licenses, than INA. Cox brought with him the AIG international growth culture.

In the early 1980s, however, the momentum changed. In 1982, INA Corporation merged with Connecticut General Insurance Corporation, an action that, in the words of INA chairman Ralph Saul, "would create one of the largest stockholder owned insurance enterprises in the world, CIGNA Corporation."

Indeed, the merger held great promise. Both companies had long and successful histories and were generally held in high esteem in the insurance industry. The two business bases were very complementary. INA had prominence and critical mass in the property and casualty (or general) insurance market. Connecticut General had a more modest position in property and casualty, but was strong in life insurance, employee benefits, and healthcare markets, for which INA had longstanding aspirations to enter in a meaningful, mainstream way. In Wall Street, a "marriage made in heaven" was the most often-heard comment.

Nevertheless, insiders working within the newly formed CIGNA Corporation soon began to notice significant differences in the two corporate cultures. In general, INA tended to be more prone to taking risks in its business endeavors and more entrepreneurial in its management style. Connecticut General took a more measured approach, and tended to be more risk averse and more bureaucratic. While early on in the merger the senior management team was pretty much balanced in terms of representation, it was not long before the Connecticut General team was dominant.

By 1984, Connecticut General personnel had assumed in CIGNA the positions of chairman, president, chief financial officer, and executive vice-president of the property and casualty group, which at the time was CIGNA's largest and in which international operations were housed. Within a year or so after the merger was consummated, several of the leading INA executives had left the company, including John Cox, who had been the driver of INA's recent international expansion.

Initially, the merger and the subsequent organizational changes had little impact on the international operation. Because Connecticut General was not a direct international player, there was no integration task to be accomplished with respect to international business. By contrast, the domestic property and casualty operations of the two companies faced a formidable integration challenge. Overlapping management teams, service offices, systems, and product strategies all had to be sorted out and a new, integrated organization established. Such a task was naturally a significant drain on managerial resources and energy.

The international division, on the other hand, was left alone to pursue its established expansion strategy. At the time, the international management team was relatively young and aggressive, and, clearly cognizant of the franchise's potential, undertook to carry forward Cox's vision. The division was also experiencing above-average growth and probability, and so was in good corporate standing.

In late 1983, AFIA (one of the three principal US-based insurers operating internationally) approached CIGNA, inquiring if the company had any interest in buying it out. At the time, AFIA's results had deteriorated significantly, largely because of a lack of controls in its London operations, which resulted in a book of questionable business, the losses from which were likely to extend well into the future. Thus, AFIA members, who were facing significant losses and cash calls, were amenable to selling. CIGNA was an obvious candidate, already possessing a sizable international business, and thus better positioned to deal with AFIA's problems. The acquisition was consummated, with CIGNA paying approximately $400 million, by far the largest acquisition to date in its history.

International success?

CIGNA was now very much in the "big league" of international insurance. Through AFIA, it had acquired an additional $800 million in gross premium, 5,000 employees, and an extensive license base including over 20 countries in which CIGNA did not have a presence. In total, CIGNA's international insurance gross premium income now exceeded US$2.1 billion, and thus the organization was comparable to AIG, another US insurance multinational that had about US$1.7 billion in property and casualty insurance premia. Essentially, both organizations were of similar size.

Let us fast forward 15 years and see what transpired, in terms of growth and development, for these two international insurance organizations. In 1998, CIGNA sold most of its international operations to ACE Group. Thus, AIG was able to emerge as one of the leading international financial institutions in the world, while CIGNA had reached the point where it retained only a relatively small international life insurance business.

What accounted for such a difference?

CIGNA's international management team, which was the architect of the AFIA acquisition, broke up less than a year later, and the division, with a new team, was repositioned at a lower level in the organization. Instead of being a stand-alone division, International was part of a large domestic general insurance division. This meant that business plans and proposals had to be cleared through managers who had no international experience. It also meant that domestic standards drove such important items such as compensation levels.

As an example, when a proposal was made to increase the compensation of a international country manager, the question would be asked: "What's the country's premium volume?" The answer would be given and the discussion would continue: "Well, that's the same as the St. Louis service office here in the USA, so why should your guy be paid any different?" In fact, the scope of an international country manager was much broader. They would typically have to understand and deal with unions, regulators, funds flows back to the USA, foreign exchange exposures, local capital requirements, and so on; tasks that his counterpart did not have to deal with or were addressed centrally. However, it was difficult to get this logic across.

The problem was not so much the people involved, but the lack of perspective. It would be hard to get a sense of the dynamism of South-East Asia unless at some point one had looked out of the window from a high-rise hotel in Singapore and seen the myriad of ships in the harbor and the construction cranes building more high-rises. Part-time international management doesn't seem to work.

In contrast, AIG started as an international business in the early 1920s when an enterprising young American, C.V. Starr, went to Shanghai and set up a life insurance operation. It was not a domestic company expanding overseas, so an international culture was established early on and became embedded. The commitment to international business development was ongoing and unwavering and the company became one of the leading financial institutions in the world. Its approach to business expansion was very aggressive. For example, after the Soviet Union disintegrated and eastern Europe opened up, AIG was quick to enter Poland, Hungary, and Estonia. AIG's international culture, commitment, and continuity have stood it in very good stead.

10

Behaving Ethically

The subject of business ethics is vast and complex. As they pursue the globalization of their commercial activities, westerners often talk of the necessity of creating a "level playing field" where trading opportunities and access to markets are equal for everyone. Favoritism, protectionism, and forms of corruption that interfere with the concept of fairness or straightforward transactions based on healthy competitiveness are taboo. One should align one's behavior to one's values – not just any old values, but ones with the highest ethical standards.

However, these definitions and assumptions may not be shared or respected by collectivist or strongly relationship-oriented cultures. Asians, particularly, conceptualize fairness, right and wrong, honesty and dishonesty in different ways from westerners such as Americans, Northern Europeans, and Australians. Even in Europe – in its eastern parts as well as in those countries bordering the Mediterranean – business ethics and respect for the law differ strikingly. In the Middle East, another set of rules and customs applies.

There is nearly universal agreement that stealing, in the form of taking or using money that does not belong to you, is unethical. Most people would agree that the exploitation of child labor in order to lower the cost of production is unethical, as well as insider trading or brutal violation of human rights (though countries such as China and Denmark would vary wildly in defining these). But if taking money that does not belong to you is wrong, what about giving it – in the form of bribes – to other people who contribute to your company's profits? And if it is not an issue of money, what about gifts? In many parts of the world – Japan, China, and the Middle East – exchanging personal gifts as part of a business transaction has a long pedigree. In Japan (surely a culture that could be described as generally honest and ethical) it is quite normal to shower gifts on customers and associates, and indeed it would be construed negatively if this custom ceased to exist.

In other parts of the world, high-trust organizations take a strong moral stand on this issue. Motorola, for example, states in its moral code:

> *employees of Motorola will respect the laws, customs and traditions of each country in which they operate, but will, at the same time, engage in no course of action which, even if legal, customary and accepted in any such country, could be deemed to be in violation of the accepted business ethics of Motorola or the laws of the United States relating to business ethics.*

It is not hard to see how some cultures and countries (including some very large and powerful ones) would view such declarations as examples of cultural imperialism. This does not imply any impropriety on the part of Motorola (the opposite is the case), but there is a big world out there, doing business as usual. President Medvedev of Russia was explicit during 2008–09 in his desire to clean up bribery issues in Russian bureaucratic circles. In the same period, then prime minister Putin told a western journalist that "anyone who succeeded in registering a business in Russia deserved a medal." In the Ukraine, a clean-up campaign in the aftermath of the Orange Revolution resulted in a ban (perhaps better described as a moratorium) on bribery. This, according to a prominent and successful Ukrainian business leader, lasted about 12 months – a period during which "nothing got done." Cash was not demanded for licenses; officials just procrastinated until money appeared. In the old Ukraine, said the businessman, you knew "who, when and how much." Bribes normally accounted for 10 percent of his costs, he told *The Economist*; about the same as gangland extortion (protection) money, he added wryly. Comfortingly, women were known for accepting lower bribes and often, disarmingly, requested donations to local schools.

International teams of several types, such as those promoting trade in different countries, launching new products, entering new markets in connection with joint ventures, sales and purchasing teams in general, or those involved in license procurement, patents, and expatriate placement are often confronted with dilemmas in seeking facilitation of their objectives. It is clear that in a very diverse and patently multicultural world, they will on occasion be in dire need of guidelines as to how to proceed through a veritable labyrinth of traditional, established ways of contracting business. These vary in every culture: there are no internationally accepted definitions of either ethical behavior or corruption.

The intention of the US Foreign Corrupt Practices Act (FCPA) is crystal clear and set out in explicit detail. Seen through American eyes, there is little or no ambiguity. But ambiguity is nevertheless endemic in Asia, not least with economic giants such as India and China. India has a 3,000-year tradition in its commercial practices where the prerogatives of hierarchy, networks of relationships, consideration of privilege, face, and dignity will inevitably override others of fairness, equality, or opportunity. Face is undoubtedly the dominant factor controlling behavior, arrangements, and accommodations in Japan and hardly less so in Korea. China does not recognize the concept of "absolute truth" or any clear definition of right and wrong, good and bad. The ubiquitous custom of *guanxi* requires unavoidable concessions and mutual granting of favors relating to any transaction. Even in Europe, the *mani pulite* ("clean hands") campaign in Italy in the 1990s was a disaster for many leading business people and politicians, who viewed the new regulations as a complete reversal of the Italian way of life. It was less than successful, as the achievements of Signor Berlusconi still signal to all.

Non-Americans view the FCPA as something of a presumptuous anomaly, as it purports to dictate behavior not only to US citizens and companies, but also to people of other countries and cultural practices. A leading French executive, asked to comply with the FCPA, pointed out that centuries-old traditions of French philosophy, literature, and commercial experience were the factors that told him how to behave and conduct business – not American legislation. New also is the idea that the blame shifts over to the person offering the bribe rather than the person or entity demanding it. This concept does not go down readily in such different countries as Russia, Indonesia, and Iran. Even in France and Germany, where bribery is illegal at home, it is not considered illicit abroad. There is an "ethics gap" between the USA and Europe. Codes of conduct were drawn up by most US firms in the 1980s and 1990s. Not more than 60 percent of British and European companies had them by the beginning of the twenty-first century. Nordic companies compared well in this respect with the Americans, but southern European enterprises are way behind.

In 2007, a leading British intercultural expert was asked to consult with a large Norwegian company that felt it was in danger of contravening the FCPA in some of its dealings in the Middle East. As the company was listed on the New York Stock Exchange, it was vulnerable to investigation by the Americans. The consultant was requested to give a seminar to a selection of the firm's managers, outlining views of different cultures regarding facilitation payments; a problem that had already manifested itself in the company's dealings in the previous months. The consultant – well-traveled and with 30 years' experience of business habits in four continents – was well prepared and ready to give an ethically oriented Norwegian audience the lowdown on all manner of under-the-table transactions he had witnessed and been involved in in a dozen countries "east of Oslo." Unfortunately, the Norwegians invited to the seminar half a dozen of their foreign managers, including a Russian, an Iranian, an Afghan, and two Arabs. The consultant was thus prevented from giving his presentation with the frankness and revelatory content he had envisaged. In spite of neutralizing his remarks as nimbly as he could, he was unable to avoid making reference to the cultural idiosyncrasies in negotiating with Russians, Arabs, and certain countries in the Middle East and Central Asia. By the time he had got through half of his presentation, it was clear (to him and to some of the Norwegians) that he had alienated the non-Nordic members of the audience.

Ironically, if he had been addressing only the easterners, he would have found no difficulty in discussing the world that they lived in and their cultural characteristics. As a part-time resident of Italy, he was used to entering the Italian cultural habitat and dealing with Italians on their own terms. In this instance, however, he had been commissioned by a Norwegian company to explain the intricacies of a sensitive subject in their terms. Cultural experts are able, chameleon-like, to adapt their message and communication style to satisfy members of any culture with which they are familiar. With a mixed audience like the one in question, this was nigh on impossible, given the delicate nature of the subject. A subsequent appointment for the speaker to address the company's staff in Tehran was hastily canceled (by the Iranians).

When an international team enters such a minefield, it is advisable for them to be familiar with the stipulations of the FCPA. In conformity with this Act, the Norwegian company itself provided all its managers with strict directives on ethical behavior. "Facilitation" payments, though sometimes legal, had to be shown explicitly in the company's accounts. "Intermediaries" were instructed to act in strict accordance with both Norwegian law and the FCPA. Lobbyists were subject to the same restrictions. The company's anticorruption compliance program was in the form of a 46-page document. All employees were instructed to report any noncompliance on the part of colleagues; passive and active corruption were both punishable, even if the advantage was passed on to a third party.

Some instances of reward were listed as allowable. These included moderate entertainment expenses in line with company policy; small, appropriate, inexpensive gifts; payments to get back one's passport; payments to secure entry or departure to or from a foreign country. However, warning was given that a single fax, letter, phone call, or email, or money transfer, to or from an individual or organization could give grounds for proof of noncompliance, as could "knowledge or willful blindness," offers, promises, authorizations, charitable donations, golf outings, loans on preferential terms, use of sports equipment, reimbursements, and so on.

When dealing with governments, the policy notes that routine governmental action such as providing police protection, processing permits by officials (some of whom have dual roles), and help in arranging travel and accommodation may require fees that are not always easy to quantify. Employees are instructed, however, to watch out for danger signs. Transparency International can give information about highly susceptible countries where local custom requires "grease" payments; 5 percent commission is regarded as a critical threshold. Other danger signs are requests by a state representative that they be paid in cash (or in a third country or tax haven). Services may be suspicious if they are not definable or quantifiable.

Managers of international teams may well find that the ball is in their court. Either they will be responsible for the decision (in blunt terms, to bribe or not to bribe), or at least they must direct their team members to steer the right course when the occasion arises. Is it possible to give general or comprehensive advice as to how to react to such situations; are certain principles to be followed; or is it always a question of case by case?

Steering a course

There are two well-tried basic approaches to the problem of conducting an intercultural dialogue on ethics effectively among people who hold diverse cultural beliefs and values. Richard Evanoff terms these the "universalist" approach and the "relativist" approach.

The universalist approach contends that it is possible to formulate a set of norms that apply equally to all countries. This "common core" of behavior or existence is exemplified by the acknowledgment that, as Anthony Giddens contends, all cultures have basic requirements with regard to eating and drinking, seeking shelter, using language, having kinship systems, engaging in religious rituals, exchanging gifts, producing works of art, and making music. These are sometimes referred to as "cultural universals," an idea that runs throughout much of the history of western thought. Aristotle and Kant both believed that ethics could be based on a set of universal principles that stood apart from culture and held true for all people, in all places, at all times.

A team following this approach may take the line that "all humans are basically the same" and, with this as comfort, seek convergence on the basis of humans having the same fundamental needs, aspirations, ambitions, knowledge, and hopefully modes of rationality. Many cross-cultural dialogues will indicate that there are similarities and differences between cultures. Some of these similarities may in fact be universal to all cultures (for instance gratitude for help) and followers of the universalist approach suggest that such similarities could be taken as a starting point for cross-cultural dialogue.

The problem with the universalist approach is that, on closer examination, many of the characteristics and values that we think initially resemble each other begin to diverge. Eating, drinking, and art are common activities, but our cuisines and art styles show great variation from culture to culture; each country has its own aspirations and ambitions (political, economic, and aesthetic); French rationality differs wildly from that of the Japanese, whose cognitive processes are unlike western ones; the forms of ethical systems we construct will vary accordingly. The fact that disputes and misunderstandings continually arise over cross-cultural ethics shows that whatever "common core" elements we latch onto in our reasonings, they are insufficient to resolve outstanding differences or anomalies.

The universalist approach has another weakness in that it is difficult, if not impossible, to nail down the values or norms of a culture exactly. Culture is not a biological constant of any particular group. It is something that is acquired or learned through experience over the centuries and changes gradually as it is passed on from generation to generation. It is a product of historical circumstance and climate and subject to change with regard to each. Climate changes slowly, but traumatic events of history can have a sudden effect on cultural behavior. The atomic bombing of Hiroshima and Nagasaki, followed by the unthinkable military defeat of Japan, produced at least two generations of Japanese whose attitude to war, peace, and international relations changed drastically. The division of Germany in 1945 and its subsequent reunification created a new cultural group – east Germans – who are still not fully assimilated with their western cousins. The complete military defeat of the Third Reich also had its impact on the German worldview and as a corollary the world image of Germany has been modified.

If the universalist approach fails in reconciling ethical points of view, a team may well take the opposite tack and operate on the premise that human beings are not similar, that cultural traits are unalike, and that we have to accept that a culture has the right to possess its own norms and behave accordingly. This means that, in order to resolve disputes, we must acknowledge the depth and durability of cultural differences and meet them head on to bring them into the open. This is the essence of the relativist approach, which holds that all cultural characteristics and values are valid, must be respected, and need to be worked around. There are no "good" and "bad" cultures, no "God's eye" perspective from which cultural traits can be evaluated or ranked. In other words, "good" and "bad," "true" and "false," "honest" and "dishonest" are all relative; that is, they must be seen in the context of a particular cultural environment or circumstance. Hollis and Lukes note that relativism can be conceptual, perceptual, rational, or moral. Moral relativism is in focus when it comes to ethical considerations.

Are we saying that a team should simply adopt a tolerant attitude toward its counterparts' (in its eyes) unethical behavior on the grounds that "that is their culture" and no further debate will be fruitful? This relativist approach would obviously preclude the possibility that something better can be hoped for and worked toward. Cultural attitudes, positions, and values are neither God given nor constants. They are strategies that have served the members of a given culture well in the past. They are not innate or inherent. They are traits that have been adopted on the basis of learning and experience. They are in fact social constructs – all societies have them. A team, with its own collection of social constructs, need not automatically accept the positioning of the other side on grounds of relative value. There is always room for development and change; and hopefully improvement. The multicultural composition of an international team is a valuable element in approaching an ethical dilemma. The team manager may look to Italian, Russian, Chinese, or Singaporean colleagues for their interpretation of the proposals. The clear-cut views of American, Nordic, and Swiss team members will provide balance.

At all events, it becomes apparent, as international negotiating grows increasingly widespread, that both the universalist and relativist approaches to ethical dilemmas fall short of producing easy solutions. Cultures are unalike and we must deal with this, though we should not accept unreservedly the ethics of a particular group as superior to others or as unchangeable. Some facilitation payments are common worldwide and figure in the negotiating patterns of many cultures and millions of individuals. However, the fact that a certain proposition or stance is ubiquitous does not mean that it is valid. There must be another approach – one that encourages reflection on the basic questions of how things ought to be done and why.

Dialogue and interaction between parties are vital. The world itself produces no concepts, only people do, and they produce them when interacting with others. Language is no use if there is no one to speak to; opinions are no use if there is no one to hear them. By entering into dialogue with other cultures, we can compare perspectives and, through critique, decide what is positive and negative in each. Our aim should be to combine the best elements of each cultural stance. Cultural attitudes that may have varied sharply throughout history may at a given propitious moment suddenly converge. The opportunity in question may arise through a political or economic development, a forthcoming merger, a change of key personnel, or a change in market conditions. The attitudes that were born in previous conditions – social constructs – can always be reconstructed to suit new circumstances.

Such opportunities will present themselves from time to time and enable negotiators to deal more effectively with certain impasses. New norms can be created, hopefully adapting themselves to particular moments in history. Payment demanded as a bribe shocks many cultures when seen in such terms. A different scenario might be more palatable, such as a scholarship or internship that offers a benefit to both sides. A clear statement from a person who is asked for a bribe would be that their company's regulations or their country's laws make it quite impossible to comply with the demand. However, they would like to know what solution could be found to resolve the impasse. How would a person of the other (briber's) culture resolve it? What are the culture's exit strategies for such dilemmas?

It is important for someone wishing to negotiate their way out of paying a bribe to be well acquainted with the cultural principles or characteristics of the person or entity making the demand. Team managers will be culturally aware and have recourse to the multicultural capabilities of their team. If a confrontation on this ethical issue takes place, they need to know what the chemistry on both sides will be. If facing a Korean, Japanese, or other Asian, they must be acutely aware that any negotiation or concession or discussion of such will be inextricably tied to the Asian's preoccupation with face. There must be a graceful exit strategy, otherwise discussion is pointless. Iranians and Arabs, not completely obsessed by face considerations, nevertheless must be allowed to maintain maximum dignity. Russians, wheelers and dealers par excellence, must never be humiliated. On the western side, individuals may seek agreement on certain conditions. While Americans are constrained by rules, they think in bottom-line terms. They want to do the deal. So do Brits, but they will negotiate in an indirect manner replete with understatement and coded speech. The French, who worship logic, will discuss the theoretical situation rather than the actual one. Any deal agreed to by the Germans must be, above all, tidy (*in Ordnung*). Finns will stick to common-sense arrangements, Australians will call a spade a spade. Italians and South Africans will be on their home ground.

There is no way I would advocate paying bribes, whatever the return. Yet, the fact remains that in large parts of the world, "business as usual" entails under-the-table considerations and activities. In countries like Indonesia, Kenya, and Bulgaria, many aspects of commercial life would come to a standstill if certain conditions were not met. Though large sums of money have been paid out in this manner by huge companies of all nationalities in the past

– and many scandals have been uncovered and punished – it is not always a question of money. Italy is a country where this type of activity is endemic, yet most accommodations between Italian individuals and middle-sized companies take place in a relatively pleasant manner, where favor is repaid by favor, and the wheels of officialdom turn faster as a result. The whole Chinese concept of *guanxi* is a world in itself where various elements of enterprises and society are closely linked by bonds of reciprocity in exchanging favors. Common on the mainland, *guanxi* is even more ubiquitous in practical Hong Kong and Taiwan, both of whom trade energetically with the wider world including the United States. Chinese see *guanxi* as a social investment, not bribery.

A final word to team managers: cross-cultural dialogue on ethics is vital in seeking a new ethical framework. This, like most social constructs, has to be negotiated in discussion where all sides are encouraged to participate and refrain from imposing their own norms. An international team is in a good position to engage in such dialogues.

CASE STUDY

The soccer World Cup, held every four years, can be described as a quadrennial exhibition of world cultures, as players from more than 50 countries contest ferociously one of the most sought-after trophies in sport. Competition is often vicious, but the 2002 World Cup was uniquely characterized principally by its harmonious atmosphere. This was probably due to the ethical behavior, on and off the field, by the two host nations, Japan and Korea, both determined to show off Asian traits at their best.

The 2002 World Cup

There are over 200 well-recognized cultures around the globe, bewildering in their multiplicity and kaleidoscopic variety. Is there

a museum holding an exhibition of world cultures, which, by jux-
taposing them, might compare and illustrate their basic features?

Such a museum may not yet exist, but a kind of exhibition does
– the soccer World Cup. Held every four years since the 1930s,
this competition, once confined to two continents, has increased
in international scope and complexity to cover the whole world.
Each World Cup has had its moments of drama, triumph, and
disaster, ferocious rivalry and competitiveness. Nevertheless, none
could match the 2002 World Cup – in fact, the least acrimonious of all – for its explicit and dazzling confirmation of the link
between national cultural characteristics and performance on the
field of play. Perhaps it was an account of the added cultural variety
of more nationals involved; almost certainly it had something to do
with the colorful split venues of Korea and Japan; but 3–4 billion
people around the world had a month-long opportunity to get a
glimpse of competing cultural endeavor in its mental and physical
aspects. It was cross-culture with a human face, observable at one
event and at one time.

One of the great successes of the 2002 World Cup was the outstanding performance of the little-fancied Japanese team, which,
unbelievably, almost reached the semi-finals. This was largely due
to the team leader (manager), who was in fact a Frenchman, and
led the team in such a skillful manner that they achieved results
that had hitherto been unimaginable.

Philippe Troussier, the manager, had several interesting insights
into the cultural link between national tradition and the behavior of players. Japanese, as is well known, show great respect to
elders and seniors. Troussier, though very experienced, was initially regarded as too young to be a manager, as he was only 43!
Japanese simply equate experience with age. Troussier was able
to establish his authority, but quickly ran up against other problems of a cultural nature. The exaggerated respect for elders meant
that Japanese players preferred to pass the ball to older players,
rather than those in good receiving positions. Furthermore, if an
older player like Nakata gained international experience by playing for a foreign club, the younger players became so mesmerized

by his reputation that it destroyed their own confidence. Before the World Cup, when Japan, after a string of impressive victories, played France, World and European Cup winners, in the Stade de France in front of a crowd of 80,000, the young Japanese team were so overawed by the fame of the French and their star player Zidane that they surrendered the game before it started. They lost 5–0.

In the 2002 World Cup, the Japanese were a different force. Troussier had discovered that while some cultural traits led to weakness against opposition, others contributed greatly to team strength. Japan is a collective society where people are discouraged from shining as individuals. This desire for the collective good is observable in the loyalty that Japanese men show to their companies; in the football world it certainly equates to team spirit. Coaches of Latin and other teams often have to combat selfishness or egoism on the part of star players; Troussier had no such problems with the Japanese. Their unselfishness was culturally programmed. If anything, he had to encourage more individuality in order to make his team's tactics less predictable for the opposition. Japanese players are extremely skillful at passing the ball accurately to each other for a whole minute or more. Against a good defense, however, somebody has to break through.

The Japanese are not good in one-to-one situations. Just as Japanese business people are reluctant to take decisions without consulting their colleagues, their football players tend to prolong harmonious passing, rather than confront a defender head-on. Troussier had to teach his players more direct aggression, including trickery and shady tactics (which the fair-minded Japanese were not keen on). Japanese have been brought up in a disciplined, orderly environment where parents, teachers, and company seniors give constant guidance. This provides a feeling of security, but dampens adventurism and the ability to tackle complicated problems. One's identity arises from one's role in the group. Troussier noticed that his goalkeeper would not leave his goal line, even when it would be advantageous to do so. The goalie did not want to break out of his protective shell – the goal line was his place.

The Japanese traditional desire to belong to a group worked in Troussier's favor and he was able to create a side that showed even better teamwork than the Germans or Swedes. There were, however, some amusing side-effects. One Saturday evening, after a splendid victory, Troussier told his players to go out on the town in groups of two and three, forget about football for a few hours, have a few drinks, and relax. Two hours later, when he had finished his paperwork, he found them all sitting in the team bus, discussing tactics. They were happiest that way, just like Japanese salarymen who sacrifice much of their home life in their attachment to the company.

There was no doubting the national pride in the team's achievements. The team regarded each victory as one for Japan itself and prayed for their ancestors during the playing of their national anthem. Japan's traditions of respect, courtesy, and ethical behavior shone through the tournament. The players did not foul unnecessarily, the public applauded losing teams as they left the field, and the Japanese team invariably went over to thank their fans after each game.

All in all, both Japan and Korea showed the world that on the field of play one can have a good time when teams – and cultures – collide.

11

Trust in the Team

In 1990, the fall of the Berlin Wall, the demise of the totalitarian regime in the Soviet Union, the lifting of the Iron Curtain, and the subsequent liberation of most states in eastern Europe seemed for a while to herald in a new era of optimistic expectations among people around the globe. Francis Fukuyama announced the End of History, suggesting that the model of the western democratic state had triumphed definitively and would, in the course of a few decades, be adopted by all and sundry. Enlightened leadership would encourage international cooperation in economic, political, and social spheres; wars would phase themselves out, deemed unnecessary or irrelevant; science would reduce the frequency of religious extremism; the globalization of trade would draw governments and giant international companies closer together; regular collaboration and insights would engender increased trust at many levels: governments, envoys, conglomerates, managers, and communities in general.

A decade is a long time in politics and the development of international relations. History, as Fukuyama admits, soon resumed shortly after he said it had ended, and the last 10 years of the twentieth century witnessed the reawakening of old traditional rivalries and enmities; blatant protectionism; the vigorous pursuit of narrow national interests; lack of concern or sympathy for poor, emerging states; and bickering between great powers such as India and Pakistan, Russia and the United States, China and Japan, even among family members of a rapidly expanding EU.

A new millennium inevitably brings with it fresh expectations for a "brave new world" and indeed, the worldwide celebrations of this significant milestone witnessed exuberant and explosive expressions of joy in such openly delighted metropoles as Rio de Janeiro, Sydney, and a myriad others. Was humankind coming of age, after 2,000 years of recorded strife and mistrust?

The events of September 11, 2001 proved a stunning shock to everyone around the world, Muslims included. Major wars in Afghanistan and Iraq followed and the first decade of the twenty-first century saw a disastrous erosion of trust between governments and political regimes, regional authorities and minorities, global firms, international bodies such as the UN, World Bank, IMF, the International Red Cross, UNESCO, Médecins sans Frontières, and other aid groups and charitable associations. Hopeful and ambitious trade groups such as ASEAN, NAFTA, and MERCOSUR struggled to maintain mutual trust among their members, not to mention the labored efforts of the EU to achieve a constitution acceptable to its 27 communities. Enlightened leaders in politics (*à la* Washington, Jefferson, Lincoln, Churchill, Gandhi, Atatürk) and business (Henry Ford, Akio Morita, Konosuke Matsushita, Wennergren, Gyllenhammer) are currently conspicuous by their absence. Lee Kuan Yew could stake a claim to have been the most successful "manager" of the last 30 years of the twentieth century; Mikhail Gorbachev, Nelson Mandela, Martti Ahtisaari, Carlos Ghosn, Jack Welch, Junichiro Koizumi, Jorma Ollila, and Richard Branson have been successful in some of their goals in recent times. The four Nordic premiers, particularly Danish Anders Fogh Rasmussen (recently elected Secretary-General of NATO), have impressed by their integrity. The jury is still out on Barack Obama, one of the most popular US Presidents of all time on election.

The diminishment of public trust applies not only to governments and political leaders, but also, acutely, to business leaders and certain categories of professions: bankers, lawyers, accountancy and insurance firms, real estate companies, and media moguls. Bad governance resulted in disgrace and bankruptcy for "star" enterprises such as Enron, WorldCom, and Arthur Andersen; their senior executives were finally jailed. The 2008–09 recession exposed the "outrageous" (to quote Obama) excesses and greed of the banks and their bonus-happy experts, who gambled (and lost) billions of other people's money. While the Madoff scandal may have been the biggest in statistical terms, other abuses of public and investors' trust run into hundreds or thousands of cases. Intergovernmental, intercompany, interbank, and interconsultant trust is at an all-time low.

What about interpersonal trust? And what about that less frequently considered phenomenon, intercultural trust? How would skeptical attitudes engendered by the misdemeanors of 2008–09 affect the level of trust between well-meaning executives of different nationalities? In particular, what would be the effect on international teams?

The effectiveness of an international team normally requires a high level of trust between its members. This is more difficult to achieve in a virtual team, though it is even more essential. People who live and work in close proximity can be expected to share similar values, preferences, aspirations, taboos, customs, and social habits. They know each other. On the basis of these shared circumstances, they can build trust (or see it eroded) according to their day-to-day experience with each other. A multicultural group starts life together the other way around: they have dissimilar values and habits and they communicate them in a variety of ways, so automatic initial trust is highly unlikely. Something has to be created before it can be either eroded or built on.

Trust between individuals may be difficult enough, but there are other complicating factors. Setting apart how one views one's compatriots, some nationalities instinctively distrust each other. There may be long-standing historical antipathies, the results of former invasions, occupations, exploitations, religious convictions, even genocide. Any form of mutual trust is practically unattainable in these cases. Other nationalities distrust each other on account of much less serious divisions. Nordics see gesticulating Latins as over-emotional and unreliable. Japanese and some other Asians are unable to trust people who do not meet their high standards of courtesy and face protection. Germans distrust people who show up late for appointments. The British distrust people who boast or talk about money. Australians distrust anyone who speaks in an authoritative or superior manner.

Intercultural communication problems affecting trust

Misunderstandings can arise in an international team through different communication patterns, even when common goals and enthusiasm are intact. Often the mode of expression causing the problem is seen as a virtue or positive contribution by the speaker. Finnish silence (usually positive) will normally be interpreted as negative. Arab loudness, to show sincerity, will frequently offend Swedes or Britons. American drive and enthusiasm will often slide into hype, certainly distrusted by Germans, Brits, and Nordics.

Coded speech	British
Hype, hard sell	US
Flexible, creative truth	Latin
Silence	Japanese, Finnish
Smiles	Asian
Humor	British, US
Verbosity	Latin
Loudness	Arab

Table 11.1 Intercultural communication problems

USA and UK: Trust, mistrust, and communication

Europeans often accuse the British of automatically following American leadership. The common language and heritage are cited as reasons for this. Britain and the USA have been allies in six out of America's last seven wars and their common stand against terrorism at this writing confirms the consistency of the political alliance. There was also a substantial Americanization of British business in the second half of the twentieth century. Yet, the two cultures do not trust each other fully. The mistrust arises out of a conflict not in values, but in modes of communication. This is illustrated in Figure 11.1.

Britons frequently feel that Americans are "over the top," either with inevitable hype or using an irritating string of naïve clichés. Americans for their part see British coded speech and hesitation

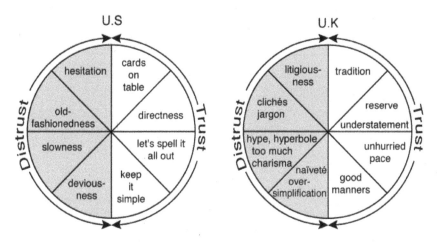

Figure 11.1 Trust and distrust in the US and UK

to commit oneself instantly as signs of deviousness. With the Americans it is cards on the table and let's move on. The British, who are often heading in the same direction, have much more tradition at stake, want to exercise their reputed reserve, and would love to rein in their reckless cousins.

Trust and loyalty in Japan and China

Trust, loyalty and allegiance in China and Japan were the subject of a study conducted by Professor Stephen White of INSEAD. In the survey, 150 managers of Japanese company subsidiaries in China were asked to comment on the degree of corporate allegiance shown by Chinese staff and managers.

Figures 11.2 and 11.3 contrast the nature of allegiance in Japanese company staff in Japan and that of Chinese employees of Japanese companies in China. In Figure 11.2, workers obey section heads, who report faithfully to department heads, who report to MDs, who report to the president. The president is virtually synonymous with the *kaisha* (company). Obedience flows smoothly from the worker base to the board. Trust flows freely from the president to the factory floor. In addition, workers feel that they have a direct link to the *kaisha*, their protector and guarantor. This spirit prevails in the great majority of Japanese companies.

JAPAN

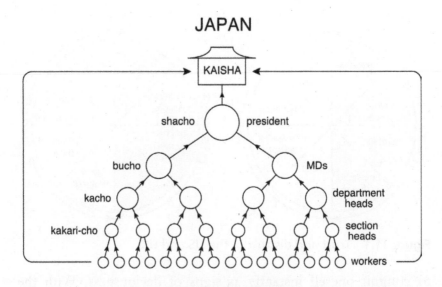

corporate allegiance

Figure 11.2 Trust and loyalty in Japan

In Japanese companies in China, usually led by a Japanese managing director, the structure was similar up to a point, but essentially different in reality. In China, workers were loyal toward lower-middle and middle managers and the allegiance flowed upward as far as department heads. Then it stopped. The managing director reported to the leadership group, but there was little, if any, concrete allegiance between department heads and the MD. In the "pyramids" leading down from department heads, mutual support was strong. Each department leader had his own personal empire (intimate circle) where promotion, reward, and careers were taken care of in a paternalistic manner. When a department head left the company for another one (a rare event in Japan), he often took the key people in the department with him; again, heresy in Japan.

What does this mean *vis-à-vis* Japanese and Chinese members of international teams? Fortunately, it is good news on both counts. The Chinese team member will regard the international team as his "intimate circle" to whom he owes allegiance and who will look after him. He will try hard to integrate himself and cooperate with

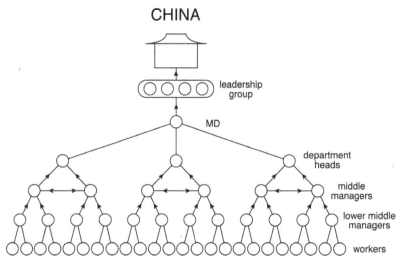

Figure 11.3 Trust and loyalty in China

the team leader. The Japanese, as usual, will try to be good team men and stay faithful to head office at the same time.

Leaders or managers of an international team are in a key position to create trust among their colleagues. In spite of the general erosion of public trust, they have a micro-world of talent and ambition at their disposal in which they can create shared mindsets. Often the quickest way to establish empathy with a different mindset is to find a third mindset that you can both laugh at or criticize.

This strategy is used in all corners of international business. It is well known in northern Europe that the quickest way to get a Finn on your side is to make fun of Swedish pomposity. Such empathy creation of course requires intimate knowledge of other cultures. Cultural black holes can interfere with team harmony. A cultural black hole (CBH) is an unswerving, indiscussable belief that blinds an individual to any contradictory arguments and swallows whole any form of enlightenment. Examples are jingoism (several varieties), the American Dream, Russian suspicion of foreigners, and communist or Islamic finality. The only antidote to a CBH is a combination of logic, common sense, and humor. A clever team leader can generally nudge a team member toward rational discourse. Excesses such as American hype, Italian verbosity, German ultra-directness, and Hispanic flexible truth can also be effectively countered with a humorous approach. Pseudo-conflicts often arise and should be dealt with speedily.

Fujitsu once had a problem with a Spanish–Japanese team over a matter of different styles of eye contact. The Spanish distrusted the Japanese, who avoided eye contact in conversation, persistently looking at their own feet. The Japanese, on the other hand, felt that the Spaniards *stared* at them all the time, "looking into their soul." When it was explained that the Spanish stare denotes sincerity and the downcast eyes of the Japanese modesty, the irritation disappeared.

Linear-active, multi-active, and reactive cultures find trust in different ways. Linear-actives generally trust institutions (laws, courts, Rotary Clubs, YMCAs, Red Cross, and so on). Multi-active cultures show less faith in the efficiency of officialdom and trust only members of their ingroup. Reactive cultures such as the Japanese have a moderate faith in state institutions, but trust more particularly their former schoolmates and until recently the company (*kaisha*) that gave them lifelong employment. As far as individuals are concerned, linear Americans, Germans, and Nordics trust people who maintain word–deed correlation and consistency. Multi-active Latins respond to compassion and physical and mental closeness, and reveal personal weaknesses to others who are expected to defend them. Reactive Asians secure trust by mutual face protection and impeccable demonstrations of courtesy.

It is said that nationals from high-trust cultures such as Denmark, Finland, Germany, and Japan will accord trust to fellow team members until they prove untrustworthy. Nationals from low-trust societies such as Italy, France, Mexico, and Korea initially withhold trust until they see that it is merited. Members of small international teams learn to trust each other quickly, though multi-actives often "test" their more placid colleagues. American and French nationals often appear inquisitive to others (they ask many personal questions) and this may lead to privacy-loving Germans, British, and Finns thinking that this shows a lack of trust. More likely it is only a conversational trait or habit. A Finnish-led team working on a Baltic project I participated in recently showed that the Finns trusted Estonians, Latvians, and Lithuanians unreservedly, but that the Balts did not trust one another.

A study of the 24 national profiles in Chapter 5 will fine-tune the reader's perception of how different people accord trust. Many subtleties are involved. An English person will tend to trust someone who uses understatement or, better still, speaks in a self-deprecating manner. A little coded speech thrown in will cement the trust. Australians look more for plain talking, want easy camaraderie, and are attracted by broad speech, even profanity. They trust underdogs and "battlers." Americans, nervous with coded speech, trust Australians more quickly than Brits, also for their decisiveness. Finns, whose priority is always reliability, are won over by succinctness of expression, automatically trusting Japanese, English, Scots, and Norwegians. Swedes accord trust to those who behave "correctly" and eschew any form of roughness or abrasiveness. Danes, tougher and more cynical, do not trust anyone easily, though they admire intelligence, especially the streetwise variety. Swiss, like Swedes, crave "properness" of conduct; as successful mediators among their German-, French-, Italian-, and Roumansch-speaking fellow nationals, they consider themselves experts at cementing trust. The French, wordsmiths as they are, are slow to trust anybody who lacks elegance of expression, though foreigners who speak fluent French can quickly gain their allegiance.

Germans, less concerned with word games, want to trust individuals who are clean, tidy, and wear new clothes. The Dutch have the same requirements and trust those who, additionally, abhor time wasting. Canadians, splendidly laid-back, trust others who are laid-back; they hate intensity. With Asians – Chinese, Japanese, Indians, Malaysians – good manners inspire trust, though these must be consistent. Russians, initially wary and suspicious, crave a human approach and offer staunch friendship in return. Belgians, especially the Flemish but also the Walloons, readily trust colleagues who shun dogmatism. Italians, Spanish, Portuguese, and Brazilian team members conjoin trust with mental closeness and are easily won over by northerners who are willing to "lower their guard." Finns, Norwegians, Japanese, Koreans, some Germans, and southern English may on occasion be reluctant to do this.

Diversity of cognitive processes and concepts of truth

Closely connected to the question of trust is how the notion of truth is conceptualized in an international team. It is normal for managers to aim for transparency among team members. Goals and objectives should be clarified, information should be shared freely, communication should be effective, directives should be straightforward. All of the above require a common concept of veracity. But truth, like trust, is essentially a cultural phenomenon, not a universal one. The notion of truth is entangled with one's particular worldview, which varies from others' owing to differences in cognitive processes.

I deal with these issues extensively in my earlier work *The Cultural Imperative*, material from which I reproduce in this section.

My extensive contact with Asians in academic, social, and business life has led me to believe that a basic difference in cognitive processes between East and West is a source of cultural diversity between the two. Reactive Asians simply do not see the universe in the pronounced linear form that Americans and northern Europeans do. They analyze visible (and invisible) phenomena in an entirely different manner, mainly because they are using different analytical and cognitive tools. The multi-actives too, with their backdrop of emotion and penchant toward dual truth, have their own particular cognitive processes, though they are closer in concept to the linear ones than to the Asian systemic thinking patterns.

To be more specific, the basic concepts of truth, logic, and reasoning in the East and the West are arrived at by completely different routes. Linear-active westerners believe in scientific truth – truth that can be established through Cartesian, Hegelian, or other logical systems. They focus on target objects (especially those that can advance their goals).

When Asians focus on objects or things, they do so holistically; that is, they refuse (or are unable) to separate them from their context or environment; they see objects as parts of a whole that cannot be manipulated or controlled piece by piece. In their eyes, the world is too complicated to be contained in linear pigeonholes or ruled deterministically. For the Chinese, there is no absolute truth – only situational and/or temporary alignments of facts that can change at the drop of a hat or indeed be contradictory yet still valid. Something can be right and wrong or black and white at the same time, as long as the outcome is virtuous and harmony is preserved. Neither are the Japanese lovers of absolute truth, which they regard as a dangerous concept, able to destroy harmony and progress. Even multi-actives such as Spaniards and Italians do not arrive at truth in a linear or logical fashion. In Italy, truth is seen as negotiable (in order to produce the best possible outcome in a given situation). Spaniards and Hispanics revel in the application of dual or double truth – one dealing with immediate necessities and the other taking into consideration the more lasting philosophical whole.

These diverse concepts of truth and reality cause the three cultural types to organize their lives in quite different ways. Everything is affected: social behavior, business methods, decision making, problem solving, communication styles, the use of time and space, considerations of hierarchy and respect, aesthetics and creativity, standards of ethics, ways of negotiating, societal obligations, sense of duty, and so on. The diversity of conduct springs from one's interpretation of how the world really is. But what cognitive or interpretative tools does one use to sense reality? Why or how do they differ from culture to culture?

Language and thought

Spoken language – indeed, a complete linguistic map or blueprint – defines reality for us. However, strikingly different maps exist. Someone embarking on life with Germans and their disciplined thought processes will have a different worldview from the linguistically freewheeling American or Australian, but the schism between them is a narrow ravine if one considers the yawning canyon between European languages and Japanese. We cannot avoid language – we are born into it. Our early mental experiences are dominated by our mother tongue, and if by chance we have a choice to speak a different language a few years later, it is already too late; the patterns of thought are already formed. Language determines thought more than the other way around. By the age of 6 or 7, our thought processes are calibrated for good by either clinically logical French, exuberant but vague Spanish, respect-oriented but even vaguer Japanese, or rigidly morphological (14 case endings) Finnish.

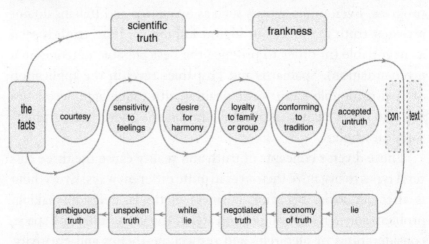

Figure 11.4   Categorical truth

Germans, Americans, and other adherents to scientific truth should bear in mind that other cultures are basically no less truthful than they (though they find this hard to swallow). Hard facts stand on their own merit, but Latins and other multi-actives live in a world where consideration of contextual circumstances, multiplicity of perspectives, and mitigating factors simply outweigh the virtues of (complacent) frankness. Reactive East Asians habitually eschew directness (bluntness) in a world where shame and loss of face are ultimate catastrophes and where gentle manipulation or rephrasing of ostensibly unavoidable truths can salvage harmony and goodwill from a risky evaluation. English coded speech has essentially the same objective.

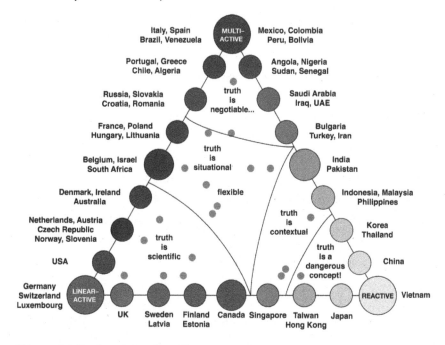

Figure 11.5 Aspects of truth

Political wrangling, shady practices, and bad governance in big business have led to public trust descending to an all-time low. Ambitious plans are being made in countries around the globe to clean up corruption and excessive greed and put the world's affairs on a more ethical footing. In the wake of the excesses that have come to light and the continued unethical behavior of many leaders and enterprises, the restitution of trust, even in business, will not happen quickly. How should international teams deal with this situation?

To begin with, there is no alternative to trusting head office. HQ must be seen as representing the interests of the shareholders and, inevitably, safeguarding the mission, integrity, and reputation of the company. In France and Sweden, where state protection of leading firms is a regular phenomenon, names such as Renault, Peugeot, Société Générale, Volvo, Saab, and Skanska are a source of pride, as are Nokia, Rolls-Royce, Unilever, DaimlerBenz, Philips, Fiat, and so on in their respective homelands. The huge bailout of bankrupt American companies in 2008–09 proved that the same applies to the USA. The postrecession era will herald in (we must assume) the restoration of integrity of troubled enterprises and the resumption of health, growth, and eventual profitability.

As has been pointed out earlier, international teams are rapidly becoming the central operating mode for global enterprises. Compared to maintaining morale in a huge conglomerate, the task of creating a trustful ambience in a small team is a relatively easy one. Once they settle down, such teams generally function smoothly and make progress in their niche areas (a difficult task for remote headquarters). As teams familiarize themselves with local markets or specific functions, they tend to become more knowledgeable than head office and often are in a position to send back more valuable information than they receive. This is of course what one hopes for from specialist groups. International teams I have worked with not only trust their colleagues, but frequently collaborate well with other teams and project groups, even at a distance. The concept of the small multinational and multicultural team augurs well for the future. Compact, manageable, and optimistic, they can become the engines of growth and progress for world commerce.

CASE STUDIES

The case studies in this chapter consider issues of creating trust between two individuals who are at loggerheads, and what happens when trust in corporate governance declines. We end with a look at the Finnish miracle of Nokia.

Kraft

Divergent core beliefs and discordant communication styles among international team members can seriously impede headway during team gatherings. Such an obstacle was encountered by a Kraft project group that met quarterly in Brussels.

Kraft is a multifaceted conglomerate in the food industry, owning such brands as Ritz crackers, Oreo, Fontaneda and Filipinos cookies, large units of United Biscuits, Fruco and Apis fruit juices, Jello gelatine desserts, Oscar Mayer frankfurters, as well as a host of Nabisco trademarks and, through its parent company Altria, the cigarette maker Philip Morris.

Always seeking to widen its international footprint, Kraft has formed dozens of multinational teams and pays considerable attention to their training and development. We were asked to facilitate a few of these teams, looking at the diversity in their composition and advising them on the salient characteristics of certain cultural groups.

One small but important sales project group consisted of a Frenchman, an Englishman, an Italian, an American, a Singaporean (Chinese) chair, and a sit-in Belgian representative from the European HQ. The individuals were talented and experienced, but the chair reported serious and recurrent internal strife that was slowing down decision making and the implementation of resolutions. During the two days we spent with the team, we were afforded several examples of dissension and group conflict.

The Italian was a peace maker, but was a lightweight. The American was visibly competent, but he was surprisingly introvert and kept out of arguments. The Frenchman and Englishman were at loggerheads. The Singaporean, unused to outspoken hostility, did not know how to manage the pair. The Belgian, representing HQ, was anxious to tread lightly and was not as influential as he could have been. The Frenchman, Tissier, unequivocally sales oriented and quite charismatic, was full of ideas and vision. His proposals were systematically torpedoed by the Englishman, Mason, who had previously been in finance and had a ready command of facts and statistics, which the Frenchman was aware of, but regarded as subsidiary or auxiliary to his bold marketing plans. The two men were wont to argue at length, reducing the input of the other talented members and creating a series of impasses that the chair was reluctant or unable to resolve.

As the first day progressed, I realized that there was no fundamental incompatibility between the Frenchman's imaginative suggestions and the Englishman's restrictive attitude. They were both productive servants of the company and shared its goals. Unfortunately, they were neutralizing each other. I sensed that Mason's stubbornness was based less on process than on personal antipathy. He just did not like his French colleague.

During coffee breaks, lunch, and dinner that night I was able to spend time with both men separately. Tissier responded well to my intervention (probably because I am fluent in French) and sought my sympathy. Mason assumed that I would see the situation through similar cultural spectacles; that is, English ones. Tissier, being continually rebuffed and reined in, was actually cutting down on his vision and charisma and was in danger of losing his value to the group. He often clammed up and sulked after being attacked.

When I talked to Mason, he confided to me that he found Tissier too nosey at social gatherings. He disliked inquisitiveness per se, being a rather private individual by nature and sharing the common British distaste for over-loquacity or shows of emotion. He found Tissier's sulkiness after being criticized rather childish. Why not be impartial, factual, and calm? He added that in the first few meetings of the group Tissier seemed to have singled him out for personal attention, asking him all sorts of questions about his family, finances, political views, plans, hopes, and aspirations. He did not like his privacy being invaded in this manner. He admitted that the interrogation had cooled off of late and that the Frenchman now replied to his arguments in a laconic, often terse manner.

I explained to Mason that it is normal for French people to question in quite a personal way colleagues with whom they are going to work. For Latins in general (Italians in particular), closeness is key to understanding and hopefully mutual trust. Though

French people require less intimacy than Italians or Spaniards in this regard, they really go to great lengths to find out what makes a foreign colleague tick. Being French, they have a very clear world-view. It is important for them to ascertain to what extent this calibrates with the horizons of their partner. Family matters, political leanings, particulars of education, attitudes to leisure, holidays, food and wine, work ethic, disparate loyalties, manners, and taboos are of great importance in putting together a profile. The better they know each other, the better they will work together.

It was probable that Tissier had singled out Mason early on as a potentially appropriate, even amiable co-worker. The French occasionally have a feeling of superiority *vis-à-vis* Italians and Belgians, as well as a streak of anti-Americanism. Putting the Asian chair aside, Tissier probably wanted Mason as an ally. His curiosity about Mason's personal affairs showed an attempt to achieve moderate closeness on which he could build trust and loyalty. French people do not ask intimate details of people in whom they are not interested.

Mason took in my remarks thoughtfully. He admitted that in the initial meetings Tissier had been more than friendly. Too friendly, he had thought, since any (southern) Englishman exhibiting the same extroversion would have been suspect. OK, Tissier was not Eton and Oxford; he (Mason) should have made allowances. By the evening I had persuaded Mason that if he demonstrated some friendliness over after-dinner drinks, he would probably find that Tissier would react with warmth. "But what shall I do?" asked Mason. "Do you both have children?" I asked. "Yes, two each." I advised Mason to show Tissier pictures of his children. Fortunately, he had some with him. Over a whisky he followed my advice, albeit a little self-consciously. Tissier was naturally engaged and scrambled for his own photographs.

The next day was a revelation. Tissier actually beamed at Mason, who slowed down his torpedoes to give the Frenchman time to think. The arguments became constructive. Conflicts began to be seen as really pseudo-conflicts. The Belgian and the Singaporean were able to relax and think constructively themselves. Nagging problems often have simple solutions. Six months later Tissier and Mason were sending their children to each other's homes for holidays. It takes two to tango, but it also takes two to set up an impasse.

G100

G100 is probably the most powerful gathering of chief executives in the world. Founded by Dennis Kozlowski and Dennis Carey, it is an exclusive group of top global CEOs of publicly traded companies. It meets semi-annually in New York's historic Pratt Building, year-round home of the Council of Foreign Relations. This unique team holds off-the-record discussions of the latest trends in mergers and acquisitions, government policy, and other corporate issues of special interest to CEOs. Most of the leading names in US business – Jack Welch, Raymond Gilmartin, Jeffrey Immelt, Dennis Kozlowski, Meg Whitman, David Dorman, among others – belong to it. The presidents of these huge corporations pay $100,000 each to network in New York and Aspen, Colorado. Sumptuous dinners are preceded by sittings of the CEO Academy. Sessions start at 8.30 am and last till 5.30 pm.

In April 2002, I was approached by Dr. Marie-Caroline von Weichs, president of G100, who asked me if I would like to give an address entitled "When Cultures Collide" to the CEO Academy meeting in New York in June. These dates are significant. Mergers and acquisitions activity in the spring of 2002 had reached fever pitch. US corporations, buying and merging with companies all over the world, were finding themselves confronted with cultural problems of great magnitude. The US firms did not have a sufficient number of international teams to deal with these issues. Raymond Gilmartin, CEO of Merck, who was chairing the G100 event, wanted this very representative body of American CEOs to be introduced to the cross-cultural aspects of international business. I accepted the assignment, gratified to see that a large number of top US business leaders would be made aware of the intercultural problems that arose in most of their companies. However, the conference itself was not held till late June and in the intervening months a series of revelations occurred that reverberated throughout the membership of G100 in a bone-shaking manner. Huge US-governed multinationals such as WorldCom, Enron, and Tyco were declared bankrupt and fell like ninepins. Their chief officers – Ebbers, Kay, Skilling, and Kozlowski – were perceived to be guilty of fraud on a previously unheard-of scale; billions of dollars had been embezzled, millions of shares became worthless overnight, the eminent executives were disgraced and arraigned, even a formerly respected name like Arthur Andersen was implicated.

The CEO Academy went ahead as planned, though several luminaries failed to attend (for obvious reasons). Kozlowski, designated as one of the CEO panel to speak after me, withdrew from the program. His subject was to have been "Investor Relations Module – Lessons from the Trenches"!

My address was well received, though I felt that minds were elsewhere. As my session was the first after Raymond Gilmartin's opening remarks, I was able to sit in on all other sessions for the rest of the day. It was a valuable opportunity for me to observe the behavior of a club of 100 American CEOs in a period of crisis. Though my module had been uncontroversial in the current climate, the subsequent modules were entitled Corporate Governance, Ethics, Leadership, Investor Relations, and Relations with the Media. In view of what had recently transpired, it is hard to imagine a more embarrassing agenda for the meeting. I was surprised that (a) it had not been changed, and (b) that they let me stay.

The media representatives present seemed to enjoy the day, too. The speakers included famous executives – Jeffrey Immelt (General Electric), Christoph Walther (DaimlerChrysler), William Weldon (Johnson and Johnson), Patricia Russo (Lucent Technologies), David Dorman (AT&T), Mark Mactas (Towers Perrins), Paul Curlander (Lexmark), Robert. J. Hurst (Goldman Sachs), John Dasburg (Burger King), Fred Hassan (Pharmacia), William Stavropoulos (Dow), Lawrence Weinbach (Unisys), Meg Whitman (then eBay), and Ray Gilmartin (Merck).

All the modules except mine had assumed new significance in the light of recent events. Nevertheless, no direct reference was made to the scandals and their victims. Hypocrisy was in the air as one good resolution succeeded another. It was a difficult meeting. The tone was necessarily cautious and guarded. Questions to the panelists were relatively diluted and uncritical, except one or two from the media, though even they were less barbed than usual. The forum was clearly one for closing ranks rather than critical investigation. Not a few of the participants present would come under scrutiny in the following months. It was comforting to take refuge in the chairmanship of squeaky-clean Ray Gilmartin and the respected Jeffrey Immelt (who had just succeeded Jack Welch as Chairman of General Electric). Quite a number of usually articulate attendees kept quiet the whole day.

The same atmosphere prevailed during cocktails and dinner. Welch was particularly accessible and benign. He was interested in my culture talk, but busied himself conversing with as many people as possible on any subject other than corporate governance. Nearly everyone had their picture taken with him.

During the gala dinner, Worth presented its 2002 Best CEO award to eBay's then CEO Meg Whitman, who made a resounding, forward-looking speech. Perhaps it compensated for the absence of Martha Stewart, who faced early inquiries into her share manipulations (which led ultimately to her imprisonment).

The G100 team set-up was later rocked by the split between its co-founder Dennis Carey and its president, Marie-Caroline von Weichs. According to *Fortune* magazine, Carey and von Weichs had carried on a three-year affair, largely subsidized by Spencer Stuart, one of America's top executive search companies. Gifts to von Weichs included jewelry ($200,000), a gold watch ($20,000), a diamond bracelet ($50,000), a free apartment, a company car, and frequent trips to and from Europe. (She was the daughter of a former Austrian ambassador.) Carey's failure to divorce his wife led von Weichs to sue him for $10 million and to tell his wife of his hidden assets. The wife then sued Carey, too, for perjury and disguising the extent of his wealth.

Nokia

In 1865 a 25-year-old Finnish mining engineer named Fredrik Idestam founded a small forest products company in the Finnish inland town of Tampere. A few years later he moved his plant 10 miles to the west along the river Nokia and called his enterprise Nokia AB, after the river. The word *nokia* in Finnish means "weasel," a somewhat less than inspiring name in translation.

After investments in wood products and rubber that had little success, Nokia decided to focus on electronics. A large number of acquisitions in consumer electronics led to its becoming one of Europe's top three television manufacturers. However, it was a disastrous move, producing eventual cumulative losses of more than $1 billion. In 1988 Nokia's chairman and chief executive Kari Kairamo committed suicide.

Nevertheless, in the following decade Nokia's group operating profit went from €144 million (1990) to €5.8 billion in 2000. The market value of all Nokia stocks at years end 1990 was €677 million; at year end 2000 it was €222 billion. At this point Nokia was Europe's largest company by market capitalization. With the sale of 130 million mobile phones in 2000 it had also achieved a unique position for a Finnish enterprise: world leader in a major industry.

Nokia's meteoric rise is an astonishing commercial phenomenon, even in a period of history marked by startling political, scientific, and evolutionary change and advancement. How was it achieved? What was the key? A simple answer, in laconic Finnish parlance, would be that Nokia stumbled across the right product (the mobile phone) in the right place (Finland) at the right time (the IT revolution). This is not untrue, but it does not address the magnitude of the transformation. There is no single key to Nokia's success. The factors are numerous and varied, but they can be grouped into three categories:

✧ External factors
✧ Agility in internal management
✧ The "home turf" factor

One huge external factor was the proximity of Russia. For hundreds of years Finland has lived in the shadow of its giant neighbor. This proximity, even in Soviet times, has not always been disadvantageous. For instance, the 1940–44 Russo-Finnish war seemed to change Nokia's luck in the context of a war-battered economy, but what actually followed was the opposite. When cruel war reparations were demanded by the Russians (in goods), Nokia was agile enough to seize the opportunity to get engaged up to the hilt. This quick decision meant that the company profited from the communist state's demand for power and relay cables, as well as cable machinery. The experience was both profitable and valuable: a centralized economy meant long lines of products; order volumes were predictable; Nokia was paid in oil; the hikes in oil prices in the 1970s doubled Nokia's exports and profits; experience with Russian bureaucrats served Nokia's executives well; they learned how to do a balancing act between east and west.

When the Soviet Union collapsed in 1991, the Nokia management reacted with agility, cost cutting vigorously and concentrating on western markets. The tremendous surge in cellular networks enabled Nokia to transfer large numbers of personnel to the mobile phone division. Matti Alahuhta, head of telecommunications, maximized the window of opportunity by concentrating on research and innovating boldly.

Nokia had often been lucky, but the visionary team of Alahuhta, Vanjoki, Ala-Pietilä, and Ollila introduced factors that guaranteed they would increase their lead over rivals. The main one was heavy and consistent investment in R&D. The Nokia Research Center was established in 1979 with 50 employees. By 2001, 35 percent of its workforce of 18,000 was employed in R&D in 54 research centers in 14 countries. In 1998 the company established a New Venture Fund with a capital investment of $100 million. Later, Ala-Pietilä set up the Nokia Ventures organization, widening the company's horizons even further. Another vital ingredient was the high level of Finnish education, producing graduates by the thousands, including a large female contingent. Kairamo's "young lions" were fresh, open-minded, adaptable, agile, bold yet humble.

So the ingredients were all there: humility, curiosity, a young country's energy, ambition, educational excellence, unselfish team-work, vision, financial experience, priority on research and inno-vation, Finnish rural values of honesty, simplicity, and tenacity, agility and speed and... some luck. Finland is a small country and Nokia's managers all knew each other and trusted their common background. The small-but-good concept reigned.

Nokia is no longer small, though it is still good. The company has lost ground in many areas to ferocious competitors who will not go away. Nokia now has too many committees – it is not as nimble as it was. Furthermore, Finnish shareholding is less than 5 percent. It will be interesting to see how Finland's champion responds to the vigorous challenges it faces. Nokia does not stand still. Its dynamic new leader, Stephen Elop, finds that his Canadian dynamism slots in well with Finnish *sisu*. Watch this space.

Appendix

Cultural Spectacles

In private, the English have a pretty good opinion of themselves. Why? Well, they consider English people to be straightforward, calm, steady, understated, loyal, democratic, honest, humorous, reserved, commonsensical, reticent, modest, laid-back, and admirably casual. They abhor pomposity, sentimentality, and too much emotion in public and try not to be too serious or over-earnest about things. They don't gabble or make a fuss, don't pry into others' affairs, and know how to queue properly. In other words, they are normal human beings.

However, the English have discovered that foreigners, unfortunately, are not normal. Sadly, they are abnormal. English see foreigners as devious, volatile, unsteady, disloyal, inquisitive, hyperbolic, over the top, undemocratic, and prone to extremes. They try to deceive and/or steal from the English and lack a sense of humor, subtlety, a modicum of reserve, a concept of fair play, and good old common sense. When conversing, they are verbose, pompous, sentimental, over-emotional, glib, and alternately intense or solemn. In general they take things too seriously (Germans); often gush and bore us by being terribly earnest about everything (Americans); pry into our private affairs (French); make a fuss in public (Latins); and are incapable of making a decent queue (everybody).

The fact is, all nationalities think they are normal – their fathers and mothers brought them up to be! When others display diametrically opposing characteristics, they appear as unsettling abnormalities. The Japanese, ultra-polite at all times, see all foreigners as (relatively) rude. Tight-lipped Finns think that everyone else gabbles. Americans see non-Americans as slow and old-fashioned. Australians see them as stuffy. French consider others intellectually inferior.

In an international team, nobody is normal. This is not as alarming as it sounds, but the team leader must bear in mind that colleagues have their own perspectives on other nationalities.

To the Germans, foreigners are: unpunctual; untidy; disorderly; inefficient; undisciplined; poorly dressed; untruthful; unreliable; unserious; flippant; disorganized; nonconformist; reckless; inquisitive; can't mind their own business; short term; poor planners; too hurried; too informal too early; lack respect, frankness, and sense of duty; over-simplify things; don't give enough context or explanation; indulge in too much small talk; can't stand criticism; lack protocol; devious and often break laws; dishonest	**To the Swiss, foreigners are:** unpunctual; undisciplined; underfunded; improper; unserious; ill prepared; lacking in planning, foresight, and frugality; untidy and neglectful of the environment; lacking correctness and propriety; often volatile and break rules; less honest
To the Dutch, foreigners are: slow; lazy and unhygienic; time wasting; untruthful; inefficient; unthrifty; intolerant; undemocratic and inexperienced internationally; lack directness, steadiness, planning, and conviction; too flexible and weak in their opinions; lacking energy, enterprise, and intercultural sensitivity; often disregarding of human rights	**To the Americans, foreigners are:** slow; old-fashioned; cautious; impractical; undemocratic; stuffy; devious; afraid of change and innovation; small thinkers; lacking in drive, ambition, energy, work ethic, and a national mission; apt to complicate simple things, fail to grab opportunities, and have too little bottom-line focus; leftish or anti-American; liable to fail to understand that everything is possible in the USA
To the Danes, foreigners are: naïve; gullible; slow thinkers lacking in rationality, humor, originality, creativity, artistry, and perspicacity; class-conscious; owners of a human rights record inferior to the Danish; intolerant and downright undemocratic; inefficient; liable to talk too much (often "over the top") and fail to understand low-key style and subtle irony; weak in history and geography	**To the Italians, foreigners are:** cold; closed; uncommunicative; distant; buttoned up; inflexible; rule bound; short-sighted; insensitive; unrealistic; uncivilized; hypocritical; tend to underestimate Italians; liable to lack compassion, imagination, delicacy, and perspicacity; not possessors of close families; likely to fail to develop "ingroups" and key relationships; over-respectful of officialdom; often selfish

To the Russians, foreigners are:	To the Norwegians, foreigners are:
small thinkers; cold; unimaginative; uncharismatic; ungenerous; selfish; unromantic; pushy; aggressive; exploitative; overbearing; anti-Russian; too smooth; too impersonal; too inflexible; too law-abiding; lacking in humanism, culture, historical perspectives, sense of justice, and good manners; liable to fail to show enough kindness to children and respect to the elderly	liable to wish they were Norwegians; wont to spend too much time indoors; slick, devious, usually corrupt, and lacking in straightforwardness, foresight, and pragmatism; often devious; unpunctual; disrespectful of women; profligate with money; generally unreliable; changeable; likely to fail to deliver
To the French, foreigners are:	**To the Canadians, foreigners are:**
inarticulate; slow; illogical; imprecise; woolly; too rule-bound; too Anglo-Saxon; closed; often boring; lacking in imagination and vision; possessors of poor dress sense; lacking in culture, historical perspective, and knowledge of France's importance and mission; non-speakers of French; money-minded; short term; often uncouth; agenda bound; accepting of mediocrity; lacking in charisma and delicacy; too informal; disrespectful; liable not to understand French uniqueness; intellectually inferior	unsteady; immoderate; unreliable; undemocratic; intense; preoccupied with the sensational; lacking in humor, trust, and morality; laid-back; impartial; low key; lacking in multicultural tolerance and sensitivity
To the Chinese, foreigners are:	**To the Indians, foreigners are:**
immodest; impatient; intolerant; loud; rude; insincere; disloyal; unkind; ungenerous; ungrateful; unscrupulous; untrustworthy; lacking a sense of duty, conscientiousness, diligence, courtesy, gentleness, and wisdom; disrespectful to their parents, the elderly in general, and hierarchical position; desirous of exploiting others, but lacking the tenacity, stoicism, and cleverness to do so; liable not to understand the power of concepts such as self-sacrifice and collective will; desirous of doing deals quickly and leaving early; immoral with blatant double standards	cool; cautious; clumsy; closed; impolite; gullible; lacking in eloquence, compassion, and sensitivity; liable to tell too many jokes based on sarcasm, the lowest form of humor; afraid of risk; possessors of weak family ties; too individualistic and selfish; lacking in breadth of vision and historical perspective

To the Japanese, foreigners are:	To the Finns, foreigners are:
impolite (even rude); loud; verbose; hurried; impatient; reckless; untidy; liable to make hasty decisions on important matters standing up; short term in their thinking; individualistic and selfish; scornful of collective behavior; disloyal to their companies, often going from one to another; confrontational; apt to fail to protect another's face; disrespectful of age; apt to fail to understand Japanese uniqueness	verbose; loud; often noisy; liable to use 100 words instead of 10; extravagant in body language; over-emotional; unreliable; volatile; lacking in directness; often untruthful, devious, and undisciplined; liable to promise too much and then fail to deliver; old-fashioned in business matters; unpunctual; indecisive; inefficient; unrealistic; woolly; hyperbolic (hard sell); slow to pay their debts; frequently pompous; lacking in *sisu*, stamina, and word–deed correlation
To the Swedes, foreigners are:	**To the Irish, foreigners are:**
hurried; loquacious; individualistic; uncaring; often incorrect and improper in their business dealings; aggressive and bulldozing; liable to make hasty decisions without adequate consultation; unable to understand the meaning of consensus or a classless society; confrontational; lacking in nurture and kindness; often corrupt	lacking in warmth, humor, and originality; often too factual and rule bound; liable to take things literally; unappreciative of Irish romanticism, poetry, artistry, and creativity; often too formal, even stiff; lacking in imagination and vision; poor at telling stories
To the South Africans, foreigners are:	**To the Australians, foreigners are:**
biased against white South Africans; lacking in multicultural sensitivity; cautious and risk averse; slow to pursue opportunities; unadventurous; not as entrepreneurial as South Africans; not as sports minded as they need to be	somewhat closed; unfriendly; ungenerous and inhospitable; products of class-conscious societies whose members are often stuffy, conceited, pompous, arrogant, bossy, perhaps outright snobs; apt to talk posh; old-fashioned; unappreciative of Australian humor and irony; lacking in clear-sightedness; liable to create and pursue complex goals and get stitched up in red tape; not as cheerful as they need to be; too solemn; boastful; unable to call a spade a spade

To the Belgians, foreigners are:	To the Spanish, foreigners are:
too opinionated and dogmatic; desirous of quick solutions to complex problems; uncomprehending of the art of compromise; liable to overlook gradualist solutions; confrontational; lacking in moderation; arrogant; apt to underestimate Belgium's economic clout and think that Belgians are either French or Dutch	cold; materialist; product oriented; money minded; rule bound; time dominated; lacking in eloquence, pride, honor, dignity, romanticism, vision, and understanding of human frailty; closed; opaque; tight-lipped; inflexible; lacking in closeness of family and relationship orientation; often critical of Hispanics; historically exploitative of them
To the Brazilians, foreigners are:	**To the Arabs, foreigners are:**
cool; closed; unimaginative; gloomy; pessimistic; short-sighted; unadventurous; small-minded; mediocre footballers; intolerant; racist; unsociable; touchy; too formal	immoral; unjust; anti-Muslim; inflexible; unsociable; sex minded; ungrateful; uncivilized; impersonal; cold-hearted; lacking in a sense of history and family closeness; inhospitable; too private
To the Singaporeans, foreigners are:	**To the Hong Kongers, foreigners are:**
inefficient; unserious; undisciplined; short-sighted; unregulated; untidy; intolerant; lacking in multicultural experience; discourteous; poor listeners; immodest; disrespectful of elders; profligate	too formal; too rule based; up to their neck in red tape; slow at business; poor adapters; too patient; unproductive; afraid of risk; inefficient; lacking in factuality; inhibited; not tenacious

The members of an international team, blessed by increasing cosmopolitanism, will see their colleagues emerge from these stereotypical attitudes or stances and often contradict their preconceptions of them; humorous Germans and Swiss do exist. An individual may even be won over by another's trait that they earlier considered negative or inappropriate; a Spaniard may learn to like aspects of German discipline. As suggested in Chapter 5, one should not ignore or disregard a stereotype, but rather get inside it and understand it. For instance, a Swede's slow decision making originates from the desire for consensus (surely positive); Norwegian stubbornness is born of a love of integrity; Russian soul searching is the product of a harsh, difficult history.

Within a team, all-round tolerance will develop and personal obstinacy will diminish. It is wise, however, for the team leader to realize that some preconceptions regarding national behavior will linger. No American can completely dissociate themselves from the

American Dream. Brits will instinctively shun over-earnestness, Finns unnecessary words, Germans mental untidiness, Dutch time wasting, Australians any trace of pomposity, Asians grating directness. Norwegians cannot rid themselves of Norway-centeredness, French of their sense of intellectual superiority. Italians, for their part, are always aware that only they really understand what makes the world go round.

Bibliography

Applegate, J.L. & Sypher, H.E. (1988) A constructivist theory of communication and culture, in Y.Y. Kim & W.B. Gudykunst (eds) *Theories in Intercultural Communication* (pp. 41–65), Newbury Park: Sage.

Barnlund, D.C. (1970) A transactional model of communication, in J. Akin, A. Goldberg, G. Myers, & J. Stewart (eds) *Language Behavior: A Book of Readings in Communication* (pp. 43–61), The Hague: Mouton.

Berry, Michael (1992) *Know Thyself and the Other Fellow Too: Strategies for Effective Cross-Cultural Communication*, Brussels: Institute for European Studies.

Fisher, Glen (1980) *International Negotiation: A Cross-Cultural Perspective*, Yarmouth, ME: Intercultural Press.

Giddens, A. (1989) *Sociology*, Cambridge: Polity Press.

Hall, Edward T. & Reed Hall, Mildred (1983) *Hidden Differences, Studies in International Communication: How to Communicate with the Germans*, Hamburg: Stern Magazine/Gruner & Jahr.

Hall, Edward T. & Reed Hall, Mildred (1990) *Understanding Cultural Differences: Germans, French and Americans*, Yarmouth, ME: Intercultural Press.

Harris, Philip R. and Moran, Robert T. (1979) *Managing Cultural Differences: High-Performance Strategies for Today's Global Manager*, Houston: Gulf.

Hatch, E. (1983) *Culture and Morality*, New York: Columbia University Press.

Hollis, M. (1979) The limits of irrationality, in B.R. Wilson (ed.) *Rationality* (pp. 214–20), Oxford: Basil Blackwell.

Hollis, M. & Lukes, S. (eds) (1982) *Rationality and Relativism*, Oxford: Basil Blackwell.

Johannesen, R. (1978) *Ethics in Human Communication*, Wayne, MI: Avery.

Lehtonen, Jaakko (1990) *Kultur, Språk och Kommunikation*, University of Jyväskylä Press.

Lewis, Richard D. (2005) *Finland, Cultural Lone Wolf*, London: Intercultural Press.

Lewis, Richard D. (2006) *When Cultures Collide*, London: Nicholas Brealey Publishing.

Lukes, S. (1973) On the social determination of truth, in R. Horton & R. Finnegan (eds) *Modes of Thought: Essays on Thinking in Western and Non-Western Societies* (pp. 230–48), London: Faber & Faber.

Nydell, Margaret K. (1987) *Understanding Arabs: A Guide for Westerners*, Yarmouth, ME: Intercultural Press.

Rearwin, David (1991) *The Asia Business Book*, Yarmouth, ME: Intercultural Press.

Richmond, Yale (1992) *From Nyet to Da: Understanding the Russians*, Yarmouth, ME: Intercultural Press.

Sapir, Edward (1966) *Culture, Language and Personality, Selected Essays*, Berkeley: University of California Press.

Segall, M. H. (1979) *Cross-cultural Psychology: Human Behavior in Global Perspective*, Monterey, CA: Brooks/Cole.

Whorf, Benjamin Lee (1956) *Language, Thought and Reality*, Cambridge, MA: MIT Press.

Wittgenstein, L. (1958) *Philosophical Investigations*, trans. G. E. M. Anscombe, 3rd edn, New York: Macmillan.

Zakaria, F. (1994) Culture is destiny: A conversation with Lee Kuan Yew, *Foreign Affairs* 73: 109–26.

Index

Acknowledgements

Just as I noted the influences of Edward and Mildred Hall and other intercultural writers and specialists in my acknowledgments in *When Cultures Collide* and *The Cultural Imperative*, I wish to mention Richard Evanoff and Antony Giddens as being particularly perspicacious with regard to their remarks on ethics. I would also like to thank Tim Cullen, Tim Flood, Atle Jordahl, and Bill Ribaudo for reviewing my manuscript and especially Iouri Bairatchnyi for his insightful introduction. Other individuals who have given me support and encouragement in my work are Sir Eldon Griffiths, Susan Donnell, Jan Karban, Annabelle Pryde, Shannon Fitzpatrick, Stephen White, Alexander Kosov, Eero Vuohula, Hans-Jan Erstad, Eivind Lorgen, Ulla Ladau-Harjulin, Ulla Ramstedt, Tapio Pihlajaniemi, Barry Tomalin, Matti Alahuhta, Klaus Cawén, Markku Vartiainen, George Simons, Michael Zarin, Andrew MacMartin, Kai Hammerich, Jorma Nevaranta, and the last three Finnish ambassadors to Britain, Pertti Salolainen, Jaakko Laajava, and Pekka Huhtaniemi.

All of the above have earned my gratitude. I have discussed many of my ideas with Michael Gates, who is an invaluable sounding-board. David Garst contributed the case study on INA/CIGNA and AIG. Rob Drayson has skillfully helped me with many of my diagrams and Ceri Erskine has given me all kinds of technical and analytical support.

Finally, I would like to thank Sally Lansdell of Nicholas Brealey Publishing for her thoughtful and meticulous editing of the book.

About the Author

Richard D. Lewis has been active in applied and anthropological linguistics for over 35 years. His work in several fields of communicative studies has involved him in the organization of courses and seminars for many of the world's leading industrial and financial companies.

In 1961 he pioneered the world's first English by Television series, produced by Suomen Television, and subsequently was script writer for the first BBC series, *Walter and Connie*, in 1962.

He has lived and worked in several European countries, where his clients included ABB, Allianz, Banco de España, Banque de France, Deutsche Bank, Ericsson, Fiat, Gillette, IBM, Mercedes Benz, Nestlé, Nokia, Saab, and Volvo.

He also spent five years in Japan, where he was tutor to Empress Michiko and other members of the Japanese Imperial Family. During this period, his services were requested by firms such as Nomura, Mitsubishi, Hitachi, Sanyo, Mitsui, and Nippon Steel.

More recently he has been heavily involved in the intercultural field, founding companies in France, Germany, Spain, Italy, and Brazil, teaching communication skills in these countries as well as in Finland, Sweden, the United Kingdom, and the United States.

Mr. Lewis, who speaks ten European and two Asian languages, is currently chairman of Richard Lewis Communications plc, an international institute of language and cross-cultural training with offices in over a dozen countries. His book *When Cultures Collide* is regarded as the classic work on intercultural issues and was the Spring main selection of the US Book of the Month Club in 1997.

Mr. Lewis, who is currently cross-cultural consultant to the World Bank, was knighted by President Ahtisaari of Finland in March 1997. In 2009 he was promoted to the rank of Knight Commander of the Order of the Lion of Finland.

Other books by Richard D. Lewis

When Cultures Collide
(2006, 2nd edn) Nicholas Brealey Publishing

Finland, Cultural Lone Wolf
(2005) Intercultural Press

Humour across Frontiers
(2005) Transcreen Publications

The Cultural Imperative
(2003) Intercultural Press

Cross-Cultural Communication: A Visual Approach
(1999) Transcreen Publications

Memoirs of a Linguist: The Road from Wigan Pier
(1998) Transcreen Publications